Table of Contents

Practice Test #1

Reading and English Language Arts

1. In the model known in reading instruction as the Three Cueing Systems, which of these relate most to how sounds are used to communicate meaning?
    a. Syntactic cues
    b. Semantic cues
    c. Phonological cues
    d. Pragmatic cues

2. Relative to reading, we should teach students to activate their prior knowledge at which time(s)?
    a. Before reading
    b. During reading
    c. After reading
    d. All of the above

3. Scholars have identified three kinds of major connections that students make when reading: connecting text to self, text to the world, and text to text. Which of the following student statements best reflect(s) the connection of text to the world?
    a. "These mythic gods have more power, but feel and act like humans."
    b. "This novel is set during a period I learned about in my history class."
    c. "I can relate to how the main character felt about being controlled."
    d. All three statements equally reflect connection of text to the world.

4. When students are taught to use effective reading comprehension strategies, they not only achieve deeper understanding, they also learn to think about how they think when reading. This is known as...
    a. Schemata.
    b. Scaffolding.
    c. Metacognition.
    d. Metamorphosis.

5. Some experts maintain that teaching reading comprehension entails not just the application of skills, but the process of actively constructing meaning. This process they describe as *interactive*, *strategic,* and *adaptable*. Which of the following best defines the *interactive* aspect of this process?
    a. The process involves the text, the reader, and the context in which reading occurs.
    b. The process involves readers' using a variety of strategies in constructing meaning.
    c. The process involves readers' changing their strategies to read different text types.
    d. The process involves changing strategies according to different reasons for reading.

6. In first-language (L1) and second-language (L2) acquisition, which of the following is true about developmental stages?
    a. L2 learners do not undergo the first stage called the Silent Period as L1 learners do.
    b. L2 learners undergo all stages, but are urged to skip the first stage more than in L1s.
    c. L2 learners do not undergo the second stage of Formulaic Speech as L1 learners do.
    d. L2 learners undergo the third stage of Structural and Semantic Simplifications later.

7. Which statement is most accurate about social contexts of L1 and L2 acquisition?
    a. Both L1 and L2 learning can occur in equally varied natural and educational contexts.
    b. L1s are only learned in natural contexts, while L2s are learned in educational contexts.
    c. Variations in L2 proficiency can result from the different contexts of learning the L2s.
    d. L2s are not a speaker's natural language and so are never learned in natural contexts.

8. An ESL student whose L1 is Chinese tends to omit plural endings and articles before nouns. Of the following, which is the best explanation for these errors?
    a. The student has not yet learned these English grammatical forms.
    b. Omission avoids having to choose among irregular English forms.
    c. Incompatible nature and rules of the L1 are transferring to the L2.
    d. The student does not understand how the L1 and L2 forms relate.

9. Which of the following is the most accurate characterization of dialects?
    a. They are non-standard versions of any language.
    b. They are often seen as less socially acceptable.
    c. They include linguistic features that are incorrect.
    d. They indicate poor/incomplete language learning.

10. Of the following, which statement is correct regarding Standard English?
    a. The formal Standard English applies to written language.
    b. Standard English is universal in English-speaking nations.
    c. Speech communities use the Standard English of writing.
    d. The Standard English construct does not include dialects.

11. The source of the silent *b* in the English word *debt* was originally…
    a. A Middle English word.
    b. A voiced Old English *b.*
    c. From Latin etymology.
    d. The Greek etymology.

12. We are familiar with the modern English meanings of the word "disaster." But in the 16th century, this word meant…
    a. Catastrophe.
    b. Star-crossed.
    c. A misfortune.
    d. Unflowerlike.

13. Which of the following is an example of a portmanteau?
    a. Fax
    b. Brunch
    c. Babysitter
    d. Saxophone

14. The English language word "quark" is an example of the result of which linguistic process?
    a. Blending
    b. Conversion
    c. Neologisms
    d. Onomatopoeia

15. The questions in this test can give you an idea of what kinds of questions you might find on the actual test; however, they are not duplicates of the actual test questions, which cover the same knowledge but may differ somewhat in form and content.
The preceding sentence is which of the following sentence types?
    a. Simple
    b. Complex
    c. Compound
    d. Compound-complex

16. Which of the following is NOT typically categorized as a prewriting process?
    a. Planning
    b. Reflection
    c. Visualization
    d. Brainstorming

17. Which of the following correctly represents the sequence of stages or steps in the writing process?
    a. Prewriting, drafting, revising, editing, publishing
    b. Prewriting, drafting, editing, publishing, revising
    c. Prewriting, editing, drafting, revising, publishing
    d. Prewriting, drafting, editing, revising, publishing

18. Research has found which of the following outcomes occur for students via revision and rewriting?
    a. Students only correct their mechanical errors in revisions.
    b. Students often incorporate new ideas when they rewrite.
    c. Students retain their original writing goals during revision.
    d. Students' planning in prewriting is unaffected in rewriting.

19. Arthur writes a paper. One classmate identifies ideas and words that resonated with her when she read it. Another describes how reading the paper changed his thinking. A third asks Arthur some questions about what he meant by certain statements in the paper. A fourth suggests a portion of the paper that needs more supporting information. This description is most typical of...
    a. A portfolio assessment.
    b. A holistic scoring.
    c. A scoring rubric.
    d. A peer review.

20. Which of the following is the best definition of Information Literacy?
    a. It is the set of skills required for reading and comprehending different information.
    b. It is the cognitive skill set necessary to amass a comprehensive base of knowledge.
    c. It is the skill set required for the finding, retrieval, analysis, and use of information.
    d. It is the set of skills necessary for effectively communicating information to others.

21. What is the primary reason the early 21st century has been referred to as the Information Age?
    a. Because educational and governmental agencies require greater information
    b. Because there are more sources and outputs of information than ever before
    c. Because students can now learn all they need to know in four years of college
    d. Because college students today are much more interested in new information

22. Of the following statements, which adheres to Information Literacy standards?
   a. Students accessing information must critically evaluate it and its sources before using it.
   b. Students accessing information can ascertain how much of it they need after they find it.
   c. Students accessing information efficiently sacrifice broader scope and incidental learning.
   d. Students accessing information ethically must eschew using it to attain specific purposes.

23. According to the MLA system for documenting sources in literature, which of the following typically combines signal phrases and parenthetical references?
   a. An MLA list of the works cited
   b. MLA in-text citations in a paper
   c. Adding MLA information notes
   d. All of the above

24. According to MLA guidelines for writing research papers, which of the following is correct regarding citations of Web sources if you cannot immediately see the name of a source's author?
   a. Assume the author is not named, as this is a common occurrence on the Web.
   b. Do not name an agency or corporation as author if it is the sponsor of the source.
   c. Author names are often on websites, but need additional looking to discover.
   d. It is not permissible to cite the book or article title in lieu of an author's name.

25. When making in-text citations in a research paper, which of the following reflects MLA guidelines for citing Web sources with regard to page numbers?
   a. If a Web source does not include pagination, you are advised to avoid citing that source.
   b. If page numbers appear on a printout from a website, include these numbers in citations.
   c. In-text citations of online sources in research papers should never include page numbers.
   d. If the Web source is a PDF file, it is recommended to cite page numbers in your citations.

26. The MLA guidelines for citing multiple authors of the same source in the in-text citations of a research paper are to use the first author's name and "et al" for the other(s) in the case of...
   a. More than one author.
   b. Two or three authors.
   c. Three or more authors.
   d. Four or more authors.

27. When you have a writing assignment, which of the following is true about your reader audience?
   a. You need not identify the audience because it is the assigning teacher.
   b. You should consider how your readers are likely to use what you write.
   c. You should know your writing purpose more than a reader's purposes.
   d. You are overthinking to wonder about readers' likely attitude/reaction.

28. Which statement is correct regarding the relationship of your audience profile to the decisions you make in completing a writing assignment?
   a. How much time you spend on research is unrelated to your audience.
   b. Your audience does not influence how much information you include.
   c. The writing style, tone and wording you use depend on your audience.
   d. How you organize information depends on structure, not on audience.

29. Which of the following statements is most accurate about writing the introduction to an essay or paper?
    a. The introduction should use the technique of starting essays with dictionary definitions.
    b. The introduction should leave the most attention-getting material for later in the work.
    c. The introduction should move from the focused and specific to the broad and general.
    d. The introduction should move from the broad and general to the focused and specific.

30. When writing a paper or essay, which of these parts of the introduction should come first?
    a. Your thesis statement for the paper or essay
    b Background on the essay or paper's purpose
    c. Something original to engage reader attention
    d. A "road map" of how you will present the thesis

31. Which of the following is true about effective ways to open the introduction of an essay or paper?
    a. You should summarize your position in your own words, not by quoting another.
    b. Citing a statistic related to the topic that is surprising can grab readers' attention.
    c. Opening with a story or anecdote is counter to the purposes of an essay or paper.
    d. Asking rhetorical questions to open an essay or paper will only frustrate readers.

32. Which of the following is the *worst* way to view the conclusion of an essay or paper you write?
    a. As a means of including all material that would not fit elsewhere
    b. As a means of reiterating the thesis you stated in the introduction
    c. As a means of synthesizing and/or summarizing your main points
    d. As a means of clarifying the context of your discussion/argument

33. In writing, _____ is the overall written expression of the writer's attitude, and _____ is the individual way in which the writer expresses the former.
    a. Voice; tone
    b. Tone; voice
    c. Style; tone
    d. Voice; style

34. _____ is the overall choice of language you make for your writing; _____ are the specific words from a given discipline that you use when writing within or about that discipline.
    a. Vocabulary; diction
    b. Vocabulary; jargon
    c. Diction; vocabulary
    d. Style; vocabulary

35. Which of the following is most accurate regarding writing style?
    a. The kind of diction you use does not affect style.
    b. You add style later to give your writing personality.
    c. Style is unrelated to your control of your content.
    d. Your purpose for writing guides your writing style.

36. When considering strategies for writing assignments, it helps to know the cognitive (or learning) objective(s) your teacher is aiming to meet with an assignment. If the assignment asks you to "describe," "explain," "summarize," "restate," "classify," or "review" some material you read, what is the cognitive objective?
    a. Knowledge recall
    b. Application
    c. Comprehension
    d. Evaluation

37. Your writing assignment asks you to do things like "organize," "plan," "formulate," "assemble," "compose," "construct," and/or "arrange" some material you have read and/or learned. Which of the following cognitive (learning) objectives is the teacher aiming to meet with this assignment?
    a. Analysis
    b. Synthesis
    c. Evaluation
    d. Application

38. Which of the following processes used in writing is the most complex?
    a. Evaluation
    b. Application
    c. Comprehension
    d. Knowledge recall

39. Of the following learning and writing processes, which strategy/strategies is (or are) the most commonly used forms of analysis in college-level writing?
    a. Comparing and contrasting
    b. Explaining cause and effect
    c. Giving support to an opinion
    d. Options A and B

40. Which of the following writing strategies is (or are) among the most commonly used forms of synthesis in college-level writing?
    a. Explaining cause and effect
    b. Comparing and contrasting
    c. Proposing a solution
    d. Using persuasion

41. Among writing projects that can develop from research, which of the following discourse aims is represented by a white paper, an opinion survey, an annotated bibliography, and a problem solution?
    a. Expressive
    b. Exploratory
    c. Informative
    d. Persuasive

42. This treatise developed from an initial idea about the way a plant develops from a seed. The preceding sentence is an example of which literary device and argument method?
    a. Analogy
    b. Allegory
    c. Allusion
    d. Antithesis

43. Of the following sentences, which one appeals to emotion?
    a. It is dangerous to use a cell phone while driving because you steer one-handed.
    b. Statistics of greater accident risk show cell-phone use while driving is dangerous.
    c. It is really stupid to use a cell phone when you drive because it is so dangerous.
    d. Many state laws ban cell-phone use when driving due to data on more accidents.

44. Which of the following gives an example of a fallacy of inconsistency?
    a. "There are exceptions to all general statements."
    b. "Please pass me; my parents will be upset if I fail."
    c. "He is guilty: there is no evidence he is innocent."
    d. "Have you stopped cheating on your assignments?"

45. Which of the following statements is most true?
    a. Introducing oral and written texts from a variety of cultures can enhance students' understanding and appreciation of language.
    b. Children typically learn language best when exposed primarily to texts exemplary of their own background or culture, thereby increasing their ability to identify personally with what they are learning.
    c. Studying other languages will impair a student's ability to develop his or her own first language.
    d. Students should be exposed to one type of text at a time to diminish genre confusion.

46. Which adult would be most effective in helping a student who frequently mispronounces sounds both in reading and in conversation?
    a. A whole language specialist
    b. A speech pathologist
    c. A paraprofessional
    d. A psychologist

47. Which of the following is least important in its effect on a child's language development?
    a. Physical development of ears, mouth, and nose
    b. The IQ and educational level of the child's parents
    c. Interaction and conversation with fluent speakers
    d. Developmental or psychological delay

48. Which choice describes a common function of reading or writing?
    a. Communication of ideas
    b. Enjoyment
    c. Language acquisition
    d. All of the above

49. A classroom is comprised of students with varying abilities in language. Some students can read fluently, while others are still just learning. Speech and language abilities also range widely among the students. Which approach best suits this class?

    a. Each student begins with reading texts slightly below their ability level and practices reading aloud with partners and teachers to build skills.

    b. The teacher consistently presents challenging material for students, knowing that when students are held to high expectations, they typically rise to meet a challenge.

    c. The teacher splits the classroom into groups based on ability and appoints a group leader to guide other students.

    d. The class is exposed to a variety of "texts," in combination with direct phonetic and vocabulary instruction, including written text, video, song, and spoken stories.

50. Learning to construct a reading response would be most beneficial in enhancing which language skill?

    a. Oral presentation

    b. Comprehension

    c. Fluency

    d. Learning a second language

51. Which exercise would be best for building fluency in young students?

    a. Allowing students to draw pictures that illustrate the texts they read if they are unable to write their responses.

    b. Using daily games and lessons to reinforce phoneme-identification skills.

    c. Placing the students into groups to read aloud to one another.

    d. Reading to the students every day from a variety of texts.

52. Mr. Harris divides his 3rd-grade English class into two sections each day. Approximately 60% of the class period is spent on phonics and sight word practice, and 40% is spent on learning comprehension strategies. Which statement is most true regarding Mr. Harris' approach?

    a. This approach neglects several important components of language instruction.

    b. This approach will bore the students and possibly create negative feelings about English class.

    c. This approach will provide the best balance of reading instruction for this age group.

    d. This approach could be improved by spending equal amounts of time on each component, as they are equally important.

53. Which of the following is the best use of technology in a language arts classroom?

    a. Providing laptops to students to achieve more effective note-taking, access to word processing programs, and access to the internet.

    b. Encouraging the use of PowerPoint or similar programs to support lectures and oral presentations, as well as to organize pertinent class concepts.

    c. Incorporating a computer-based "language lab" in which students can listen to texts and engage in interactive word-study and comprehension activities.

    d. Whenever possible, watching film interpretations based on texts studied in class.

54. Which of the following choices would be the best comprehensive project for a 4th-grade class at the end of the school year?

a. An open-book, cumulative test that measures the students' understanding of various concepts and genres through multiple choice, short-answer, and short-essay questions.

b. Assign children to a group in which they will read and adapt a short play. Each group will perform its play with costumes and staging, while the rest of the class will serve as audience members. Audience members will write short responses to what they have seen, which will be shared with the performers.

c. Each student picks a topic about which they would like to conduct independent research. The students will read a variety of texts from different sources to learn more about the topic and then use that information to create a presentation for the class. The use of technology and media is encouraged in presentations.

d. The students take a field trip to the local university to visit the English Department. The students are permitted to sit in on a class lecture and speak to professors about the program. Students also get a chance to interact with college students and find out what literacy skills are most important for a successful college experience.

55. Which choice describes an appropriate alternative to Round-robin reading?

a. All students read together, simultaneously speaking the text aloud.

b. Students break into pairs assigned by the teacher to take turns reading the text while the teacher circulates among the pairs to guide and assess the students.

c. The teacher reads aloud to the students before engaging in a class discussion about what they have learned.

d. Students work on independent assignments while the teacher listens to students read individually.

56. Which of the following choices would be the least effective example of an integrated curriculum that includes language arts instruction?

a. Ms. Smith, a language teacher, confers with Mr. Langston, a history and social studies teacher. Ms. Smith shows Mr. Langston how to model previewing and predicting skills before he introduces a new unit or assignment so that the students build their comprehension skills while reading for information.

b. A science teacher recognizes that the students are having difficulty retaining information from their science textbooks when test time arrives. She creates a study guide with leading questions designed to help jog the students' memory about important concepts before the test.

c. Ms. Shannon, an art teacher, plans a field trip to see the latest exhibit featuring a symbolic artist. A language teacher at her school joins the students at the museum to lead a discussion about the function of symbols and their meanings, as well as different methods of interpreting shared symbols in a society.

d. A 1st-grade teacher uses children's books that introduce mathematical skills. For example, she reads a book weekly that tells a story about children preparing for a picnic, adding and subtracting items they need for the trip along the way. She encourages the children to solve the math questions along with her during the story.

57. Which choice is the best method of structuring language arts curriculum and instruction?
    a. Examine all state-level or national standardized tests that students will be required to take. Structure the curriculum and lessons to address all concepts included in the tests, with an attempt to proportion the time spent in a way that mirrors the breakdown of the tests.
    b. Research the instructional methods used in supplemental education fields. Use those newer methods of introducing and reinforcing concepts in class to ensure that students are receiving consistent and standard instruction.
    c. Use the written curriculum provided by the school district or specific campus as a foundation for instruction. Schedule regular planning sessions to incorporate a variety of texts and instruction methods, as well as to coordinate instruction with teachers of other subjects.
    d. Plan sequential units of study that focus on isolated skills such as word and vocabulary study, comprehension strategies, listening, viewing, and speaking. Design lessons to focus on the mastery of one skill at a time with the goal of studying the relationship between skills toward the end of the school year.

58. Which choice describes the most complete method of displaying student achievement or progress in language arts?
    a. A written report or story that demonstrates a student's knowledge of grammar, spelling, comprehension, and writing skills.
    b. Either a norm- or criterion-referenced test that breaks language skills into small sub-sets and provides achievement levels for each skill.
    c. A portfolio containing a log of stories or books the student has read, rates of reading fluency, writing samples, creative projects, and spelling, grammar, and comprehension tests/quizzes.
    d. A year-end project in which the student presents what he or she has learned from a student-chosen book; the student must read an excerpt of the story and display a visual aid highlighting important information from the story or literary techniques used by the author.

Read the vignette below and use it to answer questions the following 2 questions:
    Amelia has been having trouble in her 1st-grade class for several months. When her teacher, Mrs. Gant, calls Amelia for one-on-one reading practice, Amelia avoids her and protests that she is working on something else at the time. Amelia knows all her letter-sounds when she sees them individually. However, she still cannot consistently decode simple words. Amelia often seems "lost" when her teacher gives her instructions or explains an activity to the group. She usually needs to ask several times for directions to be repeated and oftentimes does not understand what is being asked of her. Amelia sometimes misbehaves in class, hiding during lesson time or arguing with other students during group activities.

59. Which language disorder most closely matches Amelia's symptoms?
    a. Dyslexia
    b. Auditory processing disorder
    c. Either choice a or b
    d. Neither choice a nor b

60. Which answer choice describes the best sort of classroom modifications for Amelia, given her difficulties?
    a. A multi-sensory literacy approach using tactile, kinesthetic, visual and auditory techniques in combination with systematic instruction.
    b. Modified lessons that teach concepts without the use of reading skills.
    c. Extra practice in reading on a daily basis.
    d. Creating engaging activities that will capture Amelia's interest in reading and introducing texts that will motivate her to complete lessons.

61. A teacher designs lessons for the upcoming week. During the first part of the week, the teacher is going to divide the class into two sections. While one group is working independently on their projects, the other group will sit in a circle. The teacher has broken a story up into several sections that each student will read a section aloud. The teacher will note for her records how many errors a student makes. She will also administer a brief verbal "quiz" to which the students will respond in writing. The combination of verbal reading results and comprehension quiz results will give her a better understanding of each child's abilities and/or needs. What kind of assessment did this teacher use?
    a. Cloze-style
    b. Informal reading inventory
    c. Student response form
    d. Articulation assessment

62. Which assessment will determine a student's ability to identify initial, medial, blended, final, segmented, and manipulated 'units'?
    a. Phonological awareness assessment
    b. High-frequency word assessment
    c. Reading fluency assessment
    d. Comprehension quick-check

63. Activating prior knowledge, shared reading, and using graphic organizers are all examples of what type of instructional concept?
    a. Modeling
    b. Scaffolding
    c. Assessing
    d. Inspiring

64. Ms. Baird wants to check her students' individual comprehension skills, specifically their ability to support an idea with evidence from a text. Which scenario is the best way to accomplish her goals?

    a. Split the students into groups after reading the text as a class and allow them to work together on a worksheet activity she has designed.

    b. Play a game in which Ms. Baird posts a card with a main idea. Students read silently and independently and raise their hands to answer when they have found a piece of supporting evidence.

    c. As a class, brainstorm main ideas, topics, or concepts from a text. Allow students to choose a select number of these ideas and copy them onto separate index cards. The students then should individually review the text, recording any supporting evidence on the notecard with the applicable main idea.

    d. Administer a comprehension quiz during class. Allow students to switch papers and grade each other's work. Next, students can spend the remainder of the class period discussing the answers so that each one understands the text fully.

65. Using the correct answer from Question 41, choose the best answer for this question: The activity described would be an excellent pre-lesson for teaching which skill set?

    a. Working as a group to interpret a text and write an appropriate and realistic sequel, focusing on interpretive comprehension and creative writing.

    b. Silent reading as a form of comprehension practice.

    c. Organizing ideas for writing a cohesive and persuasive essay or research paper that asserts supported arguments with valid supporting evidence.

    d. Literal and figurative comprehension, as well as contributing to group discussions via oral communication skills.

66. Which text should a teacher choose in order to practice the skills of previewing and reviewing information?

    a. A poem
    b. A chapter from the students' science class textbook
    c. A library book of each student's own choosing
    d. A short story from language arts class

67. Which of the following choices describes the best introduction to a unit on oral traditions from around the world?

    a. Introducing games that practice new sight words, encoding words based on phonics rules, and answering short comprehension questions.

    b. Setting up video-conferencing with a school in Asia so that students can communicate with children from other countries.

    c. Inviting a guest speaker from a nearby Native American group to demonstrate oral story-telling to the class.

    d. Creating a PowerPoint presentation about various types of oral cultures and traditions and characteristics of each.

68. Which choice constitutes the best method for building conceptual vocabulary?

    a. Using word webs to organize thinking about related terms
    b. Previewing vocabulary words for upcoming units in other subjects such as science or social studies
    c. Implementing a framework for introducing students to various concepts over time
    d. Practicing sight words

69. Third-grade students typically receive their spelling word lists each Monday so that they can practice them at home before the test on Friday. While their teacher is pleased that the students usually receive high grades on spelling tests she observes that they misspell those same words when writing in journals or doing classwork. How should this teacher modify her instruction?
   a. Post a list of vocabulary words when the students are writing to help them recall correct spellings.
   b. Integrate spelling words into writing, reading, grammar, phonics, and other activities to help students learn the words in a variety of contexts.
   c. Provide more time, such as a two-week period, between tests so that students have more time to study.
   d. Review the words before certain activities to increase immediate recall of correct spellings.

Read the vignette below and use it to answer the next 2 questions:

   Following instruction time, Ms. Pitman provides each student with a small sign that can be hung around the waist or neck. Ten children in her class receive signs displaying a single weekly vocabulary word. Five students get signs with the following: "dis-;" "re-;" "pre-;" "un-;" and "mis-." The remaining students have signs with the following: "-ing;" "-ed;" "-s;" "-less;" and "-ful."

70. What is the best choice for a follow-up class activity based on this information?
   a. The students are arranged into groups to demonstrate tangibly that certain parts of the English language have fixed functions.
   b. Each student must use his or her sign to brainstorm a list of possible words that include those letters.
   c. Each time a bell is rung, students must find a new partner with whom he or she can combine signs to make a new word.
   d. Ask each student to explain what his or her sign means and how it functions in the English language.

71. How many students must be holding signs containing root words?
   a. Ten
   b. Five
   c. Twenty
   d. None of the above

72. Which of the following choices represents the smallest unit of language that possesses semantic meaning?
   a. Morpheme
   b. Grapheme
   c. Phoneme
   d. Word stem

73. Which choice describes a primary benefit of an adult's reading aloud to a group of elementary students?

    a. Students have a chance to rest their minds and enjoy oral language.

    b. The adult can model reading fluently for students still building reading skills.

    c. Students have time and opportunity to work on individual projects and assignments while listening to the story.

    d. The adult transmits a great deal of conceptual knowledge via auditory instruction, which is especially beneficial for students who are auditory learners.

74. The words chow, whoosh, and stalk all contain:

    a. Blends

    b. Digraphs

    c. Trigraphs

    d. Monoliths

75. Which of the following is not true regarding grammar instruction?

    a. Grammar is primarily important in writing; therefore, it must be taught predominantly within the context of writing instruction.

    b. Teachers must not only teach grammatical concepts in abstract, but also show students how to contextualize that knowledge and apply it to reading, writing, and speaking.

    c. Knowledge of grammar can be both declarative and procedural in nature.

    d. Many students find grammar to be "boring," necessitating engaging teaching methods and discussions about why grammatical knowledge is important.

Mathematics

1. Which of these is the least biased sampling technique?

    a. To assess his effectiveness in the classroom, a teacher distributes a teacher evaluation to all of his students. Responses are anonymous and voluntary.

    b. To determine the average intelligence quotient (IQ) of students in her school of 2,000 students, a principal uses a random number generator to select 300 students by student identification number and has them participate in a standardized IQ test.

    c. To determine which video game is most popular among his fellow eleventh graders at school, a student surveys all of the students in his English class.

    d. Sixty percent of students at the school have a parent who is a member of the Parent-Teacher Association (PTA). To determine parent opinions regarding school improvement programs, the Parent-Teacher Association (PTA) requires submission of a survey response with membership dues.

2. Which of these tables properly displays the measures of central tendency which can be used for nominal, interval, and ordinal data?

    a.

	Mean	Median	Mode
Nominal			X
Interval	X	X	X
Ordinal		X	X

    b.

	Mean	Median	Mode
Nominal			X
Interval	X	X	X
Ordinal	X	X	X

    c.

	Mean	Median	Mode
Nominal	X	X	X
Interval	X	X	X
Ordinal	X	X	X

    d.

	Mean	Median	Mode
Nominal			X
Interval	X	X	
Ordinal	X	X	X

Use the following data to answer questions 3-5:

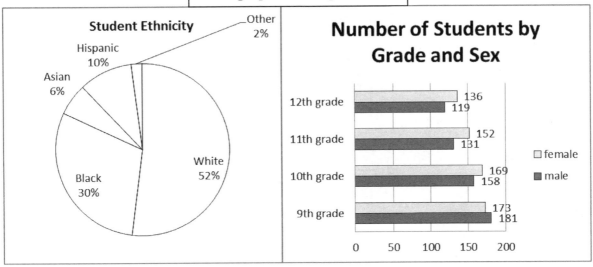

3. Which of these is the greatest quantity?
   a. The average number of male students in the 11th and 12th grades
   b. The number of Hispanic students at the school
   c. The difference in the number of male and female students at the school
   d. The difference in the number of 9th and 12th grader students at the school

4. Compare the two quantities.

Quantity A	Quantity B
The percentage of white students at the school, rounded to the nearest whole number	The percentage of female students at the school, rounded to the nearest whole number

   a. Quantity A is greater.
   b. Quantity B is greater.
   c. The two quantities are the same.
   d. The relationship cannot be determined from the given information.

5. An eleventh grader is chosen at random to represent the school at a conference. What is the approximate probability that the student is male?
   a. 0.03
   b. 0.11
   c. 0.22
   d. 0.46

The box-and-whisker plot displays student test scores by class period. Use the data to answer questions 6-8:

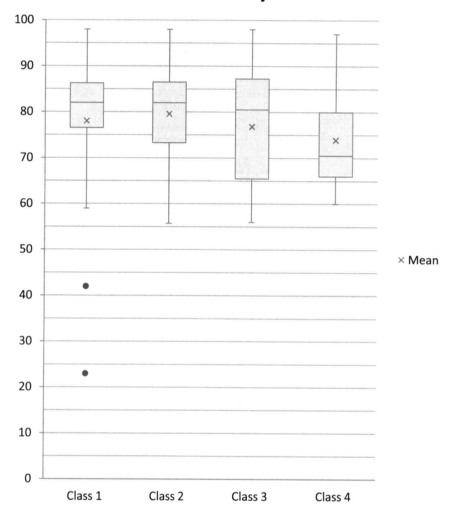

Test scores by class

6. Which class has the greatest range of test scores?
    a. Class 1
    b. Class 2
    c. Class 3
    d. Class 4

7. What is the probability that a student chosen at random from class 2 made above a 73 on this test?
    a. 0.25
    b. 0.5
    c. 0.6
    d. 0.75

8. Which of the following statements is true of the data?
  a. The mean better reflects student performance in class 1 than the median.
  b. The mean test score for class 1 and 2 is the same.
  c. The median test score for class 1 and 2 is the same.
  d. The median test score is above the mean for class 4.

9. In order to analyze the real estate market for two different zip codes within the city, a realtor examines the most recent 100 home sales in each zip code. She considered a house which sold within the first month of its listing to have a market time of one month; likewise, she considered a house to have a market time of two months if it sold after having been on the market for one month but by the end of the second month. Using this definition of market time, she determined the frequency of sales by number of months on the market. The results are displayed below.

Which of the following is a true statement for these data?

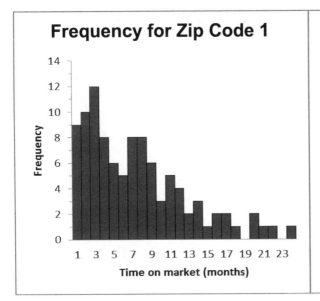 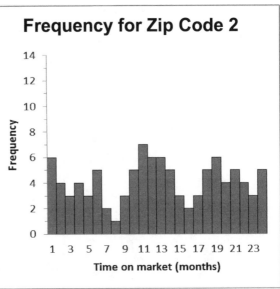

  a. The median time a house spends on the market in Zip Code 1 is five months less than Zip Code 2
  b. On average, a house spent seven months longer on the market in Zip Code 2 than in Zip Code 1.
  c. The mode time on the market is higher for Zip Code 1 than for Zip Code 2.
  d. The median time on the market is less than the mean time on the market for Zip Code 1.

10. Attending a summer camp are 12 six-year-olds, 15 seven-year-olds, 14 eight-year-olds, 12 nine-year-olds, and 10 ten-year-olds. If a camper is randomly selected to participate in a special event, what is the probability that he or she is at least eight years old?

a. $\frac{2}{9}$

b. $\frac{22}{63}$

c. $\frac{4}{7}$

d. $\frac{3}{7}$

11. A small company is divided into three departments as shown. Two individuals are chosen at random to attend a conference. What is the approximate probability that two women from the same department will be chosen?

	Department 1	Department 2	Department 3
Women	12	28	16
Men	18	14	15

a. 8.6%
b. 10.7%
c. 11.2%
d. 13.8%

12. A random sample of students at an elementary school were asked these three questions:

Do you like carrots?
Do you like broccoli?
Do you like cauliflower?

The results of the survey are shown below. If these data are representative of the population of students at the school, which of these is most probable?

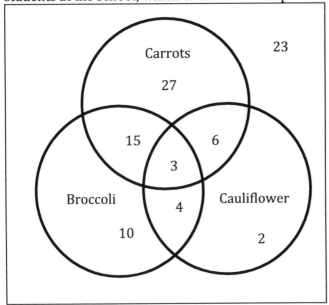

a. A student chosen at random likes broccoli.
b. If a student chosen at random likes carrots, he also likes at least one other vegetable.
c. If a student chosen at random likes cauliflower and broccoli, he also likes carrots.
d. A student chosen at random does not like carrots, broccoli, or cauliflower.

Use the information below to answer questions 13 and 14:

Each day for 100 days, a student tossed a single misshapen coin three times in succession and recorded the number of times the coin landed on heads. The results of his experiment are shown below.

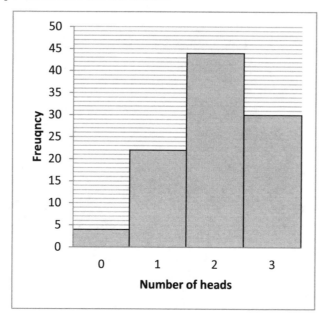

13. Given these experimental data, which of these approximates P(heads) for a single flip of this coin.

a. 0.22
b. 0.5
c. 0.67
d. 0.74

14. Which of these shows the graphs of the probability distributions from ten flips of this misshapen coin and ten flips of a fair coin?

a.

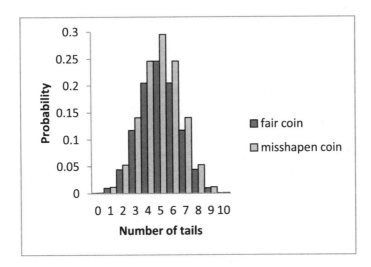

b.

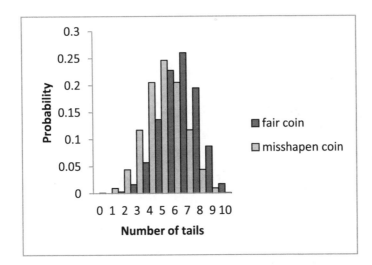

c.

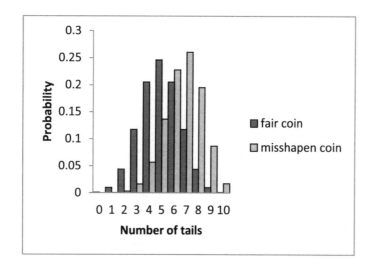

d.

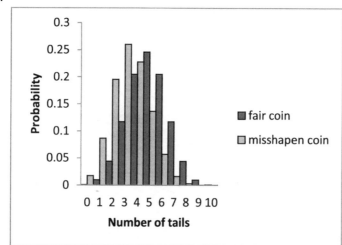

15. Which of these does **NOT** simulate randomly selecting a student from a group of 11 students?
    a. Assigning each student a unique card value of A, 1, 2, 3, 4, 5, 6, 7, 8, 9, or J, removing queens and kings from a standard deck of 52 cards, shuffling the remaining cards, and drawing a single card from the deck
    b. Assigning each student a unique number 0-10 and using a computer to randomly generate a number within that range
    c. Assigning each student a unique number from 2 to 12 ; rolling two dice and finding the sum of the numbers on the dice
    d. All of these can be used as a simulation of the event.

16. A teacher wishes to divide her class of twenty students into four groups, each of which will have three boys and two girls. How many possible groups can she form?
    a. 248
    b. 6,160
    c. 73,920
    d. 95,040

17. In how many distinguishable ways can a family of five be seated a circular table with five chairs if Tasha and Mac must be kept separated?
    a. 6
    b. 12
    c. 24
    d. 60

18. Which of these defines the recursive sequence $a_1 = -1, a_{n+1} = a_n + 2$ explicitly?
    a. $a_n = 2n - 3$
    b. $a_n = -n + 2$
    c. $a_n = n - 2$
    d. $a_n = -2n + 3$

19. What is the sum of the series 200+100+50+25+ ...?
    a. 300
    b. 400
    c. 600
    d. The sum is infinite.

20. Kim's current monthly rent is $800. She is moving to another apartment complex, where the monthly rent will be $1,100. What is the percent increase in her monthly rent amount?
    a. 25.5%
    b. 27%
    c. 35%
    d. 37.5%

21. Marlon pays $45 for a jacket that has been marked down 25%. What was the original cost of the jacket?
    a. $80
    b. $75
    c. $65
    d. $60

22. Which of the following statements is true?
    a. A number is divisible by 6 if the number is divisible by both 2 and 3.
    b. A number is divisible by 4 if the sum of all digits is divisible by 8.
    c. A number is divisible by 3 if the last digit is divisible by 3.
    d. A number is divisible by 7 if the sum of the last two digits is divisible by 7.

23. Which of the following is an irrational number?

    a. $4.\overline{2}$

    b. $\sqrt{2}$

    c. $\frac{4}{5}$

    d. $\frac{21}{5}$

24. Robert buys a car for $24,210. The price of the car has been marked down by 10%. What was the original price of the car?

    a. $25,900

    b. $26,300

    c. $26,900

    d. $27,300

25. Carlos spends $\frac{1}{8}$ of his monthly salary on utility bills. If his utility bills total $320, what is his monthly salary?

    a. $2,440

    b. $2,520

    c. $2,560

    d. $2,600

26. Jason decides to donate 1% of his annual salary to a local charity. If his annual salary is $45,000, how much will he donate?

    a. $4.50

    b. $45

    c. $450

    d. $4,500

27. A dress is marked down 45%. The cost, after taxes, is $39.95. If the tax rate is 8.75%, what was the original price of the dress?

    a. $45.74

    b. $58.61

    c. $66.79

    d. $72.31

28. Amy saves $450 every 3 months. How much does she save after 3 years?

    a. $4,800

    b. $5,200

    c. $5,400

    d. $5,800

29. Which of the following formulas may be used to represent the sequence 8, 13, 18, 23, 28, ...?

    a. $a_n = 5n + 3$

    b. $a_n = n + 5$

    c. $a_n = n + 8$

    d. $a_n = 5n + 8$

30. What is the constant of proportionality represented by the table below?

x	y
2	-8
5	-20
7	-28
10	-40
11	-44

    a. -12
    b. -8
    c. -6
    d. -4

31. Which of the following represents an inverse proportional relationship?
    a. $y = 3x$
    b. $y = \dfrac{1}{3}x$
    c. $y = \dfrac{3}{x}$
    d. $y = 3x^2$

32. Which of the following expressions is equivalent to $-3x(x-2)^2$?
    a. $-3x^3 + 6x^2 - 12x$
    b. $-3x^3 - 12x^2 + 12x$
    c. $-3x^2 + 6x$
    d. $-3x^3 + 12x^2 - 12x$

33. Which of the following is the graph of the equation $y = -4x - 6$?

a.

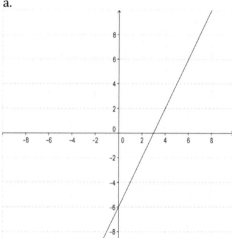

b.

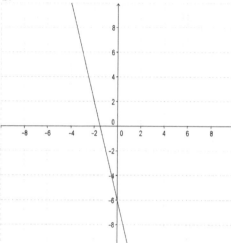

c.

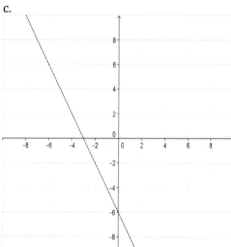

d.

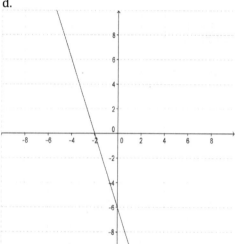

34. Elijah pays a $30 park entrance fee, plus $4 for every ticket purchased. Which of the following equations represents the cost?

a. y = 30x + 4
b. y = 34x
c. y = 4x + 30
d. y = 34x + 30

35. Which type of function is represented by the table of values below?

x	y
−2	0.25
−1	0.5
0	1
1	2
2	4

    a. linear
    b. quadratic
    c. cubic
    d. exponential

36. What linear equation includes the data in the table below?

x	y
−3	1
1	−11
3	−17
5	−23
9	−35

    a. $y = -3x - 11$
    b. $y = -6x - 8$
    c. $y = -3x - 8$
    d. $y = -12x - 11$

37. Kevin saves $3 during Month 1. During each subsequent month, he plans to save 4 more dollars than he saved during the previous month. Which of the following equations represents the amount he will save during the nth month?
    a. $a_n = 3n - 1$
    b. $a_n = 3n + 4$
    c. $a_n = 4n + 3$
    d. $a_n = 4n - 1$

38. Mandy can buy 4 containers of yogurt and 3 boxes of crackers for $9.55. She can buy 2 containers of yogurt and 2 boxes of crackers for $5.90. How much does one box of crackers cost?
    a. $1.75
    b. $2.00
    c. $2.25
    d. $2.50

39. McKenzie shades $\frac{1}{5}$ of a piece of paper. Then, she shades an additional area $\frac{1}{5}$ the size of what she just shaded. Next, she shades another area $\frac{1}{5}$ as large as the previous one. As she continues the process to infinity, what is the limit of the shaded fraction of the paper?
    a. $\frac{1}{5}$
    b. $\frac{1}{4}$
    c. $\frac{1}{3}$
    d. $\frac{1}{2}$

40. Tom needs to buy ink cartridges and printer paper. Each ink cartridge costs $30. Each ream of paper costs $5. He has $100 to spend. Which of the following inequalities may be used to find the combinations of ink cartridges and printer paper that he may purchase?

    a. $30c + 5p \leq 100$
    b. $30c + 5p < 100$
    c. $30c + 5p > 100$
    d. $30c + 5p \geq 100$

41. Hannah spends at least $16 on 4 packages of coffee. Which of the following inequalities represents the possible costs?

    a. $16 \geq 4p$
    b. $16 < 4p$
    c. $16 > 4p$
    d. $16 \leq 4p$

42. A gift box has a length of 14 inches, a height of 8 inches, and a width of 6 inches. How many square inches of wrapping paper are needed to wrap the box?

    a. 56
    b. 244
    c. 488
    d. 672

43. Aidan has a plastic container in the shape of a square pyramid. He wants to fill the container with chocolate candies. If the base has a side length of 6 inches and the height of the container is 9 inches, how many cubic inches of space may be filled with candies?

    a. 98
    b. 102
    c. 108
    d. 112

44. Eric has a beach ball with a radius of 9 inches. He is planning to wrap the ball with wrapping paper. Which of the following is the best estimate for the number of square feet of wrapping paper he will need?

    a. 4.08
    b. 5.12
    c. 7.07
    d. 8.14

45. A tree with a height of 15 feet casts a shadow that is 5 feet in length. A man standing at the base of the shadow formed by the tree is 6 feet tall. How long is the shadow cast by the man?

    a. 1.5 feet
    b. 2 feet
    c. 2.5 feet
    d. 3 feet

46. A cylindrical carrot stick is sliced with a knife. Which of the following shapes is *not* a possible cross-section?
    a. circle
    b. rectangle
    c. ellipse
    d. triangle

47. Which of the following represents the net of a triangular prism?
    a.

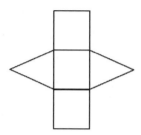

    b.

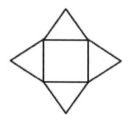

    c.

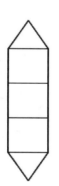

    d.

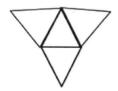

48. Which of the following transformations has been applied to ΔABC?

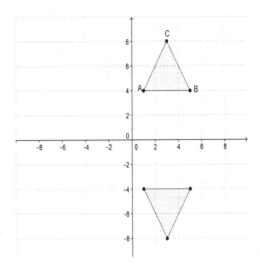

a. translation
b. rotation of 90 degrees
c. reflection
d. dilation

Social Studies

1. When the Senate held an impeachment hearing against Andrew Johnson for overstepping his authority, what did they invoke?
    a. Checks and balances
    b. Bicameralism
    c. Legislative oversight
    d. Supremacy

2. Which statement describes the authority of most local officials?
    a. Members of local government are generally elected by the people, but their authority is granted by the state
    b. Members of local government are given their authority directly from the people
    c. Members of local government have constitutionally-granted authority
    d. Members of local government are elected by the people, but the state Supreme Court determines their authority

3. A filibuster is used to delay a bill. Where can a filibuster take place?
    I.   The House
    II.   The Senate
    III.   Committees
    a. I only
    b. II only
    c. I and II
    d. I, II, and III

4. Which organization is maintained by Congress to oversee the effectiveness of government spending?
    a. The House Committee on Oversight and Government Reform
    b. The Office of Management and Budget
    c. Government Accountability Office
    d. The Department of the Interior

5. The civil rights act that outlawed segregation in schools and public places also:
    a. Gave minorities the right to vote
    b. Established women's right to vote
    c. Outlawed unequal voter registration
    d. Provided protection for children

6. How many Southern states originally ratified the 14th Amendment?
    a. Three
    b. Five
    c. One
    d. Ten

7. Senators were once chosen by state legislatures. When were they first elected by popular vote?
    a. 1912
    b. 1917
    c. 1913
    d. 1915

8. How many judges are on a panel that decides federal appeals?
   a. Five
   b. Three
   c. Nine
   d. Six

9. What petition needs to be filed to request that the Supreme Court hear a case?
   a. Writ of certiorari
   b. Writ of habeas corpus
   c. Writ of mandamus
   d. Writ of attachment

10. Every citizen 18 years of age and older has the constitutional right to vote. What do states govern in the voting process?
    a. The registration for elections
    b. The administration of elections
    c. Both A and B
    d. State governments are not involved in federal elections

11. What are campaign funds given directly to a candidate called?
    a. Soft money
    b. Hard money
    c. Bundling
    d. Independent expenditure

12. Presidential candidates are eligible for public funding if they raise $5,000 per state in how many states?
    a. Twenty
    b. Ten
    c. Twenty-five
    d. Seventeen

13. What judicial system did America borrow from England?
    a. Due process
    b. Federal law
    c. Commerce law
    d. Common law

14. Most state governments have a bicameral legislature. Which one of the following states does not?
    a. Utah
    b. Nebraska
    c. Washington
    d. Louisiana

15. What is the main difference between a primary election and a caucus?
    a. A primary election is privately run by political parties, and a caucus is held by local governments
    b. Caucuses are always held on the same day, but the dates of state primaries vary
    c. A caucus is privately run by political parties, and a primary is an indirect election run by state and local governments
    d. Primary elections are all held on the same date, but the dates of caucuses vary

16. Who negotiates treaties?
    a. The President
    b. The House of Representatives
    c. Ambassadors
    d. The Senate

17. How many intermediate directions are there?
    a. 2
    b. 4
    c. 8
    d. 16

18. Which part of a hurricane features the strongest winds and greatest rainfall?
    a. Eye wall
    b. Front
    c. Eye
    d. Outward spiral

19. Which map describes the movement of people, trends, or materials across a physical area?
    a. Political Map
    b. Cartogram
    c. Qualitative Map
    d. Flow-line Map

20. Which of the following exemplifies the multiplier effect of large cities?
    a. The presence of specialized equipment for an industry attracts even more business.
    b. The large population lowers the price of goods.
    c. Public transportation means more people can commute to work.
    d. A local newspaper can afford to give away the Sunday edition.

21. Which type of chart is best at representing the cycle of demographic transition?
    a. Pie chart
    b. Political map
    c. Line graph
    d. Flow-line map

22. The price of oil drops dramatically, saving soda pop manufacturers great amounts of money spent on making soda pop and delivering their product to market. Prices for soda pop, however, stay the same. This is an example of what?
    a. Sticky prices
    b. Sticky wages
    c. The multiplier effect
    d. Aggregate expenditure

23. John Maynard Keynes advocated what?
    a. Supply-side economics
    b. Demand-side economics
    c. Laissez faire economics
    d. The Laffer Curve

24. Assume a society has a given production possibilities frontier (PPF) representing the production of guns and butter. Which of the following would cause the PPF to move outward?
    a. The invention of a new machine that makes guns more efficiently
    b. An increase in the production of butter
    c. An increase in the production of guns
    d. A decrease in the production of guns and butter

25. Which of the following is a supply shock likely to produce?
    I.   An increase in input prices
    II.   An increase in price levels
    III.   A decrease in employment
    IV.   A decrease in GDP
    a. I and III only
    b. II and IV only
    c. I, II, and III only
    d. I, II, III, and IV

26. Which of the following would *not* cause aggregate supply (AS) to change?
    a. An increase or decrease in land availability
    b. The labor force suddenly increases dramatically
    c. A new oil discovery causes dramatic decreases in power production
    d. Worker productivity remains the same

27. Thomas Paine's Common Sense influenced which American document that ultimately helped shape the Constitution?
    a. The Articles of Confederation
    b. The Declaration of Independence
    c. Bill of Rights
    d. The Treaty of Greenville

28. Virginian _____ advocated a stronger central government and was influential at the Constitutional Convention.
    a. Benjamin Franklin
    b. James Madison
    c. George Mason
    d. Robert Yates

29. Which court case established the Court's ability to overturn laws that violated the Constitution?
    a. Miranda v. Arizona
    b. Marbury v. Madison
    c. United States v. Curtiss-Wright Export Corporation
    d. Brown v. Board of Education of Topeka

30. The first ten amendments to the Constitution are more commonly known as:
    a. The Civil Rights Act
    b. Common law
    c. The Equal Protection clause
    d. The Bill of Rights

31. Which Supreme Court case enforced the civil rights of citizens to not incriminate themselves?
    a. Marbury v. Madison
    b. Miranda v. Arizona
    c. Youngstown Sheet and Tube Company v. Sawyer
    d. United States v. Carolene Products Company

32. To be President of the United States, one must meet these three requirements:
    a. The President must be college educated, at least 30 years old, and a natural citizen
    b. The President must be a natural citizen, have lived in the U.S. for 14 years, and have a college education
    c. The President must be a natural citizen, be at least 35 years old, and have lived in the U.S. for 14 years
    d. The President must be at least 30 years old, be a natural citizen, and have lived in the U.S. for 14 years

33. The President may serve a maximum of _____ according to the ___ Amendment.
    a. Three four-year terms; 23rd
    b. Two four-year terms; 22nd
    c. One four-year term; 22nd
    d. Two four-year terms; 23rd

34. The Vice President succeeds the President in case of death, illness or impeachment. What is the order of succession for the next three successors, according to the Presidential Succession Act of 1947?
    a. President Pro Tempore of the Senate, Secretary of State, and Secretary of Defense
    b. Speaker of the House, President Pro Tempore of the Senate, and Secretary of State
    c. President Pro Tempore of the Senate, Speaker of the House, and Secretary of State
    d. Secretary of State, Secretary of Defense, and Speaker of the House

35. The President serves as Commander-in-Chief. What are the President's two limitations in that role?
    a. The President cannot declare war or oversee military regulations
    b. The President cannot enforce blockades or declare war
    c. The President cannot enforce quarantines or oversee military regulations
    d. The President cannot enforce blockades or quarantines

36. What are the official requirements for serving in the House of Representatives?
    a. A member of the House must be at least 30 years old, a U.S. citizen for a minimum of nine years, and a resident of the state and district he represents
    b. A member of the House must be at least 25 years old, a natural citizen, and a resident of the state he represents
    c. A member of the House must be at least 30 years old, a natural citizen, and a resident of the state and district he represents
    d. A member of the House must be at least 25 years old, a U.S. citizen for a minimum of seven years, and a resident of the state he represents

37. What are the official requirements for becoming a Senator?
    a. A Senator must be at least 35 years old, a U.S. citizen for a minimum of seven years, and a resident of the state he represents
    b. A Senator must be at least 30 years old, a U.S. citizen for a minimum of nine years, and a resident of the state he represents
    c. A Senator must be at least 25 years old, a U.S. citizen for a minimum of nine years, and a resident of the state and district he represents
    d. A Senator must be at least 30 years old, a natural citizen, and a resident of the state he represents

38. Senators were once chosen by state legislatures. When were they first elected by popular vote?
    a. 1912
    b. 1917
    c. 1913
    d. 1915

39. Who may write a bill?
    a. Anyone
    b. A member of the House
    c. A Senator
    d. Any member of Congress

40. Congressional elections are held every _____ years.
    a. Four
    b. Two
    c. Six
    d. Three

41. How is a tie broken in the Senate?
    a. The President Pro Tempore casts the deciding vote
    b. The Speaker of the House votes
    c. They vote again
    d. The Vice President votes

42. A newly introduced bill is first given to a _____ where it is either accepted, amended or rejected completely.
    a. Full committee
    b. Conference committee
    c. Subcommittee
    d. Senate committee

43. The House Committee on Oversight and Government Reform oversees and reforms government operations. Which Senate committee works with that committee?
    a. Senate Committee on Banking, Housing, and Urban Affairs
    b. Senate Committee on Homeland Security and Government Affairs
    c. Senate Committee on Rules and Administration
    d. Senate Appropriations Committee

Science

1. In which taxonomic group are organisms most alike?
    a. Phylum
    b. Family
    c. Class
    d. Order

2. Which division of plants produces seeds for reproduction?
    a. Anthophyta
    b. Lycophyta
    c. Sphenophyta
    d. Pterophyta

3. What do all animals belonging to the Echinodermata phylum have in common?
    a. They use multiple appendages for locomotion.
    b. They use tube feet for locomotion and feeding.
    c. They have an exoskeleton made of chitin.
    d. They must shed their outer layer of skin to grow.

4. Where are the reproductive organs of a plant?
    a. Style
    b. Stigma
    c. Flowers
    d. Sepals

5. Plants begin to break down the products of photosynthesis through respiration. What is the result of respiration?
    a. Water
    b. Oxygen and glucose
    c. Carbon dioxide and sugar
    d. Carbon dioxide and water

6. Which of the following is not an advantage angiosperms show over other types of plants?
    a. Larger leaves
    b. Double fertilization
    c. Dormant seeds
    d. Lower seed dispersal

7. How are animals of the Mollusca phylum able to respire?
    a. Through gills
    b. Through a trachea
    c. Through lungs
    d. Through muscle contraction

8. What part of a plant system responds to stimuli by releasing water via transpiration, except during adverse conditions like a drought when it closes up to prevent the plant from dehydration?
   a. Pith
   b. Stomata
   c. Guard cells
   d. Sepals

9. Which of the following animal structures is not paired to its correct function?
   a. Muscle System – controls movement through three types of muscle tissue
   b. Nervous System – controls sensory responses by carrying impulses away from and toward the cell body
   c. Digestive System – breaks down food for absorption into the blood stream where it is delivered to cells for respiration
   d. Circulatory System – exchanges gases with the environment by delivering oxygen to the bloodstream and releasing carbon dioxide

10. If a population reaches a maximum size and ceases to grow due to a limited availability of resources, the population is
   a. unstable.
   b. shrinking exponentially.
   c. at carrying capacity.
   d. moving towards extinction.

11. The following represents a simple food chain. What trophic level contains the greatest amount of energy?

   Tree -> Caterpillar -> Frog -> Snake -> Hawk -> Worm

   a. Tree
   b. Caterpillar
   c. Hawk
   d. Worm

12. Which of the following sources of fresh water is unavailable for human use?
   a. Rivers
   b. Estuaries
   c. Aquifers
   d. Glaciers

13. Which of the following words is not connected to the process of mountain building?
   a. Folding
   b. Faulting
   c. Transform
   d. Convergent

14. The formation of sedimentary rock includes all of the following processes except
   a. layering.
   b. cementation.
   c. compaction.
   d. heat.

15. Which of the following is an example of chemical weathering?
    a. Rain freezing on the roadway.
    b. Ivy growing on the side of a wooden house.
    c. Vinegar fizzing when poured on a rock.
    d. A river carrying sediment downstream.

16. Which of the following situations would result in the generation of new crust?
    a. Two crustal plates converge.
    b. Two crustal plates move apart.
    c. Two crustal plates slide past one another.
    d. A crustal plate is pushed down into the mantle.

17. Which of the following terms describes an intrusion of magma injected between two layers of sedimentary rock, forcing the overlying strata upward to create a dome-like form?
    a. Sill
    b. Dike
    c. Laccolith
    d. Caldera

18. Which statement best describes the process of absolute dating?
    a. It compares the amount of radioactive material in a rock to the amount that has decayed into another element.
    b. It measures the age of a rock by comparing it to fossils found in the same stratigraphic layer as the rock.
    c. It measures the amount of daughter elements that have broken down by half.
    d. It measures the mass loss of a rock by estimating the amount of material that has eroded due to catastrophic events.

19. Fossils are least likely to be found in
    a. sedimentary rock.
    b. metamorphic rock.
    c. igneous rock.
    d. Fossils are commonly found in all types of rock.

20. Which of the following is an example of a trace fossil?
    a. A mouse jaw
    b. A footprint
    c. A shark tooth
    d. A cast of a skull

21. Which of the following types of ocean currents would be the densest?
    a. Warm and high salinity
    b. Warm and low salinity
    c. Cold and high salinity
    d. Cold and low salinity

22. Which of the following does not control the movement of ocean currents?
    a. Wind
    b. Landmasses
    c. Earth's rotation
    d. Phase of the Moon

23. Compared to fresh water, the freezing point of sea water is
    a. higher.
    b. lower.
    c. the same.
    d. Sea water does not freeze.

24. Which of the following describes the physical or non-biological part of the carbon cycle?
    a. Phytoplankton use carbon dioxide and other nutrients to produce carbohydrates and oxygen.
    b. Cold water dissolves atmospheric carbon dioxide, stores it, and releases it back out to the atmosphere as needed.
    c. Carbon dioxide is dissolved in sea water, and is broken up to free carbon for use by marine life.
    d. Warm, surface water dissolves carbon dioxide where it is converted to nitrogen and phosphorus for use by marine life.

25. What drives weather systems to move west to east in the mid-latitudes?
    a. The prevailing westerlies
    b. The prevailing easterlies
    c. The trade winds
    d. The doldrums

26. If land cools off rapidly at night and the ocean water stays relatively warm, what type of wind is created?
    a. Sea breeze
    b. Land breeze
    c. Monsoon
    d. Trade wind

27. On a topographic map, an area where the contour lines are very close together indicates that
    a. a stream is present.
    b. the slope is very gentle.
    c. the slope is very steep.
    d. the area surrounds a depression.

28. What other planet in the solar system experiences a greenhouse effect similar to that observed on Earth?
    a. Mercury
    b. Venus
    c. Neptune
    d. Saturn

29. Which of the following is considered a non-renewable resource?
    a. Glass
    b. Wood
    c. Cattle
    d. Soil

30. Which statement best explains the importance of recycling and using alternative sources of energy?
    a. It will lead to greater production of goods and consumer spending in the future.
    b. It will ensure the health and safety of populations and the long-term sustainability of the environment.
    c. It will get rid of human disease and end economic warfare in the future.
    d. It will allow fossil fuel supplies to be replenished for their continued use in the future.

31. Which of the following creates a magnetic field?
    a. the spinning and rotating of electrons in atoms
    b. the separation of charged particles in atoms
    c. the vibrational and translational motion of atoms
    d. loosely held valence electrons surrounding an atom
    e. a neutron:proton ratio greater than one

32. Which of the following creates an electromagnet?
    a. rapidly spinning and rotating electrons inside an iron bar
    b. an iron bar moving inside a coil of wire that contains a current
    c. the movement of electrons through a complete circuit
    d. convection currents within the liquid core of Earth's interior
    e. translational and vibrational motion of atoms

33. What is the definition of work?
    a. the amount of energy used to accomplish a job
    b. the force used to move a mass over a distance
    c. the amount of power per unit of time
    d. energy stored in an object due to its position
    e. force multiplied by the time over which the force acts

34. What property of light explains why a pencil in a glass of water appears to be bent?
    a. reflection
    b. refraction
    c. angle of incidence = angle of reflection
    d. constructive interference
    e. destructive interference

35. Which of the following materials has randomly aligned dipoles?
    a. a non-magnetic substance
    b. an electromagnet
    c. a permanent magnet
    d. a horseshoe magnet
    e. a superconductor

36. A pulley lifts a 10 kg object 10 m into the air in 5 minutes. Using this information you can calculate:
    a. mechanical advantage
    b. efficiency
    c. frictional resistance
    d. power
    e. energy conservation

37. The boiling of water is an example of ____:
    a. a physical change.
    b. a chemical change.
    c. sublimation.
    d. condensation.
    e. neutralization.

38. What change occurs when energy is added to a liquid?
    a. a phase change
    b. a chemical change
    c. sublimation
    d. condensation
    e. single replacement

39. The center of an atom is called the ____. It is composed of ____.
    a. nucleus; protons and neutrons.
    b. nucleus; protons and electrons.
    c. electron cloud; electrons and protons.
    d. electron cloud; electrons and neutrons.
    e. electron cloud; electrons only.

40. What happens to gas particles as temperature increases?
    a. The average kinetic energy decreases while the intermolecular forces increase.
    b. The average kinetic energy increases while the intermolecular forces decrease.
    c. Both the average kinetic energy and the intermolecular forces decrease.
    d. Both the average kinetic energy and the intermolecular forces increase.
    e. Temperature does not affect the average kinetic energy or the intermolecular forces.

41. When heat is removed from water during condensation, new ____ form.
    a. atoms
    b. covalent bonds
    c. intermolecular bonds
    d. ionic bonds
    e. molecules

42. What laboratory practice can increase the accuracy of a measurement?
    a. repeating the measurement several times
    b. calibrating the equipment each time you use it
    c. using metric measuring devices
    d. following MSDS information
    e. reading the laboratory instructions before the lab

43. Which of the following is usually the first form of study in a new area of scientific inquiry?
    a. descriptive studies
    b. controlled experiments
    c. comparative data analysis
    d. choosing a method and design
    e. identifying dependent and independent variables

44. Which of the following is an example of a descriptive study?
    a. correlational studies of populations
    b. identifying a control
    c. statistical data analysis
    d. identifying dependent and independent variables
    e. drawing a valid conclusion

45. What is the purpose of conducting an experiment?
    a. to test a hypothesis
    b. to collect data
    c. to identify a control state
    d. to choose variables
    e. to make a valid conclusion

46. Which of the following is needed for an experiment to be considered successful?
    a. a reasonable hypothesis
    b. a well-written lab report
    c. data that others can reproduce
    d. computer-aided statistical analysis
    e. graphs and tables

47. The scientific method is a series of steps to _____.
    a. solve a problem.
    b. gather information.
    c. ask a scientific question.
    d. formulate a hypothesis.
    e. understand science.

48. Which of the following statements correctly describes a similarity or difference between rocks and minerals?
    a. Minerals may contain traces of organic compounds, while rocks do not.
    b. Rocks are classified by their formation and the minerals they contain, while minerals are classified by their chemical composition and physical properties.
    c. Both rocks and minerals can be polymorphs.
    d. Both rocks and minerals may contain mineraloids.

49. When two tectonic plates are moving laterally in opposing directions, this is called a:
    a. Transform boundary.
    b. Compressional boundary.
    c. Oppositional boundary.
    d. Lateral boundary.

50. The most recently formed parts of the Earth's crust can be found at:
    a. Subduction zones.
    b. Compressional boundaries.
    c. Extensional boundaries.
    d. Mid-ocean ridges.

The Arts, Health, and Fitness

1. Which of the following artistic elements would be found only in sculpture or decorative arts?
   a. Line
   b. Form
   c. Proportion
   d. Balance

2. Cross-hatching is a technique that is used to
   a. develop black-and-white photographs.
   b. achieve shading effects in pencil drawings.
   c. blend water-based paints.
   d. attach handles to pottery.

3. The advantage of drawing with charcoal as opposed to lead pencils is that
   a. charcoal can be smudged to create shading.
   b. charcoal does not require a fixative.
   c. charcoal is available in a variety of hues.
   d. charcoal is available in a wide range of different values, ranging from dark and soft to light and hard.

4. In oil painting, paint is traditionally applied
   a. all in one session.
   b. with the least oily layers of paint on the bottom and the oiliest layers at the top.
   c. to slate or paper.
   d. after the painting surface has been finished with a layer of varnish.

5. Drybrush is a technique that is primarily used in
   a. watercolor painting.
   b. oil painting.
   c. acrylic painting.
   d. ceramic glazing.

6. The fiber art technique that involves condensing, or matting, fibers together is called
   a. flocking.
   b. felting.
   c. macramé.
   d. plaiting.

7. The threads that are stretched taut across the loom before weaving begins are called the
   a. warp.
   b. weft.
   c. loom.
   d. twill.

8. Which of the following is not considered a type of digital art?
   a. Videography
   b. Cinematography
   c. Three-dimensional computer animation
   d. Pixel art

9. Which of the following artistic elements is most commonly used to create the illusion of depth in a painting?
   a. Balance
   b. Line
   c. Contrast
   d. Symmetry

10. Which of the following factors would plausibly explain two observers' differing evaluations of the same painting?
   a. Differing levels of artistic knowledge
   b. Different vantage points
   c. Different cultural beliefs and values
   d. All of the above

11. With respect to actor placement onstage, the term "upstage" means what?
   a. The actor is toward the back of the stage, away from the audience
   b. The actor is positioned at the front of the stage, close to the audience
   c. The actor is exactly at the center of the stage
   d. The actor is standing on an X on the stage that was put in place by the director

12. Mood and setting can often be confused with one another. What is the main distinction between the two terms?
   a. Mood is created solely by the characters and their actions. Setting is the physical location of the play
   b. Sensory details determine the mood, allowing the audience to feel certain emotions. Setting is what the audience sees in terms of set design
   c. Mood is created by a lighting designer, while setting is created by a set designer
   d. Setting is entirely dependent on the mood. They cannot exist without one another

13. All of the following are examples of widely studied ancient theatre forms except:
   a. Greek.
   b. Roman
   c. English Renaissance
   d. Medieval

14. The English Renaissance is a time period most known for its:
   a. Operas
   b. Comedians
   c. Playwrights
   d. Classical musicians

15. Analyzing each character in a script, studying biographical information, and understanding each characters' strengths and weaknesses are important aspects of:
   a. Developing character relationships
   b. Script analysis
   c. Plot development
   d. Psychological dissection

16. An eighth-grade theatre teacher asks her class to inhale by yawning, and then let out all the air by sighing as loudly as possible. This is an example of:
    a. Vocal projection
    b. Pitch development
    c. Vocal warm-up
    d. Breath control

17. If a drama teacher wanted to deepen his students' understanding of human emotions and characterization, he might bring which of the following to class?
    a. Costumes
    b. Commedia half-masks
    c. Comedy/tragedy masks
    d. Character masks

18. The director of a production has many duties. All of the following are assumed duties of a director except:
    a. Vocal coaching
    b. Encouraging cohesion among cast mates
    c. Interpreting and approving scripts
    d. Collaborating with crew members

19. To ensure maximum dramatic effect, a director places actors onstage precisely where he wants them. What is this called?
    a. Positioning
    b. Staging
    c. Choreography
    d. Blocking

20. When is a theatre production company required to pay royalty fees to a playwright for using his work?
    a. On opening night
    b. Every time admission is charged
    c. Any time the play is performed for an audience
    d. When the admission price exceeds five dollars per audience member

21. In order for a director to get an idea of a performer's capabilities and talent, he might ask the performer to read a script he or she has never seen before. This is called:
    a. Blind reading
    b. Preliminary reading
    c. Cite reading
    d. Cold reading

22. A theatre director hoping to produce a low-cost series of experimental skits would benefit from using which type of theatrical stage?
    a. Proscenium
    b. Black box
    c. Arena
    d. Thrust

23. What is the difference between a thrust stage and an arena?
    a. An audience can sit on three sides of a thrust stage; they can sit on all four sides of an arena
    b. A thrust stage cannot utilize a backstage, whereas an arena can
    c. An audience can only sit in front of a thrust stage; they can sit on three sides of an arena
    d. A thrust stage can be an unused room or warehouse converted into a theatre; an arena is also known as a platform stage

24. A director might hire a dramaturg for what purpose?
    a. To apply special effects makeup to the actors' faces and/or bodies
    b. To analyze dramatic text and research relevant historical facts in order to determine the artistic requirements of a specific production
    c. To incorporate lighting and sound effects to enhance the mood for the audience
    d. To aid in marketing efforts and increase ticket sales

25. What is theatre gel used for?
    a. It is a safety precaution in case someone gets burned by a stage light; theatre gel is applied to the skin to prevent scarring
    b. Lighting technicians use theatre gels, or small transparent pieces of colored film, to change the mood with lighting
    c. Sound technicians use theatre gels, or thick sound-resistant pads, to muffle sounds that are too loud
    d. Costume designers use theatre gels, or adhesive liquids, to mend clothing when it tears or needs a quick hem

26. A large instrument used for lighting that consists of a lamp socket and is surrounded by a reflector is called what?
    a. A specific light
    b. A general light
    c. A strip light
    d. A floodlight

27. When there are budget constraints, some directors and/or set designers will use a certain type of set that can be changed by merely adding one or two set pieces, which makes the set very versatile. What is this type of set called?
    a. Unit set
    b. Convertible set
    c. Multi set
    d. Uniform set

28. What style of music traditionally is played by a sextet—a group consisting of two violins, a piano, a double bass, and two bandoneóns?
    a. Tango
    b. Salsa
    c. Flamenco
    d. Tejano

29. The folk music of which of the following cultures or countries is primarily percussive in nature?
    a. Finnish
    b. Peruvian
    c. Mongolian
    d. Ewe

30. The Hammond organ originally was used by
    a. U.S. churches in the 1930s
    b. blues, rock, and jazz musicians in the 1960s
    c. Baroque composers in the 1640s
    d. English composers in the 1890s

31. In which of the following musicals would one expect to hear klezmer music?
    a. Fiddler on the Roof
    b. The Sound of Music
    c. Oklahoma!
    d. A Chorus Line

32. Which of the following composers was known best for creating operettas?
    a. Wolfgang Amadeus Mozart
    b. Giacomo Puccini
    c. Sir Arthur Sullivan
    d. Giuseppe Verdi

33. Which of the following musical genres was *one* of the influences in the development of Tejano music?
    a. Incan music
    b. African music
    c. Peruvian music
    d. German music

34. The MP3 format allows a CD track to be stored at a fraction of its original size because the process
    a. copies the original file at a lower sound volume
    b. removes selected vocal or instrument tracks
    c. removes selected information, including frequencies that are too high or too low for humans to hear
    d. converts the digital information to analog information

35. Music of the Renaissance began relying on what interval as a consonance, which previously had been regarded as dissonant?
    a. second
    b. third
    c. fifth
    d. None of these, because intervals were not used until the Baroque period.

36. Which of the following pairs of composers lived and worked during the same time period?
    a. Antonio Vivaldi and Friedrich Chopin
    b. Gustav Holst and Johann Sebastian Bach
    c. Johann Pachelbel and Franz Liszt
    d. Pyotr Ilyich Tchaikovsky and Edvard Grieg

37. Of the commonly accepted and understood time periods into which Western classical music has been divided, which period is associated most strongly with musical nationalism?
    a. Baroque
    b. Classical
    c. Romantic
    d. Contemporary

38. Which of the following describes the best method for determining the proper-sized violin for a student musician?
    a. Choosing a violin that is about a quarter as long as the student is tall
    b. Allowing the student to choose an instrument based on what "feels right"
    c. Choosing a violin whose scroll extends just to the base of the student's hand
    d. Choosing a violin that allows the student's fingers to curl comfortably around the scroll and allows the elbows to bend slightly

39. Which are the best tuning pitches before a rehearsal or performance?
    a. Concert C # and Concert A, with exception of French horns
    b. Concert D and Concert B ♭, with the exception of flutes
    c. Concert B ♭ and Concert F, with the exception of saxophones
    d. Concert F and Concert A ♭, with the exception of clarinets

40. What is the normal compass of a timpani?
    a. a minor third
    b. a perfect fourth
    c. a perfect fifth
    d. a major seventh

41. How often should brass players oil the valves of their instruments in order to prevent sticking?
    a. once a day
    b. about once a week
    c. once a month
    d. only when the valves begin to stick

42. Which of the following statements is true about the viola?
    a. It is tuned the same as a violin.
    b. It is a mainstay of the symphony but is rarely used in chamber music.
    c. It uses alto or "viola" clef, a clef that is otherwise rarely used.
    d. It is larger than the violin, but it uses a finer bow.

43. Foods that are rich in fiber include:
    a. turkey and shellfish.
    b. yogurt and eggs.
    c. beans and whole-wheat bread.
    d. skim milk and orange juice.

44. An adolescent with a body-mass index (BMI) of 22 would be considered:
    a. underweight.
    b. normal.
    c. overweight.
    d. obese.

45. Stretching and warming up before participating in strenuous physical activity is beneficial for all of the following EXCEPT:
    a. improving performance.
    b. gaining muscle mass.
    c. increasing flexibility.
    d. decreasing risk of injury.

46. Bulimia differs from binge-eating disorder in that bulimics:
    a. display a preoccupation with food.
    b. frequently withdraw from family and friends.
    c. often show signs of depression.
    d. have a distorted image of their own bodies.

47. Which of the following illustrates the specificity of training principle?
    a. Someone who wants to attain higher levels of fitness work is more successful working under a specific plan than another person who lacks a specific plan.
    b. Someone training to be an excellent basketball player trains by first mastering specific individual basketball skills.
    c. Someone who wants to become healthier proceeds by tailoring different activities for different areas of physical health (such as cardiovascular fitness).
    d. Someone who swims three times a week has difficulty exercising at the same intensity when he or she switches to running three times a week.

48. When is it a good idea to have students perform circuit training?
    a. when students are used to regular physical activity
    b. at all fitness levels, from beginning to advanced
    c. when students are just beginning to exercise regularly
    d. only when students are recovering from injuries

49. What is a main difference between complex carbohydrates and simple carbohydrates?
    a. Simple carbohydrates have fiber, and complex carbohydrates don't.
    b. It is easier to digest simple carbohydrates.
    c. It is easier to maintain good blood sugar levels with simple carbohydrates.
    d. Simple carbohydrates are more nutritious.

50. How do you perform a skinfold test?
    a. Use calipers to measure how thick particular skinfolds are.
    b. Send an electric current through skinfolds to estimate body fat.
    c. Determine in certain places how much fat can be pinched between the fingers.
    d. Compare the thickness of skinfolds to a person's weight and height.

51. Which of the following is generally the LEAST important factor in physical performance among teenagers?
    a. the amount of sleep a teenager gets
    b. a teenager's age
    c. adequate nutrition or lack thereof
    d. which school a teenager attends

52. Which of the following should NOT be a factor in designing a physical education course?
    a. emphasizing visual learning
    b. fun
    c. evaluating student progress
    d. safety

53. Lecturing is BEST suited for teaching which of the following?
    a. exercises for flexibility
    b. the rules of a game/sport
    c. the ethics of steroid use
    d. basic motions in a sport

Answers and Explanations

Reading and English Language Arts

1. C: Phonological cues are based on the speech sounds in words and their alphabetic representations in print. Readers can identify words by knowing sound-to-letter correspondences. Syntactic cues (A) are based on how words are arranged and ordered to create meaningful phrases, clauses and sentences. Semantic cues (B) are based on the meanings of morphemes and words and how they combine to create additional meanings. Pragmatic cues (D) are based on the readers' purposes for reading and their understanding of how textual structures function in the texts that they read.

2. D: Reading instructors should teach students to activate their prior knowledge because it will improve their reading comprehension. Before reading choice A, teachers should discuss and model connections with existing knowledge to prepare students by helping them consider what they already know about the subject of the text. While they read option B, students can make better sense of the text by considering how it fits with what they already know. After reading choice C, teachers can lead discussions helping students focus on how the connections they made between the text and their previous knowledge informed their understanding of the text, and on how the text helped them build their foundations of existing knowledge.

3. A: The student making this observation is connecting reading of a mythological text (presumably Greek or Roman) s/he reads to the world—in this instance, to human nature—by noting that despite greater powers, the gods' emotional reactions and behaviors are like those of humans. The student statement in choice B reflects a connection of text to text—fiction (a novel) to historical accounts of a period (for example, see Dickens's *A Tale of Two Cities)*. The student statement in option C reflects a connection of text to self: the student can relate to the feelings of a character in the text. Because each choice reflects a different one of the three kinds of student connections named, choice D is incorrect.

4. C: Thinking about thinking, or understanding our own cognitive processes, is known as metacognition. Explicitly teaching effective reading comprehension strategies does more than deepen student understanding of reading: it also promotes higher-order, abstract cognitive skill of metacognition. Schemata (A) (plural, singular *schema*) is Piaget's term for mental constructs we form to understand the world. Piaget said we either assimilate new information into an existing schema or alter an existing schema to accommodate the new knowledge. Reading instruction experts may refer to experience or background knowledge as schemata because students undergo this cognitive process when they fit what they read to their existing knowledge/experience. Scaffolding (B), a term coined by Jerome Bruner, means the temporary support given to students as needed while they learn and is gradually reduced as they become more independent. Reading instruction experts may also describe students' connections of text to prior experience as scaffolding. Metamorphosis (D) is a term meaning a transformation—literally in biology as with caterpillars into butterflies, or figuratively, as in Franz Kafka's *The Metamorphosis,* wherein protagonist Gregor Samsa becomes a cockroach.

5. A: The process of actively constructing meaning from reading is interactive, in that it involves the text itself, the person reading it, and the setting in which the reading is done: the reader interacts with the text, and the text interacts with the reader by affecting him/her; the context of reading

interacts with the text and the reader by affecting them both; and the reader interacts with the reading context as well as with the text. Choice B is a better definition of the *strategic* aspect of the process. Options C and D are better definitions of the *adaptable* aspect of the process.

6. B: Researchers find that learners of both their native language (L1) and a second language (L2) go through all three developmental stages, which means that choices A and C are both incorrect. However, learners of a second language are often urged by teachers and others to skip the Silent Period, whereas young children acquiring their native languages are not similarly expected to speak immediately. L2 learners are not likely to undergo the third stage later (D) but sooner than or at a similar time as L1 learners, due either to having not yet learned all linguistic forms of the L2 or to being unable to access all of the L2's forms as they produce language.

7. C: L2s can be learned in a number of educational contexts, such as being segregated from the L1, formally taught via the medium of the L1, through submersion, or within the language classroom but not used to communicate outside it, among many others. They can also be taught/learned in several natural contexts: as the majority language to members of ethnic minority groups, as the official language of a country where learners speak a different language, or for international communication purposes separate from the L1 or official language. Therefore, it is not accurate that L2s are never learned in natural contexts (B and D). Unlike L2s, L1s are always first acquired in natural contexts, meaning choice A is inaccurate.

8. C: Omitting articles (for example, *a/an, the, these*) and plural endings (*–s*), which is common among Chinese ESL students, is not because they have not yet learned the English forms (A) or words for these. Nor are these omissions a way to avoid having to choose the correct form among various English irregularities (C). These errors are also not due to the student's not understanding the relationship between the Chinese and English versions of the forms (D). Rather, Chinese does not include articles or plural endings the way English does, so the student has no frame of reference or comparison. Therefore, the student's ESL pattern of absent articles and plurals reflects the nature and rules of the L1, which have transferred to the L2 but are incompatible with it.

9. B: As linguists have long pointed out, dialects are NOT non-standard versions of a language (A). In linguistics, dialects are *differing* varieties of any language, but these may be vernacular (nonstandard) OR standard versions of a language. They are often considered less socially acceptable, especially in educational, occupational and professional settings, than whichever standard version is most accepted. The linguistic features of dialects are not incorrect (C), but simply different. Their use does not indicate poor or incomplete language learning (D).

10. A: The formal version of Standard English is reflected in dictionaries and grammar books and applied in written language. In speech, Standard English is NOT universal (B): it differs in pronunciation between the northern and southern regions of North America and between native English speakers in England, Ireland, Australia, India, and other English-speaking areas. Speech communities use a more flexible variety of *informal* Standard English rather than the Standard English of writing (C). The construct of Standard English actually includes a range of dialects (D) because formal Standard English is used in writing and not speech, which by nature dictates a less formal, more flexible version.

11. C: The etymology, or origin, of the English word *debt* is the Latin word *debitum*. It came into English during the Middle English form of the language. Therefore, this word was not originally a Middle English word (A) but a Latin word. Because it came from Latin into Middle English, it did not exist as an Old English word with a voiced *b* (B) as Old English preceded Middle English. The origin

of this word was not Greek (D) but Latin. NOTE: Early scribes and printers, described by some as "inkhorn scholars," introduced many silent letters to English spellings to indicate their Latin or Greek roots, as in this case.

12. B: In Old Italian, the word *disastro* meant unfavorable in one's stars. It was commonplace to attribute bad fortune to the influences of the stars in the Medieval and Renaissance eras. The Old Italian word came into English in the late 1500s as "disaster" and was used by Shakespeare (cf. *King Lear*). The word's Latin root is *astrum*, meaning "star," and the Latin prefix *dis-*, meaning "apart" and signifying negation. *Catastrophe* (A) and *misfortune* (C) are both Modern English meanings of the word "disaster," whereas the "ill-starred" meaning used in Elizabethan times has now become archaic or obsolete. The root means "star," not the aster flower (D).

13. B: The word "brunch" is a blend of "breakfast" and "lunch". Blends of two or more words are known as portmanteau words. (*Portmanteau* is a French word meaning a suitcase.) "Fax" (A) is an example of clipping, or shortening a word, from its original "facsimile." "Babysitter" (C) is an example of compounding, or combining two or more words into one. "Saxophone" (D) is an example of proper noun transfer: A Belgian family that built musical instruments had the last name of Sax, and this wind instrument was named after them. These represent some of the ways that new words have entered—and still do enter—the English language.

14. C: Neologisms (from *neo-* meaning "new"), also known as "creative coinages," are new words sometimes invented by people which then become parts of our vocabulary. The word "quark" was first coined by the great Irish author James Joyce; he used it in his last novel, *Finnegans Wake.* The physicist Murray Gell-Mann then chose this word from Joyce's work to name the model of elementary particles he proposed (also proposed concurrently and independently by physicist George Zweig) in 1964. Blending (A) is another way new words come into our language; for example, "moped" is a blend of the respective first syllables of "motor" and "pedal." Conversion (B), also called functional shift, changes a word's part of speech. For example, the common nouns "network," "microwave," and "fax," along with the proper noun "Google" have all been converted to verbs in modern usage. Onomatopoeia (D) means words that imitate associated sounds, such as "meow" and "click." New words are also created this way.

15. D: This is an example of a compound-complex sentence. A simple (A) sentence contains a subject and a verb and expresses a complete thought. Its subject and/or verb may be compound (e.g., "John and Mary" as subject and "comes and goes" as verb). A complex (B) sentence contains an independent clause and one or more dependent clauses. The independent and dependent clause(s) are joined by a subordinating conjunction or a relative pronoun. A compound (C) sentence contains two independent clauses—two simple sentences—connected by a coordinating conjunction. A compound-complex (also called complex-compound) sentence, as its name implies, combines both compound and complex sentences: it combines more than one independent clause with at least one dependent clause. In the example sentence given, the first two clauses, joined by "however," are independent, and the clause modifying "actual test questions," beginning with "which cover," is a relative, dependent clause.

16. B: Typically, after students write something, their teachers may ask them to reflect upon what they wrote, which would mean that this is NOT a prewriting activity. In writing exercises, teachers will typically ask students to plan (A) what they will write in order to clearly define their main topic and organize their work. Many teachers find it helps students to visualize (C) what they are reading and/or want to write about, and make drawings of what they visualize as preparation for writing.

Brainstorming (D) is another common prewriting activity designed to generate multiple ideas from which students can then select to include in their writing.

17. A: After prewriting (planning, visualizing, brainstorming), the correct sequence of steps in the writing process are drafting, in which the writer takes the material generated during prewriting work and making it into sentences and paragraphs; revising, where the writer explores any changes in what one has written that would improve the quality of the writing; editing, in which the writer examines his or her writing for factual and mechanical (grammar, spelling, punctuation) errors and correcting them; and publishing, when the writer finally shares what he or she has written with others who will read it and give feedback.

18. B: Researchers have found that the writing processes both form a hierarchy and are observably recursive in nature. Moreover, they find that when students continually revise their writing, they are able to consider new ideas and to incorporate these ideas into their work. Thus they do not merely correct mechanical errors when revising (A), they also add to the content and quality of their writing. Furthermore, research shows that writers, including students, not only revise their actual writing; during rewrites, they also reconsider their original writing goals rather than always retaining them (C), and they revisit their prewriting plans rather than leaving these unaffected in rewriting (D).

19. D: This description is most typical of the process of peer review. Classmates read Arthur's paper and then they identify values in it, describe it, ask questions about it, and suggest points for revision. These are types of helpful feedback identified by experts on writing and collaborative writing. The other choices, however, are not typically collaborative. For a portfolio assessment (A), the teacher collects finished work products from a student over time, eventually assembling a portfolio of work. This affords a more authentic assessment using richer, more multidimensional, and more visual and tactile products for assessment instead of using only standardized test scores for assessment. Holistic scoring (B) is a method of scoring a piece of writing for overall quality (evaluating general elements such as focus, organization, support, and conventions) rather than being overly concerned with any individual aspect of writing. A scoring rubric (C) is a guide that gives examples of the levels of typical characteristics in a piece of writing that correspond to each available score (for example, scores from 1-5).

20. C: According to the Association of College and Research Libraries, Information Literacy is the set of skills that an individual must have for finding, retrieving, analyzing, and using information. It is required not just for reading and understanding information (A). Information Literacy does not mean learning and retaining a lot of information (B), or only sharing it with others (D), but rather knowing how to find information one does not already have and how to evaluate that information critically for its quality and apply it judiciously to meet one's purposes.

21. B: The early 21st century has been dubbed the Information Age primarily because, with widespread Internet use and other innovations in electronic communications and publishing, there are more sources of information and greater output of available information than ever before. While some agencies might require more information (A), this is only possible because such information is more readily available now. Professionals in higher education and research find that with this new explosion of information, college students cannot possibly gain enough information literacy by just reading texts and writing research papers, and cannot learn all they need to know in four years (C). This period is also not called the Information Age due to an increased student interest in acquiring information (D), but due to the increased access to information.

22. A: It is a standard of Information Literacy (IL) that students must use their own critical thinking skills to evaluate the quality of the information and its sources before they use it. Another standard is that the student should ascertain how much information s/he needs for his/her purposes first; deciding this after uncovering excessive information is inefficient (B). An additional IL standard is to access necessary information in an efficient and effective way. However, none of these standards include the idea that students will lose incidental learning or broadness of scope by doing so (C). IL standards include the principle that students *should* use the information they find in ways that are effective for attaining their specific purposes (D).

23. B: The MLA (Modern Language Association) system for documenting literary sources defines in-line citations in a paper as combining signal phrases, which usually include the author name and introduce information from a source via a fact, summary, paraphrase, or quotation; parenthetical references following the material cited, frequently at the end of the sentence; and, except for web sources that are unpaginated, page number(s). MLA defines a list of works cited (A) as an alphabetized list found at the end of a research paper that gives the information sources referenced in the paper, including each source's publication information , quotations, summaries, and paraphrases. Guidelines for preparing the list of works cited are provided in the *MLA Handbook*. MLA information notes (C) are an optional addition to the MLA parenthetical documentation system. These notes can be used to add important material without interrupting the paper's flow, and/or to supply comments about sources or make references to multiple sources. They may be endnotes or footnotes. Option D is incorrect.

24. C: On the Internet, it often occurs that the name of the author of an article or book is actually provided but is not obviously visible at first glance. Web sources frequently include the author's name, but on another page of the same site, such as the website's home page; or in a tiny font at the very end of the web page, rather than in a more conspicuous location. In such cases, students doing online research may have to search more thoroughly than usual to find the author's name. Therefore, they should not immediately assume the author is not named (A). Also, many Web sources are sponsored by government agencies or private corporations and do not give individual author names. In these cases, the research paper *should* cite the agency or corporation name as author (B). Finally, it is much more common for online sources to omit an author's name than it is in print sources. In these cases, it is both permitted and advised by the MLA to cite the article or book title instead (D).

25. D: When online sources you are citing in your research paper are in PDFs and other file formats that have stable pagination, the MLA advises including the page number in the research paper's in-text citation because these numbers are valid and do not change. If a Web source has no pagination, as often happens, the MLA does NOT advise avoiding the citation (A); it advises simply making the citation without a page number because there is not one available. Unlike in PDFs (above), when citing a source from a printout, the MLA advises NOT including page numbers even if you see them because the same page numbers are not always found in all printouts (B). It is not true that in-text citations should never include page numbers (C).

26. D: The MLA guidelines for citing multiple authors of the same work in in-text citations (for both print and online sources) dictate using the first author's name plus "et al" for the other authors when there are four or more authors. If there are two (options A and B) or three (options B and C) authors, the guidelines say to name each author, either in a signal phrase [for example, "Smith and Jones note that... (45)" or "Smith, Jones, and Gray have noted... (45)"] or in a parenthetical reference ["(Smith, Jones, and Gray 45)."].

27. B: For any writing assignment, you should first target an audience, perform an audience analysis, and develop an audience profile to determine what you should include in and omit from your writing. Even though the assigning teacher may be the only one to read your writing, you should not assume s/he is your main audience (A) because the teacher may expect you to write for other readers. In addition to first knowing your purpose for writing before beginning, you should also consider what purpose your writing will meet for your readers (C) and how they are likely to use it. Considering what your audience's attitudes toward what you will write and their likely reactions to it is also important to shaping your writing and is NOT overthinking (D).

28. C: The kind of audience for whom you are writing, as well as your purpose for writing, will determine what style, tone, and wording you choose. Knowing who your audience is will enable you to select writing strategies, a style and tone, and specific word choices that will be most understandable and appealing to your readers. Knowing the type of audience will also dictate how much time to spend on research (A). Some readers will expect more supporting evidence, while others will be bored or overwhelmed by it. Similarly, you will want to include more or less information depending on who will be reading what you write (B). And while the structure of your piece does inform how you organize your information, you should also vary your organization according to who will read it (D).

29. D: It is best to begin an essay or paper with a broader, more general introduction to the topic, and move to a more focused and specific point regarding the topic—not vice versa (C)—by the end of the introduction. This point is your thesis statement. Writing experts advise *against* the technique of beginning an essay with a dictionary definition (A) because it has been so overused that it has become ineffective and uninteresting. To engage the reader's interest in your topic, it is best to *begin* with some very attention-getting material rather than leaving it for later (B).

30. C: The first part of the introduction to an essay or paper should be some original, fresh material that will engage the attention of readers enough so they are interested in continuing to read it. Following this should be the transitional portion of the introduction, which gives some pertinent background information about the piece's particular purpose (B). This informs the reader of your reason for focusing on your paper or essay's specific topic. The transitional portion moves the piece to the third part of the introduction: the thesis statement (A), which is a clear expression of the main point you are trying to make in your essay or paper. An optional addition in the introduction is an explanation of how you will defend your thesis, giving readers a general idea of how your essay or paper's various points will be organized. This is sometimes described as a "road map" (D).

31. B: One recommended technique for beginning the introductory part of a paper or essay is to cite a statistic related to your paper/essay's topic that readers are likely to find surprising. This will get the readers' attention, while also giving some information about the topic to be discussed in the rest of the piece. Another effective technique for starting the introduction is to use an interesting quotation that summarizes your position. This adds interest, support, and power; it is not true that you should use only your own words instead of quoting another (A). It is also not true that opening with a story or anecdote is contrary to the purposes of an essay or paper (C): when you as the writer have some personal interest in your topic, this technique is useful for getting the readers as emotionally engaged in the subject matter as you are. It is not true that asking rhetorical questions will only frustrate readers (D): this is a technique that helps readers imagine being in different situations so they can consider your topic in new ways.

32. A: While students may sometimes regard the conclusion of their essay or paper as simply the last paragraph that includes all the pieces that they could not fit into earlier parts of the piece, this

- 63 -

is an inadequate treatment of the conclusion. Because the conclusion is the last thing the audience reads, they are more likely to remember it. Also, the conclusion is an excellent opportunity to reinforce your main point, remind readers of the importance of your topic, and prod readers to consider the effects of the topic in their own lives and/or in the world at large. A good conclusion should restate your original thesis statement (B), pull together and/or summarize the main points you made (C), and make clear(er) your discussion's or argument's context (D).

33. B: Tone is the way in which the writer writes overall to express his or her attitude. Voice is who the reader hears speaking in the writing, the individual way the writer uses to express his or her tone—not vice versa (A). Style (options C and D) is the effect a writer creates through language, mechanics, and attitude or the sound (formal or informal) or impressions (seriousness, levity, grace, fluency) of the writing.

34. C: Diction refers to your overall choice of language for your writing, while vocabulary refers to the specific words in a discipline that you use when writing in or about that discipline—not vice versa (A). Jargon (B) is very specialized terminology used in a discipline that is not readily understood by readers outside of that discipline. It is hence less accessible than the vocabulary of the discipline, and only used in writing intended only for those who are already familiar with it. Diction and vocabulary are elements of writing style (D).

35. D: Knowing your purpose for writing means knowing what you want to achieve with the content of your writing, and knowing this will determine your writing style. Your choice of words and how formal or informal your writing is—your diction—*does* affect your style (A). Diction and tone should be consistent in your writing style, and should reflect vocabulary and writing patterns that suit your writing purpose best. Style is not added later to give writing personality (B). It develops from your purpose for writing, or what you want to accomplish with your writing. Style *is* directly related to your control of the content (C) of your writing.

36. C: The verbs quoted all refer to interpreting information in your own words. This task targets the cognitive objective of comprehension. Tasks targeting the cognitive objective of knowledge recall (A) would ask you to name, label, list, define, repeat, memorize, order, or arrange the information. Tasks targeting the cognitive objective of application (B) would ask you to calculate, solve, practice, operate, sketch, use, prepare, illustrate, or apply the material. Tasks targeting the cognitive objective of evaluation (D) would ask you to judge, appraise, evaluate, conclude, predict, score, or compare the information.

37. B: The verbs quoted all refer to taking pieces or parts of information or knowledge and bringing them together to create a whole, and to building relationships among the parts to fit new or different circumstances. Analysis (A) is the opposite of synthesis—breaking information down into its component parts and demonstrating the relationships among those parts. An assignment for analysis would ask you to compare, distinguish, test, categorize, examine, contrast, or analyze information. Evaluation (C) is making judgments of information based on given criteria, confirming or supporting certain preferences, and persuading the reader. An assignment targeting evaluation would use words like evaluate, predict, appraise, conclude, score, judge, or compare. Application (D) is using knowledge in new contexts. The assignment would ask you to apply, prepare, practice, use, operate, sketch, calculate, solve, or illustrate.

38. A: Evaluation is the most complex of the thinking/writing strategies listed in these choices because it commonly incorporates the other thinking strategies. Knowledge recall (D) requires showing mastery of information learned. Comprehension (C) requires showing understanding of

the information learned. Application (B) requires taking the information learned and using it in new or different circumstances. These processes are not as complex as evaluating (or making critical judgments) the information learned. Analysis, synthesis, and evaluation are more complex than knowledge recall, comprehension, and application. Of analysis, synthesis, and evaluation, evaluation is the most complex.

39. D: Comparing and contrasting, explaining cause and effect relationships, and analyzing are the most commonly used forms of analysis in college-level writing. Supporting an opinion (C) you have stated in your writing is one of the most commonly used forms of *synthesis*, not analysis, in college-level writing.

40. C: Proposing a solution to some problem or situation is one of the most commonly used forms of synthesis strategies in college-level writing. The other most commonly used synthesis writing strategy is stating an opinion and supporting it with evidence. Explaining cause and effect (A) and comparing and contrasting (B) are two of the most commonly used *analysis* (not synthesis) writing strategies. Using persuasion (D) to convince the reader is typically used together with the other strategies named to add credibility and acceptance to the position stated by the writer.

41. B: A white paper, opinion survey, annotated bibliography, and problem solution are all examples of the exploratory discourse aim. So are definitions, diagnoses, marketing analyses, feasibility studies, and literature (*not* literary) reviews. The expressive (A) discourse aim is reflected in things like vision statements, mission statements, proposals, constitutions, and legislative bills. Examples of writing reflecting the informative (C) discourse aim include news and magazine articles, reports, and encyclopedia articles. Examples of writing reflecting the persuasive (D) discourse aim include political speeches; editorials; ad campaigns; and works of artistic, social, or political criticism.

42. A: This sentence is an analogy, which compares similarities between two concepts to establish a relationship. Analogy can enhance comprehension of a new concept via comparison to an older/more familiar concept. Allegory (B) uses symbolism to represent a more abstract concept with a more concrete concept. Examples of literary works which are overall allegories include Dante's poem *Divine Comedy* and the novels *Animal Farm* by George Orwell (1945) and *Lord of the Flies* by William Golding (1954). Allusion (C) is a passing reference to a literary work/place/person/event, wherein the reader must make the connection. For example, saying "Susan loves to help and care for other people so much that her friends call her Mother Teresa" is an allusion to a famous person exemplifying Susan's personal qualities. Antithesis (D) juxtaposes words/phrases/sentences with opposite meanings, balancing these to add insight. A good example is Neil Armstrong's statement during his and Buzz Aldrin's moon landing: "That's one small step for man, one giant leap for mankind."

43. C: This sentence appeals to the reader's emotions by stating simply that it is dangerous and "really stupid" to use a cell phone while driving; it does not provide any evidence or logic to support the statement. Choice A offers a logical, common-sense argument in that steering one-handed makes driving more dangerous. Choice B refers to statistics of greater accident risk to support the statement that cell phone use while driving is dangerous. Such supporting evidence is an appeal to logic. Choice D cites the fact that many state laws ban cell phone use while driving to support the idea that it is dangerous, and also refers to data on more accidents from doing so. These pieces of supporting evidence also appeal to logic rather than emotion.

44. A: A fallacy of inconsistency exists in a statement that contradicts itself or defeats itself. Saying there are exceptions to all general statements is itself a general statement; therefore, according to the content, this statement must also have an exception, implying there are NOT exceptions to all general statements. Option B is an example of a fallacy of irrelevance: passing or failing is determined by course performance, so asking to pass because parents will be upset if one fails is an irrelevant reason for appealing to a teacher for a passing grade. Choice C is an example of a fallacy of insufficiency: a statement is made with insufficient evidence to support it. A lack of evidence of innocence is not enough to prove one is guilty because there could also be an equal lack of evidence of guilt. Option D is an example of a fallacy of inappropriate presumption: asking someone if s/he has stopped cheating presumes that s/he has cheated in the past. The person being asked this question cannot answer either "yes" or "no" without confirming that s/he has indeed been cheating. If the person being asked has not been cheating, then the person asking the question is making a false assumption.

45. A: Students are completely capable of understanding and appreciating oral traditions and written texts from other world cultures, as well as those originating from cultures in the students' own community. In fact, introducing a variety of material can increase some students' appreciation of language and literature, as it enables them to learn about the world around them. Language skills emerge at a point in most children's development during which students are fascinated with learning new concepts. Introducing a variety of texts also benefits students in a classroom who belong to other cultures; these students are able to learn concepts from texts that represent their family, culture, or country of origin.

46. B: There are many different adults who can assist children in acquiring various types of language. If a child inconsistently mispronounces certain sounds in reading, he or she may simply need a reminder or instruction from a teacher. Often, children will not acquire knowledge of certain letters or sounds until a certain age. However, the child in this scenario mispronounces words consistently both in reading and in conversation. This combination suggests that the child is not physically able to make certain speech sounds. A speech-language pathologist can assist in determining whether or not the child's mispronunciations indicate the need for therapy. This type of therapist can also work directly with the child to help him or her learn how to make certain sounds.

47. B: Children develop language skills, both oral and written, based on a variety of physical, psychological, emotional and environmental factors. In order to speak, a child must have a developed physiology of the mouth, ears, nose, and other relevant physical features. Children will also learn to speak and read when they interact and receive instruction from fluent adults or older children. There are also times when a developmental or psychological delay can impair language acquisition. However, the IQ and education level of a child's parents is not necessarily relevant to the child's ability to acquire language (although parental intelligence or education may affect the type of exposure a child will encounter outside of school).

48. D: Reading can achieve a variety of purposes. Initially, students learn to read as a form of language acquisition. This process also enables them to learn about various concepts through written texts, both inside and outside of school. Individuals will write and read to share thoughts, stories, and ideas with others. As language develops, many individuals will view reading as a common form of entertainment or enjoyment, regardless of the text's perceived instructional value or content. Each answer choice describes a widely-accepted purpose of the reading process.

49. D: Classrooms will most always consist of students at different levels of ability. The physical and psychological processes needed for reading evolve simultaneously over time and do so at different rates for each individual. No two students will match up perfectly with respect to language skills. Language skills also incorporate a variety of other processes, including speaking, listening, thinking, viewing, writing, and reading. By pairing direct instruction with various types of cognitive processes, all students receive varied instruction and will make progress. By being introduced to different types of text, students will develop skills according to their own strengths at that particular time.

50. B: Reading responses can take various forms. The most common form of reading response is likely to be targeted student writing. Students may use journals, worksheets, or other formats to construct written responses to something they have read. The purpose of this type of assignment can range from fostering an appreciation of written text to helping a student prepare for an activity in class. Students may also engage in creating an oral reading response in the form of a presentation or debate. Ultimately, reading response increases a student's capacity to understand what he or she has read and to analyze personal responses to the text.

51. B: Reading fluency combines accuracy, speed, and inflection while reading aloud. As children are learning to read, they work on all of these skills simultaneously with writing, thinking, viewing, listening, and comprehension. By using daily games or specific lessons, a teacher can directly affect students' ability to read the individual sounds in words (phonemes). As students identify more sounds correctly, they will read more accurately. Practicing reading aloud can increase fluency, but only if the child's reading partner is able to correct and encourage him or her to read more accurately. By reading aloud to the students, a teacher models correct speed and inflection, but this will affect the students' skills less directly than lessons and games in phonetics.

52. A: In order to achieve a balanced language program, a teacher must spend time on many different skills that have been mentioned in previous questions and answers. Language skills cannot be reduced to the process of reading (fluency plus comprehension). Students develop their language skills over a long period of time, and they do so across multiple domains. Students' ability to listen and speak, write, view, respond, synthesize information, and read for a variety of purposes all must be included in daily instruction. By practicing only fluency and comprehension, students will not fully understand the various functions of language skills and may even lack an appreciation for them.

53. C: There is currently a wide variety of technology resources available that can support class instruction. However, teachers must choose carefully in order to ensure that the technology is useful and relevant to his or her intended learning outcomes for the class. The language lab described allows students to experience text through listening *and* reading, thereby utilizing different processes in the brain. The interactive modules also support decoding and comprehension skills that go along with the texts. This use of technology reinforces important skills in a way that will be unique and interesting for the students.

54. B: In this project, students will engage in almost every aspect of literacy in a group context. Students must first accurately read and comprehend a short play; they will also use their writing skills to adapt the play to their specific purposes by cutting or adding text. The teacher can gauge the students' interpretive skills by the way they perform their play. By splitting the students into groups, the teacher can provide each student the chance to interpret and perform, as well as to experience the performances. Audience members receive additional practice with listening and

interpreting when they generate responses to the performances. Group members can evaluate the effectiveness of their performances based on responses from the audience.

55. B: The intention of Round-robin reading is to provide practice reading aloud with appropriate fluency. This practice is also used to cover a large quantity of text with the entire class during the class period. By pairing the students, each child will get more practice reading aloud. He or she will also be more likely to stay engaged when working with only one partner, as there will be less time and fewer opportunities to become distracted. The teacher can then circulate amongst the groups to encourage focus and concentration, as well as provide guidance on fluency and comprehension of the text. As long as the students are paired carefully, this strategy is most likely preferable to the Round-robin method.

56. B: Integrated curriculum is vital to student growth and to fostering a love of learning. In reality, all subject areas are related, and a good teacher will find ways to highlight the connection of concepts across the curriculum. In choice B, the science teacher provides a way to help students study for a test. However, she would probably be better advised to work with the students on comprehension and retention before test time arrives. She could use a variety of previewing and reviewing skills, as well as creative ways to bring the information to life during class discussions and activities. This teacher might also benefit from discussing the situation with a language arts teacher to get ideas on how to build skills in reading for information, main ideas, and supporting concepts.

57. C: All private and public schools will provide some sort of curriculum guidance, which usually takes the form of a list of concepts that must be covered within a certain time frame. Teachers must use this provision as a guideline for planning instruction. However, with time and creativity, teachers can bring these concepts to life using various types of material (oral, written, media, performance) and engaging instructional methods. Teachers can also find ways to integrate instruction and concepts with teachers of other subjects to ensure that students understand that language skills are not only interrelated, but also applicable to all areas of learning.

58. C: Literacy skills are various and include a number of different sub-skills: reading fluency, comprehension, application of knowledge, listening, speaking, grammar, spelling, writing, and more. It is important for teachers to track student development for lesson design and to communicate with the student, future teachers, and parents. Therefore, it is best to keep samples of a variety of assessments, including descriptions of reading fluency, writing samples, projects, and formal assessments of grammar, spelling, and other skills. All of these skills develop simultaneously, but at different rates. Therefore, it is impossible to judge a student's literacy based only on one measure of assessment.

59. B: Amelia exhibits some very specific symptoms in this vignette She has trouble decoding sounds in words, cannot follow verbal directions or instructions, and displays both avoidance behaviors and oppositional behavior during difficult language tasks. All of these symptoms are characteristic of auditory processing problems in which a student cannot accurately and consistently understand written or verbally-presented information. Amelia's symptoms may also suggest that she could have dyslexia, a reading disorder that affects the student's ability to read, write, do mathematics, or process information accurately. An educational specialist should be capable of pinpointing the causes of Amelia's difficulty.

60. A: Most traditional methods teach reading via aural and visual techniques. However, students with auditory processing problems or dyslexia will not learn to read effectively with these methods,

no matter how much practice is provided. Therefore, most students with this type of difficulty will benefit from a multi-sensory technique in which they can make use of all their senses. Combined with systematic instruction and a great deal of practice, the multi-sensory technique is very effective in building reading and processing skills in students with this kind of life-long learning difference.

61. B: The teacher used an informal reading inventory to gain insight into the students' abilities in a larger group setting. While some informal reading inventories, or IRI's, are administered between one teacher and one student, these inventories usually work best in a group setting. The benefit of this type of assessment is that it provides insight within the context of an entire class or large group in a short period of time. This assessment does not provide specific or generalized information about the students' progress, but rather allows the teacher to gauge her students' needs at any given point during instruction.

62. A: The words in this question prompt are most often used to refer to *sounds* made while reading. Initial/onset, medial, and final sounds are decoded in the beginning, middle, and end of words. When a teacher needs to assess an emergent or struggling reader's ability to differentiate between sounds in words, he or she may use a phonological awareness assessment. This tool will provide the teacher with information about the student's current ability to decode or encode words.

63. B: Scaffolding refers to any kind of special instruction designed to help students learn a new or challenging concept. There are countless forms of scaffolding techniques. The three techniques mentioned in the question prompt are all used to facilitate student understanding of a given text or a concept taught within the text. Scaffolding should not be confused with modeling strategies, which refer to the process of demonstrating how something should be done before a student tries it on his or her own.

64. C: The question prompt states that Ms. Baird wants to make sure her students understand certain concepts on an individual basis, rather than as a group. Choice C describes a scenario in which the students support each other in creating a foundation for the activity. They help each other and are scaffolded by their teacher in determining the main ideas. However, Ms. Baird utilizes the practice of silent reading to ensure that students are practicing the skill of finding supporting evidence on an individual level. She will be able to gauge each student's comprehension levels by checking their notecards after the lesson.

65. C: In the previous question, the best method of teaching was to incorporate group brainstorming as a model of analyzing text, followed by practice supporting the main ideas with evidence from the text. Once the students' notecards have been checked and edited for accuracy, they can easily be used to demonstrate the process of organizing ideas in an essay or research paper. Students can use their notecards as aids for making their outlines. They simply have to arrange the notecards in an appropriate order and add pertinent information to bridge the ideas together in their writing.

66. B: Previewing and reviewing are skills that assist in learning detailed or large amounts of information. Using these concepts, students learn skills such as skimming and outlining to get an idea of what the text is about before actually reading it. After reading, the students learn to review the information they learned and compare it to their initial previews. This method is particularly helpful when individuals are reading in order to learn new information, as they would be when reading their science texts.

67. C: Oral language is a vital aspect of any language arts instruction. Often, the first concepts of language are transmitted via oral and auditory processes. The first Americans also possessed a rich oral culture in which stories and histories were passed down through generations via storytelling. Inviting a guest speaker who is part of this culture helps students understand more about cultures in their world, as well as the value of oral language and storytelling. This introduction gives students a relevant personal experience with which to connect what they will be learning in class.

68. A: "Conceptual vocabulary" terms are related in meaning and often have complex meanings. For instance, the term "community" may refer simply to a group of people living in close proximity to one another. However, there are many ideas that can be associated with this concept: neighbors, helping, spending time with one another, roles within a community, and so on. Word webs can be used to show a central term and its related concepts, demonstrating the relationship between words based on meaning. Using this type of graphic organizer provides a tangible way to show students that some words have complex meanings and are interconnected with other aspects of language.

69. B: Spelling is often taught in a systematic way. Students receive words and memorize them for quizzes and tests. However, spelling is related to many aspects of language and must be treated as a dynamic subject. Integrating the words into other parts of language instruction will help students not only learn how to spell correctly, but also to recall meanings of words and various rules of English spelling and grammar. By using the same words in different subjects, the students will retain the information more readily than if they study the words intensely for one week in only one context.

70. C: One half of the class receives signs showing vocabulary words, which are probably used as root words. Remaining students are split into two general groups: those with prefixes on their signs and those with suffixes. The best approach is to get the students moving, listening, and talking in order to solidify their understanding of how roots, suffixes, and prefixes work together to make new meanings out of various root words. This approach also allows the students to participate in a game in a group context, making the activity more fun and engaging.

71. A: Based on the vignette, it is not possible to say exactly what words are listed on the ten children's signs, since the words are called "vocabulary." However, the second group obviously holds signs that are prefixes, or a group of letters added to the beginning of a root word in order to change its meaning. The final group possesses suffixes, which are used at the end of root words to change their meanings. Therefore, the students using vocabulary words must hold the root words, since prefixes and suffixes do not possess relevant meaning unless paired with a root.

72. A: A phoneme is a unit of language that represents the smallest unit of sound. For instance, the *k* in "kit" or the *ph* in "graph" both represent English phonemes. Graphemes are written phonemes and can be alphabetic letters, numbers, characters, punctuation marks, and so on. Neither phonemes nor graphemes have semantic meaning unless they are used as part of a larger unit of language, such as the morpheme. Morphemes can be roots, prefixes and suffixes. The word "rechargeable" is comprised of three morphemes: "re," "charge," and "able." Each component of this word has a meaning unto itself, but when combined with the others, each one is used to make a new word with a new meaning.

73. B: When adults or other skilled readers take time to read aloud to students, they can model (or demonstrate) what it means to read fluently. Students are still learning about grammar, spelling, decoding, comprehending, speaking, and listening. Therefore, it can be difficult for them to read

aloud consistently with appropriate speed, accuracy, and inflection since there are multiple cognitive processes taking place in the student's brain. By listening to an experienced reader, students will better understand how fluent reading is intended to sound and how fluency can affect comprehension in reading or listening.

74. B: The term "blend" is commonly used to refer to a grapheme consisting of two sounds, such as the /fl/ in *flip*. In this word, the /f/ and /l/ sounds are distinctly audible. However, the words from the question prompt contain phoneme combinations in which a completely new sound is formed. The /ch/ sound is similar to neither the /c/ nor /h/. This type of combination is called a "digraph," which is a kind of blended sound.

75. A: It is true that many students report grammar instruction as being "boring" or even irrelevant. However, knowledge of correct grammar can improve students' reading fluency, comprehension, writing, speaking, and other language skills. Therefore, it is important to help students understand the importance of learning grammatical rules and how they can be applied in various contexts. All language skills are interrelated and cannot be taught separately from one another, since they evolve simultaneously. A skilled teacher will make grammar interesting by conveying its importance and finding innovative ways to incorporate fun activities into instruction.

Mathematics

1. B: In choice A, the teacher surveys all the members of the population in which he is interested. However, since the response is voluntary, the survey is biased: the participants are self-selected rather than randomly selected. It may be that students who have a strong opinion are more likely to respond than those who are more neutral, and this would give the teacher a skewed perspective of student opinions. In choice B, students are randomly selected, so the sampling technique is not biased. In choice C, the student uses convenience sampling, which is a biased technique. For example, perhaps the student is in an honors class; his sampling method would not be representative of the entire class of eleventh graders, which includes both students who take and who do not take honors classes. Choice D also represents convenience sampling; only the opinions of parents in the PTA are examined, and these parents' opinions may not reflect the opinions of all parents of students at the school.

2. A: Nominal data are data that are collected which have no intrinsic quantity or order. For instance, a survey might ask the respondent to identify his or her gender. While it is possible to compare the relative frequency of each response (for example, "most of the respondents are women"), it is not possible to calculate the mean, which requires data to be numeric, or median, which requires data to be ordered. Interval data are both numeric and ordered, so mean and median can be determined, as can the mode, the interval within which there are the most data. Ordinal data has an inherent order, but there is not a set interval between two points. For example, a survey might ask whether the respondent whether he or she was very dissatisfied, dissatisfied, neutral, satisfied, or very satisfied with the customer service received. Since the data are not numeric, the mean cannot be calculated, but since ordering the data is possible, the median has context.

3. A: The average number of male students in the 11th and 12th grades is 134 males. The number of Hispanic students at the school is 10% of 1219, which is 122 students. The difference in the number of male and female students at the school is $630 - 589 = 41$, and the difference in the number of 9th and 12th grade students at the school is $354 - 255 = 99$.

4. C: 52% of the student population is white. There are 630 female students at the school out of 1219 students, so the percentage of female students is $\frac{630}{1219} \cdot 100\% \approx 52\%$. The percentages rounded to the nearest whole number are the same.

5. D: 131 of 283 eleventh graders are male. Given that an 11th grader is chosen to attend the conference, the probability that a male is chosen is $\frac{\text{number of males}}{\text{number of 11th graders}} = \frac{131}{283} \approx 0.46$. Note that this is **NOT** the same question as one which asks for the probability of selecting at random from the school a male student who is in eleventh grade, which has a probability of $\frac{131}{1219} \approx 0.11$.

6. A: The range is the spread of the data. It can be calculated for each class by subtracting the lowest test score from the highest, or it can be determined visually from the graph. The difference between the highest and lowest test scores in class A is 98-23=75 points. The range for each of the other classes is much smaller.

7. D: 75% of the data in a set is above the first quartile. Since the first quartile for this set is 73, there is a 75% chance that a student chosen at random from class 2 scored above a 73.

8. C: The line through the center of the box represents the median. The median test score for classes 1 and 2 is 82.

Note that for class 1, the median is a better representation of the data than the mean. There are two outliers (points which lie outside of two standard deviations from the mean) which bring down the average test score. In cases such as this, the mean is not the best measure of central tendency.

9. D:

Time on market	Frequency for Zip Code 1	Frequency for Zip Code 2	Time·Frequency for Zip Code 1	Time·Frequency for Zip Code 1
1	9	6	9	6
2	10	4	20	8
3	12	3	36	9
4	8	4	32	16
5	6	3	30	15
6	5	5	30	30
7	8	2	56	14
8	8	1	64	8
9	6	3	54	27
10	3	5	30	50
11	5	7	55	77
12	4	6	48	72
13	2	6	26	78
14	3	5	42	70
15	1	3	15	45
16	2	2	32	32
17	2	3	34	51
18	1	5	18	90
19	0	6	0	114
20	2	4	40	80
21	1	5	21	105
22	1	4	22	88
23	0	3	0	69
24	1	5	24	120
SUM	100	100	738	1274

Since there are 100 homes' market times represented in each set, the median time a home spends on the market is between the 50th and 51st data point in each set. The 50th and 51st data points for Zip Code 1 are six months and seven months, respectively, so the median time a house in Zip Code 1 spends on the market is between six and seven months (6.5 months), which by the realtor's definition of market time is a seven month market time. The 50th and 51st data points for Zip Code 2 are both thirteen months, so the median time a house in Zip Code 2 spends on the market is thirteen months.

To find the mean market time for 100 houses, find the sum of the market times and divide by 100. If the frequency of a one month market time is 9, the number 1 is added nine times (1·9), if frequency of a two month market time is 10, the number 2 is added ten times (2·10), and so on. So, to find the average market time, divide by 100 the sum of the products of each market time and its corresponding frequency. For Zip Code 1, the mean market time is 7.38 months, which by the realtor's definition of market time is an eight month market time. For Zip Code 2, the mean market time is 12.74, which by the realtor's definition of market time is a thirteen month market time.

The mode market time is the market time for which the frequency is the highest. For Zip Code 1, the mode market time is three months, and for Zip Code 2, the mode market time is eleven months.

The statement given in choice D is true. The median time a house spends on the market in Zip Code 1 is less than the mean time a house spends on the market in Zip Code 1.

10. C: The probability of an event is the number of possible occurrences of that event divided by the number of all possible outcomes. A camper who is at least eight years old can be eight, nine, or ten years old, so the probability of randomly selecting a camper at least eight years old is $\frac{\text{number of eight-, nine-, and ten-year old campers}}{\text{total number of campers}} = \frac{14+12+10}{12+15+14+12+10} = \frac{36}{63} = \frac{4}{7}$.

11. B:

	Department 1	Department 2	Department 3	Total
Women	12	28	16	56
Men	18	14	15	47
Total	30	42	31	103

There are three ways in which two women from the same department can be selected: two women can be selected from the first department, or two women can be selected from the second department, or two women can be selected from the third department. The probability that two women are selected from Department 1 is $\frac{12}{103} \cdot \frac{11}{102} = \frac{132}{10506}$, the probability that two women are selected from Department 2 is $\frac{28}{103} \cdot \frac{27}{102} = \frac{756}{10506}$, and the probability that two women are selected from Department 3 is $\frac{16}{103} \cdot \frac{15}{102} = \frac{240}{10506}$. Since any of these is a discrete possible outcome, the probability that two women will be selected from the same department is the sum of these outcomes: $\frac{132}{10506} + \frac{756}{10506} + \frac{240}{10506} \approx 0.107$, or 10.7%.

12. B: The number of students who like broccoli is equal to the number of students who like all three vegetables plus the number of students who like broccoli and carrots but not cauliflower plus the number of students who like broccoli and cauliflower but not carrots plus the number of students who like broccoli but no other vegetable: $3 + 15 + 4 + 10 = 32$. These students plus the numbers of students who like just cauliflower, just carrots, cauliflower and carrots, or none of the vegetables represents the entire set of students sampled: $32 + 2 + 27 + 6 + 23 = 90$. So, the probability that a randomly chosen student likes broccoli is $\frac{32}{90} \approx 0.356$.

The number of students who like carrots and at least one other vegetable is $15 + 6 + 3 = 24$. The number of students who like carrots is $24 + 27 = 51$. So, the probability that a student who likes carrots will also like at least one other vegetable is $\frac{24}{51} \approx 0.471$.

The number of students who like cauliflower and broccoli is $4 + 3 = 7$. The number of students who like all three vegetables is 3. So, the probability that a student who likes cauliflower and broccoli will also like carrots is $\frac{3}{7} \approx 0.429$.

The number of students who do not like carrots, broccoli, or cauliflower is 23. The total number of students surveyed is 90. So, the probability that a student does not like any of the three vegetables is $23/90 \approx 0.256$.

13. C: Since each coin toss is an independent event, the probability of the compound event of flipping the coin three times is equal to the product of the probabilities of the individual events. For example, $P(HHH) = P(H) \cdot P(H) \cdot P(H)$, $P(HHT) = P(H) \cdot P(H) \cdot P(T)$, etc. When a coin is flipped three times, all of the possible outcomes are HHH, HHT, HTH, HTT, THH, THT, TTH, and TTT. Since the only way to obtain three heads is by the coin landing on heads three times,

$$P(three\ heads) = P(HHH) = P(H) \cdot P(H) \cdot P(H).$$

Likewise,

$$P(no\ heads) = P(T) \cdot P(T) \cdot P(T).$$

Since there are three ways to get one head,
$$P(one\ head) = P(HTT) + P(THT) + P(TTH) = P(H)P(T)P(T) + P(T)P(H)P(T) + P(T)P(T)P(H)$$
$$= P(H)[(3P(T)^2],$$

And since there are three ways to get two heads,
$$P(two\ heads) = P(HHT) + P(HTH) + P(THH)$$
$$= P(H)P(H)P(T) + P(H)P(T)P(H) + P(T)P(H)P(H) = P(H)^2[3P(T)]$$

Use these properties to calculate the experimental probability P(H):
30 out of 100 coin tosses resulted in three heads, and $P(three\ heads) = P(H) \cdot P(H) \cdot P(H) = P(H)^3$. So, experimental P(H) can be calculated by taking the cube root of $\frac{30}{100}$. $\sqrt[3]{0.3} \approx 0.67$.

Similarly, $P(no\ heads) = P(T) \cdot P(T) \cdot P(T) = \frac{4}{100}$. $P(T) = \sqrt[3]{0.04} \approx 0.34$. $P(H) + P(T) = 1$, $P(T) = 1 - P(H)$. Thus, $P(H) = 1 - P(T) \approx 0.66$.

Notice that these calculated values of P(H) re approximately the same, Since 100 is a fairly large sample size for this kind of experiment, the approximation for $P(H)$ ought to consistent for the compiled data set. Rather than calculating $P(H)$ using the data for one head and two heads, use the average calculated probability to confirm that the number of expected outcomes of one head and two head matches the number of actual outcomes.

The number of expected outcomes of getting one head in three coin flips out of 100 trials $100\{0.665[3(1 - 0.665)^2]\} \approx 22$, and the expected outcome getting of two heads in three coin flips out of 100 trials three flips is $100\{0.665^2[3(1 - 0.665)]\} \approx 44$. Since 22 and 44 are, in fact, the data obtained, 0.665 is indeed a good approximation for P(H) when the coin used in this experiment is tossed.

14. C: A fair coin has a symmetrical binomial distribution which peaks in its center. Since choice B shows a skewed distribution for the fair coin, it cannot be the correct answer. From the frequency histogram given for the misshapen coin, it is evident that the misshapen coin is more likely to land

on heads. Therefore, it is more likely that ten coin flips would result in fewer tails than ten coin flips of a fair coin; consequently, the probability distribution for the misshapen would be skewed to the left with respect to the fair coin's distribution it is less likely to land on tails. Choice A shows a probability distribution which peaks at a value of 5 and which is symmetrical with respect to the peak, which verifies that it cannot be correct. (Furthermore, in choice A, the sum of the probabilities shown for each number of tails for the misshapen coin is not equal to 1.) The graph shown in choice D is skewed toward the right and must therefore also be incorrect. Choice C shows the correct binomial distribution for the fair coin and the appropriate shift for the misshapen coin.

Another way to approach this question is to use the answer from the previous problem to determine the probability of obtaining particular events, such as no tails and no heads, and then compare those probabilities to the graphs. For example, for the misshapen coin, P(0 tails)=P(10 heads) $\approx (0.67)^{10}$, or 0.018, and the P(10 tails) $\approx (0.33)^{10}$, which is 0.000015. For a fair coin, P(0 tails)=$(0.5)^{10}$=P(0 heads). To find values other than these, it is helpful to use the binomial distribution formula $(_nC_r)p^r q^{n-r}$, where n is the number of trials, r is the number of successes, p is the probability of success, and q is the probability of failure. For this problem, obtaining tails is a success, and the probability of obtaining tails is $p = 0.33$ for the misshapen coin and $p = 0.5$ for the fair coin; so, $q = 0.67$ for the misshapen coin and $q = 0.5$ for the fair coin. To find the probability of, say, getting three tails for ten flips of the misshapen coin, find
$(_nC_r)p^r q^{n-r}=(_{10}C_3)(0.33)^3(0.67)^7=\frac{10!}{3!7!}(0.33)^3(0.67)^7 \approx 0.261$. The calculated probabilities match those shown in choice C.

15. C: When rolling two dice, there is only one way to roll a sum of two (rolling a 1 on each die) and twelve (rolling 6 on each die). In contrast, there are two ways to obtain a sum of three (rolling a 2 and 1 or a 1 and 2) and eleven (rolling a 5 and 6 or a 6 and 5), three ways to obtain a sum of four (1 and 3; 2 and 2; 3 and 1) or ten (4 and 6; 5 and 5; 6 and 4), and so on. Since the probability of obtaining each sum is inconsistent, choice C is not an appropriate simulation. Choice A is acceptable since the probability of picking A, 1, 2, 3, 4, 5, 6, 7, 8, 9, or J from the modified deck cards of cards is equally likely, each with a probability of $\frac{4}{52-8} = \frac{4}{44} = \frac{1}{11}$. Choice B is also acceptable since the computer randomly generates one number from eleven possible numbers, so the probability of generating any of the numbers is $\frac{1}{11}$.

16. B: If each of the four groups in the class of twenty will contain three boys and two girls, there must be twelve boys and eight girls in the class. The number of ways the teacher can select three boys from a group of twelve boys is $_{12}C_3 = \frac{12!}{3!(12-3)!} = \frac{12!}{3!9!} = \frac{12\cdot11\cdot10\cdot9!}{3!9!} = \frac{12\cdot11\cdot10}{3\cdot2\cdot1} =220$. The number of ways she can select two girls from a group of eight girls is $_8C_2 = \frac{8!}{2!(8-2)!} = \frac{8!}{2!6!} = \frac{8\cdot7\cdot6!}{2!6!} = \frac{8\cdot7}{2\cdot1} =28$. Since each combination of boys can be paired with each combination of girls, the number of group combinations is $220 \cdot 28 = 6,160$.

17. B: One way to approach this problem is to first consider the number of arrangements of the five members of the family if Tasha (T) and Mac (M) must sit together. Treat them as a unit seated in a fixed location at the table; then arrange the other three family members (A, B, and C):

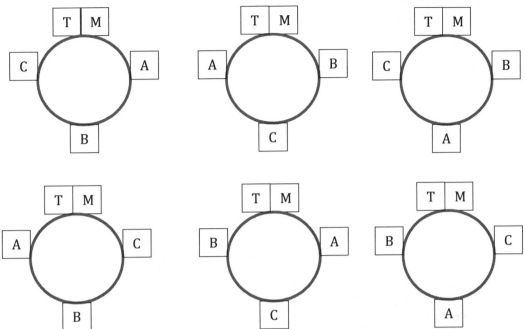

There are six ways to arrange four units around a circle as shown. (Any other arrangement would be a rotation in which the elements in the same order and would therefore not be a unique arrangement.) Note that there are $(n-1)!$ ways to arrange n units around a circle for $n > 1$.

Of course, Mac and Tasha are not actually a single unit. They would still be sitting beside each other if they were to trade seats, so there are twelve arrangements in which the two are seated next to one another. In all other arrangements of the five family members, they are separated. Therefore, to find the number of arrangements in which Tasha and Mac are not sitting together, subtract twelve from the possible arrangement of five units around a circle: $(5-1)! - 12 = 12$.

18. A: The recursive definition of the sequence gives the first term of the series, $a_1 = -1$. The definition also defines each term in the series as the sum of the previous term and 2. Therefore, the second term in the series is $-1 + 2 = 1$, the third term in the series is $1 + 2 = 3$, and so on.

n	a_n
1	-1
2	1
3	3

The relationship between n and a_n is linear, so the equation of the sequence can be found in the same way as the equation of a line. The value of a_n increases by two each time the value of n increases by 1.

n	$2n$	a_n
1	2	-1
2	4	1
3	6	3

Since the difference in $2n$ and a_n is 3, $a_n = 2n - 3$.

n	$2n - 3$	a_n
1	2-3	-1
2	4-3	1
3	6-3	3

19. B: The series is an infinite geometric series, the sum of which can be found by using the formula $\sum_{n=0}^{\infty} ar^n = \frac{a}{1-r}, |r| < 1$, where a is the first term in the series and r is the ratio between successive terms. In the series 200+100+50+25+ ..., $a = 200$ and $r = \frac{1}{2}$. So, the sum of the series is $\frac{200}{1-\frac{1}{2}} = \frac{200}{\frac{1}{2}} = 400$.

20. D: The percent increase is represented as $\frac{1100-800}{800}$, which equals 0.375 or 37.5%.

21. D: The original cost may be represented by the equation $45 = x - 0.25x$ or $45 = 0.75x$. Dividing both sides of the equation by 0.75 gives $x = 60$.

22. A: If a number is divisible by 2 and 3, it is also divisible by the lowest common multiple of these two factors. The lowest common multiple of 2 and 3 is their product, 6.

23. B: The decimal expansion of an irrational number does not terminate or repeat. The decimal expansion of $\sqrt{2}$ does not terminate or repeat.

24. C: The original price may be represented by the equation $24{,}210 = x - 0.10x$ or $24{,}210 = 0.9x$. Dividing both sides of the equation by 0.9 gives $x = 26{,}900$.

25. C: His monthly salary may be modeled as $\frac{1}{8}x = 320$. Multiplying both sides of the equation by 8 gives $x = 2{,}560$.

26. C: The amount he donates is equal to $0.01(45{,}000)$. Thus, he donates $450.

27. C. The original price may be modeled by the equation, $(x - 0.45x) + 0.0875(x - 0.45x) = 39.95$, which simplifies to $0.598125x = 39.95$. Dividing each side of the equation by the coefficient of x gives $x \approx 66.79$.

28. C: There are 36 months in 3 years. The following proportion may be written: $\frac{450}{3} = \frac{x}{36}$. The equation $3x = 16200$, may be solved for x. Dividing both sides of the equation by 3 gives $x = 5{,}400$.

29. A: The sum of 3 and the product of each term number and 5 equals the term value. For example, for term number 4, the value of 23 is equal to $5(4) + 3$, or 23.

30. D: The constant of proportionality is equal to the slope. Using the points, $(2, -8)$ and $(5, -20)$, the slope may be written as $\frac{-20-(-8)}{5-2}$, which equals -4.

31. C: An inverse proportional relationship is written in the form $y = \frac{k}{x}$, thus the equation $y = \frac{3}{x}$ shows that y is inversely proportional to x.

32. D: The expression $(x - 2)^2$ may be expanded as $x^2 - 4x + 4$. Multiplication of $-3x$ by this expression gives $-3x^3 + 12x^2 - 12x$.

33. B: Each of the graphs shows the correct y-intercept of -6, but only graph B shows the correct slope. Using the points $(0, -6)$ and $(-2, 2)$, the slope of graph B may be written as $m = \frac{2-(-6)}{-2-0}$, which simplifies to $m = -4$.

34. C: The slope is equal to 4, since each ticket costs $4. The y-intercept is represented by the constant fee of $30. Substituting 4 for m and 30 for b into the equation $y = mx + b$ gives $y = 4x + 30$.

35. D: The table represents a geometric sequence, with a common ratio of 2. Geometric sequences are modeled by exponential functions.

36. C: Using the points $(-3, 1)$ and $(1, -11)$, the slope may be written as $m = \frac{-11-1}{1-(-3)}$ or $m = -3$. Substituting the slope of -3 and the x- and y-values from the point $(-3, 1)$, into the slope-intercept form of an equation gives $1 = -3(-3) + b$, which simplifies to $1 = 9 + b$. Subtracting 9 from both sides of the equation gives $b = -8$. Thus, the linear equation that includes the data in the table is $y = -3x - 8$.

37. D: This situation may be modeled by an arithmetic sequence, with a common difference of 4 and initial value of 3. Substituting the common difference and initial value into the formula, $a_n = a_1 + (n - 1)d$, gives $a_n = 3 + (n - 1)4$, which simplifies to $a_n = 4n - 1$.

38. C: The situation may be modeled by the system $\begin{array}{c} 4x + 3y = 9.55 \\ 2x + 2y = 5.90 \end{array}$. Multiplying the bottom equation by -2 gives $\begin{array}{c} 4x + 3y = 9.55 \\ -4x - 4y = -11.80 \end{array}$. Addition of the two equations gives $-y = -2.25$ or $y = 2.25$. Thus, one box of crackers costs $2.25.

39. B: The sequence $\frac{1}{5}, \frac{1}{25}, \frac{1}{125}, \frac{1}{625}, \ldots$, may be used to represent the situation. Substituting the initial value of $\frac{1}{5}$ and common ratio of $\frac{1}{5}$ into the formula $S = \frac{a}{1-r}$ gives $= \frac{\frac{1}{5}}{1-\frac{1}{5}}$, which simplifies to $S = \frac{\frac{1}{5}}{\frac{4}{5}}$ or $S = \frac{1}{4}$.

40. A: The inequality will be less than or equal to, since he may spend $100 or less on his purchase.

41. D: Since she spends at least $16, the relation of the number of packages of coffee to the minimum cost may be written as $4p \geq 16$. Alternatively, the inequality may be written as $16 \leq 4p$.

42. C: The surface area of a rectangular prism may be calculated using the formula $SA = 2lw + 2wh + 2hl$. Substituting the dimensions of 14 inches, 6 inches, and 8 inches gives $SA = 2(14)(6) + 2(6)(8) + 2(8)(14)$. Thus, the surface area is 488 square inches.

43. C: The volume of a pyramid may be calculated using the formula $V = \frac{1}{3}Bh$, where B represents the area of the base and h represents the height. Since the base is a square, the area of the base is equal to 6^2, or 36 square inches. Substituting 36 for B and 9 for h gives $V = \frac{1}{3}(36)(9)$, which simplifies to $V = 108$.

44. C: The surface area of a sphere may be calculated using the formula $SA = 4\pi r^2$. Substituting 9 for r gives $SA = 4\pi(9)^2$, which simplifies to $SA \approx 1017.36$. So the surface area of the ball is approximately 1017.36 square inches. There are twelve inches in a foot, so there are $12^2 = 144$ square inches in a square foot. In order to convert this measurement to square feet, then, the following proportion may be written and solved for x: $\frac{1}{144} = \frac{x}{1017.36}$. So $x \approx 7.07$. He needs approximately 7.07 square feet of wrapping paper.

45. B: The following proportion may be written and solved for x: $\frac{15}{5} = \frac{6}{x}$. Solving for x gives $x = 2$. Thus, the shadow cast by the man is 2 feet in length.

46. D: The cross-section of a cylinder will never be a triangle.

47. A: The net of a triangular prism has three rectangular faces and two triangular faces. This is true of both A and C, but net C cannot be folded into a triangular prism, because the two rectangular faces on the end cannot be made to join each other. So only A can be folded into a triangular prism.

48. C: The original triangle was reflected across the x-axis. When reflecting across the x-axis, the x-values of each point remain the same, but the y-values of the points will be opposites. $(1, 4) \rightarrow (1, -4), (5, 4) \rightarrow (5, -4), (3, 8) \rightarrow (3, -8)$.

Social Studies

1. A: Checks and balances were established to keep one branch of government from taking too much authority. When Johnson violated the Tenure of Office Act by replacing Secretary of War Edwin Stanton, Johnson was impeached, but the final vote in the Senate trial came up one vote short of the number needed to convict him.

2. A: The citizens usually elect members of the local government such as mayors and city council. However, the state grants local governments their authority. State and local governments work independently and do not share authority the way the federal and state governments share power.

3. B: The House has strict rules that limit debate. A filibuster can only occur in the Senate where Senators can speak on topics other than the bill at hand and introduce amendments. A filibuster can be ended by a supermajority vote of 60 Senators.

4. C: The Government Accountability Office was originally called the General Accounting Office and was established in 1921 to audit the budget, Congress, and the Director of the Treasury. The Government Accountability Office now oversees the effectiveness of government spending in every branch.

5. C: The Civil Rights Act of 1964 affected the Jim Crowe laws in the Southern states. Many minorities suffered under unfair voting laws and segregation. President Lyndon Johnson signed the Civil Rights Act of 1964 into law after the 1963 assassination of President Kennedy, who championed the reform.

6. C: Tennessee was the only Southern state to ratify the 14th Amendment. Although Southern states that ratified this amendment could be readmitted to the Union with more reform, President Andrew Johnson, who was at odds with Congress, advised them against it.

7. C: The 17th Amendment was ratified in 1913. This amendment allowed the citizens to choose their Senators by holding elections and participating in a popular vote.

8. B: The appellant presents arguments in a brief that explains to the three judges on the panel why the trial court was wrong. The respondent explains why the trial court made the right decision. The appeals court usually makes the final decision, unless they send it back to trial.

9. A: A writ of certiorari is filed if a case is lost in appeals or the highest state court. The writ of certiorari is a request for the Supreme Court to hear the case, but it does not guarantee the case will be heard.

10. C: Nebraska does not require voter registration, but all other states do and have their own process. State and local officials administer federal elections, and though each state has its own method for holding elections, federal elections are always held at the same time.

11. B: Money given directly to a party candidate is hard money. The Federal Election Commission monitors hard money because of limitations on the amount and the money's source.

12. A: Presidential candidates are eligible for a match from the federal government (with a $250 per contribution limit) if they can privately raise $5,000 per state in twenty states. Candidates who

accept public money agree to limit spending. Candidates who do not accept matching funds are free to use the money they raise privately.

13. D: America is a common law country because English common law was adopted in all states except Louisiana. Common law is based on precedent, and changes over time. Each state develops its own common laws.

14. B: All states have bicameral legislatures, except Nebraska. The bicameral legislatures in states resemble the federal legislature, with an upper house and a lower house.

15. C: A caucus is a private event run by political parties, and a primary is an indirect election run by state and local governments. Voters may award delegates to candidates for the national conventions, depending on state laws.

16. A: The President has the authority to negotiate and sign treaties. A two-thirds vote of the Senate, however, is needed to ratify a treaty for it to be upheld.

17. B: There are four intermediate directions. They are northwest, northeast, southwest, and southeast. The intermediate directions are midway between each set of adjacent cardinal directions. The cardinal directions are north, south, east, and west. On a compass rose, the cardinal directions are typically indicated by large points, while the intermediate directions are represented by smaller points.

18. A: The eye wall of a hurricane has the strongest winds and the greatest rainfall. The eye wall is the tower-like rim of the eye. It is from this wall that clouds extend out, which are seen from above as the classic outward spiral pattern. A hurricane front is the outermost edge of its influence; although there will be heavy winds and rain in this area, the intensity will be relatively small. The eye of a hurricane is actually a place of surprising peace. In this area, dry and cool air rushes down to the ground or sea. Once there, the air is caught up in the winds of the eye wall and is driven outward at a furious pace.

19. D: A flow-line map describes the movement of people, trends, or materials across a physical area. The movements depicted on a flow-line map are typically represented by arrows. In more advanced flow-line maps, the width of the arrow corresponds to the quantity of the motion. Flow-line maps usually declare the span of time that is being represented. A political map depicts the man-made aspects of geography, such as borders and cities. A cartogram adjusts the size of the areas represented according to some variable. For instance, a cartogram of wheat production would depict Iowa as being much larger than Alaska. A qualitative map uses lines, dots, and other symbols to illustrate a particular point. For example, a qualitative map might be used to demonstrate the greatest expansion of the Persian Empire.

20. A: One example of the multiplier effect of large cities would be if the presence of specialized equipment for an industry attracted even more business. Large cities tend to grow even larger for a number of reasons: they have more skilled workers, they have greater concentrations of specialized equipment, and they have already-functioning markets. These factors all make it easier for a business to begin operations in a large city than elsewhere. Thus, the populations and economic productivity of large cities tend to grow quickly. Some governments have sought to mitigate this trend by clustering groups of similar industries in smaller cities.

21. C: The cycle of demographic transition is best illustrated by a line graph. Demographic transition is a phenomenon in which a region's growth rate increases rapidly, peaks, and then decreases slowly over a long time. In the early phase of a region's development, both the birth and death rates are high, which can cause the population to fluctuate. As the people of the region become settled, the growth rate calms down, and the region enters a period of rapid increase. Political maps are better at depicting borders and the locations of cities, while pie charts are better at representing proportions. Flow-line maps are good for illustrating the movement of people, goods, or trends across a physical area.

22. A: The phenomenon of "sticky prices" refers to prices that stay the same even though it seems they should change (either increasing or decreasing).

23. B: John Maynard Keynes argued that government could help revitalize a recessionary economy by increasing government spending and therefore increasing aggregate demand. This is known as demand-side economics.

24. A: The production possibilities frontier shows the different possible combinations of goods (and/or services) a society can produce. If all other factors are even, producing more of Good A leads to a decreased production of Good B. If the PPF moves outward, that means a change in the factors of production that allows the economy to produce more goods—economic growth—has occurred. Only Answer A is an example of economic growth.

25. D: A supply shock is caused when there is a dramatic increase in input prices. This causes an increase in price levels and decreases in employment and GDP. A supply shock causes the AS curve to move to the left (in).

26. D: A change in productivity, such as workers becoming more or less productive, would affect how many goods can be supplied. No change in worker productivity would cause no change in AS. Items A, B, and C would all affect input prices and therefore would all affect AS.

27. B: Published in early 1776, Common Sense condemned hereditary kingship. The pamphlet was popular in Colonial America, and even George Washington noticed its effect on the general population. Later that same year, Jefferson drafted the Declaration of Independence.

28. B: James Madison was a close friend of Thomas Jefferson and supported a stronger central government. George Mason and Robert Yates were both against expanding federal authority over the states. Benjamin Franklin was a proponent of a strong federal government, but he was from Massachusetts.

29. B: President John Adams appointed William Marbury as Justice of the Peace, but Secretary of State James Madison never delivered the commission. Marbury claimed that under the Judiciary Act of 1789, the Supreme Court could order his commission be given to him. The Supreme Court denied Marbury's petition citing that the Judiciary Act of 1789 was unconstitutional, although they believed he was entitled to his commission.

30. D: The Bill of Rights was drafted by Congress to limit the authority of the government and protect the rights of individual citizens from abuse by the federal government. It was the first document to detail the rights of private citizens.

31. B: The Supreme Court ruled that statements made in interrogation are not admissible unless the defendant is informed of the right to an attorney and waives that right. The case of Miranda v. Arizona was consolidated with Westover v. United States, Vignera v. New York, and California v. Stewart.

32. C: The President must be a natural citizen, be at least 35 years old, and have lived in the U.S. for 14 years. There is no education requirement for becoming President. Truman did not have a college education, but most Presidents have degrees.

33. B: Most Presidents have only served two terms, a precedent established by George Washington. Ulysses S. Grant and Theodore Roosevelt sought third terms; however, only Franklin D. Roosevelt served more than two terms. He served a third term and won a fourth, but died in its first year. The 22nd Amendment was passed by Congress in 1947 and ratified in 1951. It officially limited the President to two terms, and a Vice President who serves two years as President only can be elected for one term.

34. B: The Presidential Succession Act lists the Speaker of the House, President Pro Tempore of the Senate, and Secretary of State next in succession after the Vice President. However, anyone who succeeds as President must meet all of the legal qualifications.

35. A: The President of the United States serves as Commander-in-Chief, but the writers of the Constitution, who feared how authority was used by monarchs, limited the President's power in this role. The President cannot declare war or oversee military regulations, although Presidents have traditionally authorized the use of force without war being declared.

36. D: A member of the House must be at least 25 years old, a U.S. citizen for a minimum of seven years, and a resident of the state he represents. Members of the House do not necessarily need to reside in the districts they represent.

37. B: A Senator must be at least 30 years old, a U.S. citizen for a minimum of nine years, and a resident of the state he represents. Every state elects two Senators, and individual districts are represented in the House of Representatives.

38. C: The 17th Amendment was ratified in 1913. This amendment allowed the citizens to choose their Senators by holding elections and participating in a popular vote.

39. A: Anyone may write a bill, but only a member of Congress can introduce a bill. The President often suggests bills. Bills can change drastically throughout the review process.

40. B: Members of the House are elected for two-year terms. Senators serve six-year terms, but the elections are staggered so roughly one-third of the Senate is elected every two years.

41. D: The Vice President also serves as the President of the Senate. If a tie occurs in the Senate, the Vice President casts his vote to break the tie.

42. C: A bill is usually first reviewed by the appropriate subcommittee. The subcommittee can accept the bill, amend the bill, or reject the bill. If the subcommittee accepts or amends the bill, they send it to the full committee for review. Expert witnesses and testimony are all part of committee review.

43. B: The Senate Committee on Homeland Security and Government Affairs is a standing committee that oversees and reforms government operations and exercises the congressional power of government oversight.

Science

1. B: Family. Organisms that belong to the same taxonomic group of family are most alike. In biological taxonomy, the ranks in descending order are Life, Domain, Kingdom, Phylum, Class, Order, Family, Genus and Species. The ranks become more exclusive and specific as the classification descends. Phylum, class, and order, are all higher than the family group. The higher the rank, the fewer requirements it takes to be a member. Two mnemonics for taxonomy are Kings Play Cards On Fat Green Snakes or King Philip Cuts Open Five Green Snakes.

2. A: Anthophyta. Anthophyta is a division of plants that produces seeds as part of reproduction. Anthophyta are also known as the group that contains flowering plants. It is the largest and most diverse grouping of plants and includes many food, clothing and medicinal uses for humans. Grains, beans, nuts, fruits, vegetables, spices, tea, coffee, chocolate, cotton, linen and aspirin are all derived from plants from anthophyta. Lycophyta is a small group of plants including club mosses and scale trees. Sphenophyta contains about 30 species including horsetails, foxtails, or scouring rushes. Pterophyta contains non-seed plants like ferns. Lycophyta, sphenophyta, and pterophyta all use spores to reproduce sexually.

3. B: They use tube feet for locomotion and feeding. Animals belonging to the phylum Echinodermata have tube feet for locomotion and feeding. About 7,000 species are extant in this phylum, including starfish and sand dollars. Tube feet are an organ system that provides locomotion, respiration, feeding and sensory functions. Not all echinoderms have appendages. Having an exoskeleton made of chitin is characteristic of arthropods. Not all echinoderms must shed their outer layer of skin to grow.

4. C: Flowers. Flowers are the reproductive organs of a plant. Flowering plants reproduce by sexual reproduction where the gametes join to form seeds. Pollen is sperm. Pollinators help transfer the sperm to the ovule, the egg. The style is the part of the female reproduction system that transports the sperm between the stigma and the ovary, all part of the pistil. The stigma is the sticky tip of the style on which the pollen lands. Sepals are usually small leaves between or underneath the petals and are not as obvious or as large and colorful as the petals.

5. D: Carbon dioxide and water. Respiration produces carbon dioxide and water. The net equation of respiration is the reverse of the equation for photosynthesis. Respiration is a series of reactions that consume glucose and oxygen to release energy and produce carbon dioxide and water. Oxygen and glucose are the substances that are broken down in respiration.

6. D: Lower seed dispersal. Lower seed dispersal is not an advantage that angiosperms show over other types of plants. Gymnosperms, for example, have plentiful amounts of pollen, but it does not always hit its mark. Angiosperms are the most recently evolved plant division and contain at least 260,000 extant species. They are very diverse and occupy many habitats. Many other species in other plant divisions do not have true leaves. Gymnosperms have modified leaves in the form of needles. Double fertilization refers to how one sperm cell fuses with an ovule, forming the zygote. The second sperm forms into a triploid endosperm that provides energy for the embryo.

7. A: Through gills. Animals of the phylum Mollusca respire through gills. Respiration is the process of taking in oxygen and releasing carbon dioxide. Mollusks include five classes that include species as diverse as chitons, land and marine snails, and squid. This represents a diverse range of body structures. Many mollusks have a mantle that includes a cavity that is used for both breathing and excretion. Within the mantle are gills (ctenidia). Mollusks do not have tracheas. Some land snails

have reduced gills that feature a respiratory cavity but are not true lungs. Muscle contraction is not required for ventilation of the gills. Other structures, such as cilia, work to pass water over the gills.

8. B: Stomata. A stoma is the part of a plant system that responds to stimuli by releasing water via transpiration. It can also close during adverse conditions like a drought to prevent the plant from dehydration. Stomata closure can also be triggered by the presence of bacteria. Pith refers to the central, spongy part of the stem in vascular plants. Guard cells flank stomata and regulate the opening. Sepals are modified leaves that protect the flower bud before it opens.

9. D: Circulatory System – exchanges gases with the environment by delivering oxygen to the bloodstream and releasing carbon dioxide, is not paired correctly. It is the respiratory system that exchanges gases with the environment by delivering oxygen to the bloodstream and releasing carbon dioxide. The circulatory system transports nutrients, gases, hormones, and blood to and away from cells. The muscle system controls movement through three types of muscle tissue. The nervous system controls sensory responses by carrying impulses away from and toward the cell body. The digestive system breaks down food for absorption into the blood stream where it is delivered to cells for respiration.

10. C: at carrying capacity. A population that reaches maximum size and ceases to grow due to a limited availability of resources is said to be at carrying capacity. The carrying capacity of a species is influenced by many factors such as the amount of land or water available, food supply and predators. Unstable and moving towards extinction are not correct as carrying capacity does not necessarily mean it is unstable or becoming extinct. Shrinking exponentially is also incorrect as the question says it has stopped growing, not that it is reducing in size.

11. A: Tree. In the food chain of Tree -> Caterpillar -> Frog -> Snake -> Hawk -> Worm, the tree is at the trophic level with the greatest amount of energy. Trophic level refers to the position of an organism in a food chain. Energy is lost according to the laws of thermodynamics as one moves up the food chain because it is converted to heat when consumers consume. Primary producers, such as autotrophs, are organisms who are at the base and capture solar energy. Primary consumers are herbivores that feed on the producers. Secondary consumers consume primary consumers and so on. Decomposers get their energy from the consumption of dead plants and animals.

12. D: Glaciers. Glaciers and ice caps are fresh water unavailable for human use as they are frozen. The hydrologic cycle refers to all the water on planet Earth. Some water is in forms that humans do not tend to use, such as oceans (too salty and expensive to desalinate) and glaciers. Water suitable for drinking can be found as surface water and in ground water, which is obtained through wells. Rivers, Estuaries, and Aquifers are all examples of surface water that are available to humans.

13. C: Transform. Transform is not connected to the process of mountain building. Orogeny, or mountain building, occurs at the Earth's lithosphere or crust. Folding, or deformation, is a process that occurs to make mountains where two portions of the lithosphere collide. One is subducted and the other is pushed upward forming a mountain. This action produces various types of folding. Faulting can be characterized by a brittle deformation where the rock breaks abruptly (compared with folding). Faulting and fault types are associated with earthquakes and relatively rapid deformation. Convergent is a more general term used to describe plates interacting.

14. D: heat. The formation of sedimentary rock does not include heat. Of the three types of rock igneous, sedimentary and metamorphic, heat is essential to two: igneous and metamorphic. Sedimentary rocks are formed by sediments that get deposited and then compacted or cemented

together. Sedimentary rocks are classified into detrital, organic or chemical sediments. Layering is correct since sediments can be deposited or otherwise formed in layers. Cementation is also called lithification. Compaction refers to the pressure forming sedimentary rock leading to cementation.

15. C: Vinegar fizzing when poured on a rock is an example of chemical weathering. Mechanical and chemical weathering are processes that break down rocks. Mechanical weathering breaks down rocks physically, but does not change their chemical composition. Frost and abrasion are examples. Water, oxygen, carbon dioxide and living organisms can lead to the chemical weathering of rock. Vinegar is a weak acid and will undergo a chemical reaction, evidenced by fizzing, with the rock. Rain freezing on the roadway is an example of the phase change of water from a liquid to a solid and may lead to physical weathering. Ivy growing on the side of a wooden house is incorrect since the house is not a rock. A river carrying sediment downstream is an example of erosion.

16. B: Two crustal plates move apart. When two crustal plates move apart, magma welling up could result in the formation of new crust. This has been shown to be occurring on the ocean floor where places of the crust are weaker. The crust spreads apart at these trenches, pushing outward and erupting at the ridges. When two crustal plates converge, sublimation occurs as one plate runs under another pushing it up. Two crustal plates sliding past one another is an example of a transform fault, which does not create new crust. A crustal plate being pushed down into the mantle does not form new crust but perhaps recycles the old one.

17. C: Laccolith. A laccolith is formed when an intrusion of magma injected between two layers of sedimentary rock forces the overlying strata upward to create a dome-like form. Eventually, the magma cools, the sedimentary rock wears away and the formation is exposed. Sills and dikes are both examples of sheet intrusions, where magma has inserted itself into other rock. Sills are horizontal and dikes are vertical. A caldera is a crater-like feature that was formed from the collapse of a volcano after erupting.

18. A: It compares the amount of radioactive material in a rock to the amount that has decayed into another element. This best describes the process of absolute dating. Answer B is not usually done. Usually the stratigraphic layer of rock is used to date the fossils, referred to as relative dating. Answer C is incorrect as this would not lead to a correct date since the daughter elements may have a different half life than the parent material.

19. C: igneous rock. Fossils are least likely to be found in igneous rock. Igneous rock is formed by extreme heat as magma escapes through the Earth's crust and cools. The remains of plants and animals in fossil form are not usually preserved under these conditions. Sedimentary rock is where the abundance of fossils are found. Sedimentary rock is formed more slowly and is very abundant. Since soft mud and silts compress into layers, organisms can also be deposited. Metamorphic rock is rock that has undergone change by heat and pressure. This usually destroys any fossils, but occasionally fossil remains are distorted and can be found in metamorphic rock.

20. B: A footprint. A trace fossil is that which shows evidence of existence, but is not an organism itself. A trace fossil can be contrasted with a body fossil, which has been formed from an organism. Other examples of trace fossils include eggs, nests, burrows, borings and coprolites (fossilized feces). A mouse jaw and a shark tooth are examples of body fossils. A cast of a skull is a replica and neither a body nor a trace fossil.

21. C: Cold and high salinity. Ocean currents that are cold and have high salinity are the densest. Sea water with a higher salinity is denser that lower salinity sea water. The density of ocean water can

- 88 -

also affect currents. Water from denser areas will flow to areas of lower density. Denser ocean water sinks and becomes cooler. As the depth of the water increases, the pressure and density also increase.

22. D: Phase of the Moon. Ocean currents are not controlled by the phase of the moon. The phases of the moon refer to our viewpoint from Earth of the sun's illumination of the moon. Half the moon is illuminated by the sun at any given time. For example, a new moon is one we do not see because the side being lit by the sun is not facing us. The revolution of the moon around the earth affects the ocean tides, providing two highs and two lows at any given point during the day. Wind affects the surface currents of the ocean. Landmasses affect ocean currents as well. Earth's rotation affects the deep currents.

23. B: lower. The freezing point of sea water is lower than that of fresh water as sea water is denser. It is denser because it has more dissolved salts. The freezing point changes with salinity, pressure, and density, but can be as low as -2°C (28.4°F), compared with 0°C (32°F) for fresh water.

24. B: Cold water dissolves atmospheric carbon dioxide, stores it, and releases it back out to the atmosphere as needed. This describes the physical or non-biological part of the carbon cycle. The carbon and nutrient cycles of the ocean are processed in part by the deep currents, mixing, and upwelling that occurs. Carbon dioxide (CO_2) from the atmosphere is dissolved into the ocean at the higher latitudes and distributed to the denser deep water. When upwelling occurs, CO_2 is brought back to the surface and emitted into the tropical air.

25. A: The prevailing westerlies. The prevailing westerlies drive weather systems to move west to east in the mid-latitudes. The direction refers to that which the wind is coming from. The polar easterlies that travel from the northeast occur between 90-60 degrees north latitude. The ones from the southeast are between 90-60 degrees south latitude. The trade winds refer to those occurring near the equator in the tropics moving east. The doldrums are also in the tropics, but refer to an area of low-pressure where frequently the winds are light and unpredictable.

26. B: Land breeze. When land cools off rapidly at night and the ocean water stays relatively warm, it creates a land breeze. Sea breeze, or onshore breeze, occurs when the land heats the air above it. This heated, warmer air is less dense and rises. The cooler air from above the sea and higher sea level pressure creates a wind flow in the direction of the land. Coastal areas often have these cooler breezes. A monsoon is a seasonal wind in southern Asia that blows southwest in one season and northeast in another. The southwest winds in the summer bring heavy rain. The trade winds are the steady easterlies about the equator.

27. C: the slope is very steep. On a topographic map, an area where the contour lines are very close together indicates that the slope is very steep. Lines very far apart would indicate a more gradual change in elevation. Contour lines help represent the actual shape of the Earth's surface features and geographic landmarks like rivers, lakes and vegetation. Topographic maps also show man made features such as roads, dams and major buildings. They are based on aerial photography and the quadrangle maps are produced in various scales. The 7.5 minute quadrangle is very common and provides a 1:24,000 scale, where 1 inch represents 2,000 feet.

28. B: Venus. Venus experiences a greenhouse effect similar to that observed on Earth as its dense atmosphere traps the solar radiation and creates a greenhouse effect. The greenhouse gases, including ozone, carbon dioxide, water vapor and methane, trap infrared radiation that is reflected back toward the atmosphere. Human activity generates more of the greenhouse gases than

necessary. Some practices that increase the amount of greenhouse gases are burning natural gas and oil, farming, which leads to more methane and nitrous oxide, deforestation, which decreases the amount of offset oxygen, and population growth in general, which increases the volume of greenhouse gases. Increased gases mean more infrared radiation is trapped and the overall temperature at the Earth's surface rises.

29. A: Glass. Glass is considered a non-renewable resource. Glass is manufactured and can be recycled, but is considered a non-renewable resource. Wood is considered a renewable resource because with proper management, an equilibrium can be reached between harvesting trees and planting new ones. Cattle are managed in herds and a balance can be achieved between those consumed and those born. Soil is the result of long-term erosion and includes organic matter and minerals needed by plants. Soil found naturally in the environment is renewed. Crops can be rotated to help maintain a healthy soil composition for farming.

30. B: It will ensure the health and safety of populations and the long-term sustainability of the environment. Recycling and using alternative sources of energy reduce the amount of pollutants introduced into the ecosystem, reduce the potential for disease-related human maladies, and reduce the reliance on non-renewable resources. Greater production of goods and consumer spending in the future would probably be good for the economy, but not necessarily the environment. Fossil fuels are considered to be a non-renewable energy resource.

31. A: A magnetic field is created by a spin magnetic dipole moment and the orbital magnetic dipole moment of the electrons in atoms. Therefore, it is the spinning and rotating of electrons in atoms that creates a magnetic field. Choice B describes the nucleus and electron clouds within an atom. Choice C creates thermal energy. Choice D creates a good electrical conductor. Choice E creates a radioactive atom.

32. B: An iron bar moving inside a coil of wire that contains a current would create an electromagnet. Choice A creates a magnetic field. Choice C creates an electric current. Choice D creates the Earth's magnetic field. Choice E creates thermal energy.

33. B: Work is defined as the force used to move a mass over a distance. Choice a may be a secular (non-scientific) definition of work. Choice c is the definition of power. Choice d is the definition of potential energy. Choice e is the definition of impulse.

34. B: Light travels in straight lines. As light moves from one substance to another, the light rays bend according to the refractive index of each substance. As the light travels through the air, it hits the non-submerged portion of the pencil. The light is reflected from the pencil and this is what we see. However, as the light travels *into* the water, the light waves are bent (refracted), and that light is subsequently reflected and travels to our eyes. What we perceive is a pencil that is no longer whole and straight, but broken and bent. It is refraction (choice b) that causes this perception. Although the other distractors are also properties of waves, they are not the reasons why the observer perceives the pencil as bent.

35. A: Magnetic poles occur in pairs known as magnetic dipoles. Individual atoms can be considered magnetic dipoles due to the spinning and rotation of the electrons in the atoms. When the dipoles are aligned, the material is magnetic. Choices b, c, d, and e are all magnetic materials. Therefore, the magnetic dipoles in these materials are NOT randomly aligned. Only choice a has randomly aligned dipoles.

36. D: Power = work / time. The mass of the object (10 kg) and the distance (10 m) can be used to calculate work. The value for time is also provided.

37. A: Phase changes are physical changes, not chemical changes (b). Sublimation (c) occurs when a solid turns directly to a gas without passing through the liquid state. Condensation (d) occurs when a gas turns to liquid. Neutralization (e) is an example of a chemical change.

38. A: The addition of energy causes a phase change. Phase changes are physical changes, not chemical changes. While sublimation is an example of a phase change, it occurs when a solid turns directly to a gas without passing through the liquid state. Condensation, another phase change, occurs when a gas turns to liquid. Single replacement reactions are one category of chemical change.

39. A: The center of an atom is known as the nucleus. It is composed of protons and neutrons.

40. B: Temperature is a measure of the kinetic energy of particles. As temperature increases the average kinetic energy also increases. As the gas particles move more rapidly they occupy a larger volume. The increase in speed of the individual particles combined with the greater distance over which any intermolecular forces must act results in a decrease in the intermolecular forces.

41. C: A physical change occurs when water condenses. The only thing formed during condensation is new intermolecular bonds. Therefore, no new molecules form (e) and no new covalent bonds form (b). The only time new atoms form is during a nuclear reaction (a). The water molecule is not ionizing, so no new ionic bonds form (d).

42. A: Repeating a measurement several times can increase the accuracy of the measurement. Calibrating the equipment (b) will increase the precision of the measurement. None of the other choices are useful strategies to increase the accuracy of a measurement.

43. A: Descriptive studies are usually the first form of study in a new area of scientific inquiry. Others are also forms of scientific study, but are completed after initial descriptive studies.

44. A: A correlational study of a population is an example of a descriptive study. Answer choices b, c, and e are examples of the controlled experimentation type of scientific investigation. Answer choice d is an example of the comparative data analysis type of scientific investigation.

45. A: The purpose of conducting an experiment is to test a hypothesis. Answer choices b, c, d, and e are steps in conducting an experiment designed to test a hypothesis. .

46. C: For an experiment to be considered successful, it must yield data that others can reproduce. Answer choice a may be considered part of a well-designed experiment. Answer choices b, d, and e may be considered part of an experiment that is reported on by individuals with expertise.

47. A: The scientific method is a series of steps to solve a problem. Answer choices b, c, d, and e are all parts of the scientific method.

48. B: It is true that rocks are classified by their formation and the minerals they contain, while minerals are classified by their chemical composition and physical properties. Answer A is incorrect because rocks may contain traces of organic compounds. Answers C and D are incorrect because only minerals can be polymorphs and only rocks contain mineraloids.

49. A: When two tectonic plates are moving laterally in opposing directions, this is called a transform boundary. When there is friction at transform boundaries and pressure builds up, it can result in shallow earthquakes (usually at a depth of less than 25 meters). California's San Andreas Fault is an example of a transform boundary.

50. D: The most recently formed parts of the Earth's crust can be found at mid-ocean ridges. New crust forms here when magma erupts from these ridges and pushes pre-existing crust horizontally towards the continental plates. Such ridges include the Mid-Atlantic Ridge and the East Pacific Rise.

The Arts, Health, and Fitness

1. B: Form is an artistic element that would only apply to three-dimensional art forms, such as sculptures or decorative arts. Two-dimensional works of art have the element of shape, which refers to their length and width, while three-dimensional works of art have the element of form, which refers to their length, width, and depth. Proportion and balance are both *principles* of art that would apply to both two- and three-dimensional works. Line is an artistic element that would be applicable to both types of art.

2. B: Cross-hatching is a technique that is used to achieve shading effects in pencil drawings. When using cross-hatching, the artist loosely sketches a series of parallel lines in one direction, and then another series of parallel lines perpendicular to the first set. Each new set of lines changes the value of the sketch to create varied shading. This technique is used with media, such as pencil, that cannot be otherwise blended.

3. A: The advantage of drawing with charcoal as opposed to lead pencils is that charcoal can be smudged to create shading. Because of its loose, chalky texture, charcoal requires a fixative, unlike lead pencil. Neither pencils nor charcoal is available in different hues, but both can be purchased in a range of values.

4. B: Oil paint has traditionally been applied using the rule of "fat over lean." This means that less oily paint is used for the initial layers of paint, while oilier paint is used on the top layers to prevent drying and cracking. Oil painting was traditionally done in layers over long periods of time, and it was most commonly applied to canvas or other fabric surfaces.

5. A: Drybrush is a technique that is primarily used in watercolor painting. It involves using a fine, nearly dry brush that is dipped in undiluted watercolor paint. It is used to create precise brushstrokes—an effect that is otherwise very difficult to achieve in this medium.

6. B: The fiber art technique that involves condensing, or matting, fibers together is called felting. Flocking involves applying small fibers to the surface of a fabric to enhance its texture. Macramé fabric is produced by knotting yarns or threads. Plaiting (also known as braiding) involves intertwining multiple threads in a consistent pattern.

7. A: The threads that are stretched taut across the loom before weaving begins are called the warp. The weft threads are the threads that are woven across the warp, and the loom is the apparatus used for weaving. Twill is a weaving technique that produces a weave with parallel, diagonal lines.

8. B: Cinematography is not a type of digital art. Unlike videographers, who record images in digital form, cinematographers record images on traditional film. Three-dimensional computer animation involves the creation of animation using digital techniques, as does pixel art.

9. B: Line is the artistic element most commonly used to create the illusion of depth in a painting. For instance, an artist could use line to convey depth by incorporating an object, such as a road, that stretches from the foreground to the background of a painting. Balance is a principle of art that involves creating an impression of stability in a work; contrast and symmetry would not function to create the illusion of depth.

10. D: Two observers' differing levels of artistic knowledge, different vantage points, and different cultural beliefs and values could all plausibly explain their differing evaluations of the same

painting. An audience's perception of artwork depends on many factors, both physical and psychological. Physical factors include the audience's vantage point (close, far, left, right, above, or below the work of art). Psychological factors include audience members' level of prior knowledge of art and any cultural beliefs or values that might influence their expectations of art.

11. A: Here is an easy way to remember stage directions: There is an old wives' tale about stage construction that claims that stages used to be built on a slope (the back end was higher than the front). When a director wanted an actor to stand at the back of the stage, he literally meant, "Go *up* the stage." If the director wanted an actor positioned toward the front of the stage, he would say, "Go *down* the stage." Eventually, these directions were shortened to "upstage" and "downstage."

12. B: Mood relates to emotional responses. Audience members must use their senses to determine certain feelings, such as happiness, anger, sadness, and confusion. The director can evoke certain emotions through set design, costuming, and lighting choices. Setting can help determine mood. However, setting is concrete, as it is what the audience actually sees and hears. Mood is more abstract. Answer choice B best describes the difference between mood and setting.

13. C: The first form of theatre originated in ancient Greece. Some experts believe this happened as far back as 500 BC. The Romans developed their own form of theatre shortly after the decline of the Greek government, imitating many aspects of Greek theatre. Medieval theatre, which relied heavily on religious undertones, came next. There are other forms of ancient theatre, but Greek, Roman, and Medieval are the most commonly studied. The English Renaissance is too young to be considered "ancient," as it originated in the 16th century.

14. C: The English Renaissance is commonly known as "the age of Shakespeare." However, William Shakespeare was not the only famous playwright of this time period. Christopher Marlow, Francis Beaumont, Thomas Middleton, and countless other authors and playwrights emerged on the scene during the English Renaissance. There were also notable operas, comedies, and classical musicians, but this particular time period can *best* be distinguished by its playwrights.

15. A: Analyzing and studying characters are important aspects of script analysis, but script analysis is much too broad to be the correct answer here. Plot development focuses on the storyline and occurs during the developmental stages before the script is complete. Psychological dissection is not a term that is used in theatre. The question is clearly asking for an answer that is related to better understanding a work's characters and their relationships with one another.

16. C: There are many types of vocal techniques in theater, including warm ups, strengthening exercises, and developmental exercises. It is important to distinguish them from each other. Vocal projection would not be the correct answer here because the teacher is asking her students to *yawn,* not necessarily use their full vocal capacity. Pitch development would require certain musical notes, and breath control would require increments of time. Therefore, answer choice C is the best answer.

17. D: In order for a student to understand human emotions and characterization, he must be able to recognize facial expressions. Character masks are full masks, each representing a different emotion, such as happy, sad, surprised, mad, etc. Costumes are typically not indicators of emotion, so answer choice A is incorrect. Commedia half-masks display *some* emotion, but their main purpose is to allow for the use of text, so answer choice B is not the best choice. Comedy/tragedy masks are limited in the expressions they can convey, only showing happiness and sadness. Therefore, answer choice D is not the best choice.

18. A: The operative word in the question is *assumed.* While a director of a production *might* lend a hand to a performer in need of vocal coaching, it is not one of his expected duties. Answer choice A is the one that does not belong. Encouraging cohesion among cast mates, interpreting and approving scripts, and collaborating with crew members are all regularly assumed duties that a successful director must perform.

19. D: Director placement of an actor onstage could be considered *positioning,* but the technical theatre term is *blocking,* so answer choice A is incorrect. Staging is related to set design and prop placement, and has nothing to do with the placement of actors. Therefore, answer choice B can be eliminated. Choreography is related to actor placement onstage, but only when specific dance movements are involved, making answer choice C incorrect.

20. C: A theatre is required to pay royalty fees to a playwright any time the play is performed in front of an audience. This includes dress rehearsals or trial runs that are conducted so actors can get a feel for performing in front of others. Often, spectators are not charged an admission. The question of when royalties should be paid has nothing to do with opening night or how much admission is charged, so answer choices A, B, and D are incorrect.

21. D: Blind reading is not used in the theatre industry, so answer choice A can be eliminated. While a cold read is indeed preliminary in nature, answer choice B is incorrect because the technical term is *cold.* Cite reading is when a performer runs through a piece of sheet music for the first time. It is not related to script reading, so answer choice C is incorrect.

22. B: Experimental theatre is often performed in what is called a black box theatre. This type of theatre can be a converted classroom, an abandoned warehouse, or even an old coffee shop. Usually, there are very few (if any) costs involved with holding performances in a black box theatre. Prosceniums, arenas, and thrusts would be more appropriate for productions that require structured and technical aspects, such as lighting and sound.

23. A: Simply put, a thrust can be described as something that is shoved or *thrust* into an audience from the back wall. Because a thrust is attached to the back wall, audience members can only sit on three sides of the stage. An arena, on the other hand, is typically positioned in the middle of a very large space. Audience members can see a performance from all four sides.

24. B: Answer choice A is incorrect because applying special effects makeup is the responsibility of a makeup designer. Answer choice C is incorrect because incorporating lighting is the responsibility of a lighting designer. Taking care of sound effects is the responsibility of a sound designer. Marketing and increasing ticket sales are the responsibilities of either a house manager or a marketing manager; so, answer choice D is also incorrect. A dramaturg is a person hired to analyze text and research historical facts relevant to a production.

25. B: Theatre gels, also known as *color gels*, are small pieces of film used to change lighting color. Gels have nothing to do with safety, nor are they in actual *gel* form, so answer choice A is incorrect. Sound technicians have no need for color gels, so answer choice C is incorrect. Costume designers would not have a need for color gels, so answer choice D is also incorrect.

26. D: Specific lighting refers to a small, controlled area of light. Therefore, answer choice A is incorrect. General lighting involves a much vaster area than specific lighting. An entire stage can be illuminated with general lighting, and would obviously involve the use of more than one

instrument. Therefore, answer choice B is incorrect. Strip lights are long troughs made of metal that are divided into components. Strip lights do not contain reflectors, so answer choice C is also incorrect.

27. A: A unit set is aptly titled because it consists of separate *units* that can easily be switched around to change the layout of a set. A unit set is *convertible* and can take on *multiple* shapes, but *unit set* is the technical theatre term. Therefore, answer choices B and C are incorrect. The term *uniform* indicates consistency, or something that is constant and not ever-changing. Therefore, answer choice D is incorrect.

28. A: Tango, traditionally played to accompany its distinctive style of dance. Salsa, Flamenco, and Tejano music have varying influences and, as such, use a wide variety of instruments in their performance. Only Tango music is strongly associated with the specific combination of two violins, a piano, double bass, and two bandoneóns.

29. D: Ewe. The Ewe culture is West African and has a folk musical form based primarily on drums played with complex rhythms and meter. All of the other answers, A, B, and C, are incorrect, since they use many musical instruments in addition to percussion instruments. Finnish music, for example, uses instruments such as the harmonium, flute, and fiddle. Peruvian music predominantly features its iconic flutes and the charango, a type of mandolin. Mongolian folk music is famous for its use of the *morin khuur*, or horse-head fiddle. Therefore, of forms listed above, only Ewe is an appropriate answer.

30. A: U.S. churches in the 1930s. Laurens Hammond developed this instrument in 1934 and marketed it to churches as a low-cost alternative to the large and expensive pipe organs then used for religious services. The Hammond organ emerged after the Baroque period; therefore, answer C is incorrect. Answer D is incorrect for the same reason. Finally, while the Hammond did in fact see widespread use with popular musicians starting in the 1960s, jazz, blues, and other performers were not the instrument's original market. Widespread Hammond use among jazz, blues, and other performers did not emerge until the instrument had been on the market for almost thirty years.

31. A: *Fiddler on the Roof,* a musical that follows the struggles of a Jewish father trying to keep his faith and traditions alive. Klezmer, a Jewish musical tradition and form often performed with instruments such as the clarinet, accordion, and piano, is featured predominantly in the musical. As none of the other answers—B, *The Sound of Music*, C, *Oklahoma!,* or D, *A Chorus Line*—is necessarily a celebration of Jewish culture, heritage, or music, none of these are correct.

32. C: Sir Arthur Sullivan. While both operas and operettas involve actors on a stage singing their lines to a musical score, operetta generally is lighter in tone and substance than its weightier cousin. One of the most well-known composers of operettas is Sir Arthur Sullivan, who, with his collaborator, Sir William Gilbert, wrote fourteen operettas, including *The Pirates of Penzance* and *H.M.S. Pinafore.* Answer A, Wolfgang Amadeus Mozart; B, Giacomo Puccini; and D, Giuseppe Verdi; were all composers of opera rather than operetta and therefore incorrect answers.

33. D: German music. The word *Tejano* refers to someone from Texas of Latino and/or Hispanic descent. While Tejano music has strong cultural ties to neighboring Mexico, it also draws a heavy influence from the music of German and Czech settlers in the region. Europeans brought with them musical elements such as the polka, accordion, and waltz. Fusing these with styles such as mariachi gradually resulted in Tejano music. While it might be tempting to choose Peruvian music, answer A,

for this question, Peru's distinctive Incan roots have nothing to do with influencing Tejano music, nor does African or Celtic music. For this reason, answers A, B, and C are incorrect.

34. C: MP3 removes selected information, including frequencies from the original file too low or too high for humans to hear. This process results in a lower-quality recording small enough for storage en masse on computers and/or MP3 players. Shrinking the file size is key to converting a file to MP3, but this shrinking cannot be achieved by recording at a lower volume, so answer A is incorrect. Copying a file with selected vocal or instrumental tracks removed is not the idea of MP3, so converting the digital information to analog, would be incorrect.

35. B: The use of the third. Prior to the Renaissance, the use of the third was regarded as dissonant, but with increased vocal range gradually began to be used as consonance. The use of the second always has been considered dissonant in Western music, so answer A is incorrect. Also incorrect is answer C, the fifth, which was used as consonance more toward the end of the Renaissance and the beginning of the Baroque. Finally, because intervals had been used long before the Renaissance, answer D is incorrect.

36. D: Pyotr Ilyich Tchaikovsky and Edvard Grieg. Grieg and Tchaikovsky lived and composed during the same time period, the mid- to late 19th century, and, in the case of Grieg, into the early 20th. Indeed, they met in 1888. The rest of the composers that form the answers to this question did not live during the same eras and therefore never could have met. In the case of answer incorrect answer A, Vivaldi died in 1741, while Chopin was not born until 1810. Answer B is incorrect, since Holst was not born until 1874, 124 years after the death of Bach. Finally, Pachelbel died in 1706, 105 years before the birth of Liszt.

37. C: The Romantic period. Partly as a response to the widely perceived dominance of German music and composers during the Classical period that preceded it, the Romantic period is most strongly associated with musical nationalism; that is, composers from a given nation wrote music meant to invoke their native lands, peoples, and cultures. Noted examples include the music of Bedřich Smetana, Antonín Dvořák, and Jean Sibelius. While the other periods—Baroque, Classical, and Contemporary—would have seen selected composers and pieces which could be argued as nationalistic, the Romantic period *most strongly* is associated with musical nationalism and is therefore the correct answer.

38. D: Choosing a violin that allows the student's fingers to curl comfortably around the scroll, with the elbow slightly bent. While taller children and teens tend to have longer arms, arm lengths vary even among students of the same height, so the method described by answer A is ineffective. Answer B is also incorrect, since student musicians are still learning proper technique and may not yet have a feel for the best instrument. A violin that extends to the base of a student's hand (Answer C) would be too small. This process of elimination leaves answer D, which would yield an instrument that allows the student to hold and play the violin comfortably.

39. C: Concerts B ♭ and F, with the exception of saxophones. Concert B ♭ is a good tuning note for the majority of instruments, as it is well within their range. Concert F is excellent for horns, and in fact is better than B ♭, and also is excellent for clarinets. Nonetheless, these concert pitches are not suitable for tuning saxophones.

40. C: A timpani has a normal compass of a perfect fifth. Although a timpani can be stretched to a minor sixth, this would require the use of plastic heads. As such, all of the other answers would be incorrect. Answers A and B, a minor third and a perfect fourth, require a smaller compass than that

permitted by a timpani; a major seventh is too large, even with an instrument fitted with plastic heads.

41. A: Brass valves should be oiled once a day. Doing so keeps the valves in good working order, and prevents sticking and damage to the valve mechanism. Once per week is incorrect, as the valves will need lubrication before a week has elapsed, so B is incorrect. Also incorrect is C, once a month; it is doubtful that a brass instrument played with any regularity, could go a full month without some oiling. Waiting until the valves begin to stick, answer D, is incorrect, since sticking valves can disrupt a rehearsal, practice, or, worse, a performance, and should be oiled regularly to prevent this from occurring.

42. C: The viola uses the alto or "viola" clef, which is rarely used for other instruments or compositions. To the untrained eye, the viola is easily mistaken for its smaller cousin, the violin, but many differences exist between the instruments. The viola is tuned a perfect fifth below the violin, and whereas the violin's four strings are tuned to GDAE, the viola's tuning is CGDa. Therefore, answer A is incorrect. While the viola is indeed a mainstay of most symphony orchestras, it is also an integral part of most chamber pieces, rendering answer B incorrect. In addition, the viola is larger than the violin *and* it uses a correspondingly larger bow, which is also wider than that of the violin. Therefore, answer D is incorrect.

43. C: Fiber-rich foods include whole grains and legumes as well as most fruits and vegetables.

44. B: According to the National Heart, Lung and Blood Institute, a normal BMI, which describes weight relative to height, is between 19 and 24.9. Obesity is defined as a BMI over 30.

45. B: Warming up properly is important for the reasons cited in choices A, C, and D, but it does not build muscles.

46. D: While compulsive overeaters resemble bulimics in the ways mentioned in choices A, B, and C, they do not generally induce vomiting or exercise obsessively in an effort to change their bodies. Despite the serious health risks associated with obesity, binge-eaters face fewer immediate health consequences than do bulimics, who consistently binge and purge.

47. D: According to the specificity of training principle, just because a person has trained in one area or in one kind of physical activity does not mean that the skills the person has acquired readily transfer over to a different area or different kind of physical activity. Option D is an illustration of this principle: in this case, the person's capabilities regarding swimming at a certain intensity for a given number of times each week did not mean that the person could also run at that intensity for that number of times each week. Options A, B, and C do not illustrate the specificity of training principle.

48. A: Circuit training – training that involves alternating strengthening activities with other strengthening activities, without rests in between – is more strenuous than other kinds of weight training. It should be reserved for students who are already accustomed to regular physical exercise (otherwise it might be too strenuous). Option B incorrectly states that circuit training is good for beginning students; which is incorrect. Option C can be rejected for similar reasons. Option D can be rejected because circuit training is better for advanced students in general – it is not reserved for students recovering from injury (in addition, it is not likely to be beneficial for students recovering from an injury).

49. B: It is easier to digest simple carbohydrates than complex carbohydrates. All other options are false. For example, complex carbohydrates do have dietary fiber (so, option A can be rejected). That is one reason that complex carbohydrates are more nutritious than simple carbohydrates. Because complex carbohydrates are more nutritious than simple carbohydrates, option D is false and can be rejected. Regarding option C, simple carbohydrates are more likely to raise one's blood sugar levels than complex carbohydrates; they do not make it easier to maintain good blood sugar levels. So, option C can be rejected.

50. A: The skinfold test is one way of estimating a person's body fat (what percentage of a person's body is fat). It is performed by using calipers to measure how thick particular skinfolds are (such as skinfolds on the upper thigh). It does not give an exact measurement of the percentage of body fat, however. Option B is false (although electronic impedance involves sending a low electric current through the body to determine body fat percentage). Options C and D also give incorrect descriptions of the skinfold test, which does not involve determining how much skin can be pinched between the fingers, or comparing the thickness of skinfolds to a person's weight and height.

51. D: The school a teenager attends is generally less important in affecting his or her physical performance than the amount of sleep a teenager gets, a teenager's age, and the quality of nutrition the teenager receives. These last three factors are very likely to affect a teenager's physical performance (they also affect non-teenagers, of course). Therefore, options A, B, and C can be rejected. Lack of sleep is likely to hinder a teenager's physical performance; a teenager's age will affect his or her physical development (such as a size and strength), which in turn will affect physical performance. Lastly, nutrition plays a key role in physical performance; an undernourished person is likely to lack the energy needed for optimum physical performance.

52. A: All other factors should be included in designing a physical education course. Regarding A, of course an instructor should include teaching methods that appeal to visual learners; however, an instructor should not emphasize such methods, anymore than kinesthetic or auditory learning should be emphasized. Rather, the instructor should use a variety of teaching tactics to appeal to diverse styles of learning. Regarding options B, C, and D, a course should both be safe and fun, as well as involve some way (or ways) of tracking student progress.

53. B: Many educators in physical education believe that lecture is often a poor way of teaching in physical education. However, it is suited for some purposes, such as teaching basic information that requires expertise (such as the rules of a game or sport). It is not generally suited for teaching motor skills, which eliminates options A and D (effective teaching of which would more likely involve leading the student in activities that practice the relevant motor skills). Option C is not really a matter of basic information; since ethical issues are generally more subjective and complex, they are more suited for a more interactive kind of teaching, such as guided discussion.

Practice Test #2

Reading and English Language Arts

1. A student says, "We learned that knowledge and understanding of language is important." This is an example of an error in which of these?
   a. Phonology
   b. Semantics
   c. Syntax
   d. Pragmatics

2. English language learner (ELL) students typically are able to develop which type of English language skills the soonest?
   a. They typically develop BICS much sooner than CALP.
   b. They typically develop CALP more quickly than BICS.
   c. They typically develop both at about the same rates.
   d. They develop these at individually varying speeds.

3. A child in kindergarten is *most* likely to be referred to a speech-language pathologist if s/he does not correctly produce which of the following phonemes?
   a. /p/ as in pepper or poppies
   b. /ʒ/ as in mirage or measure
   c. /v/ as in velvet, valve, value
   d. /s/ as in see, yes, or asking

4. For a group of preschool children whose oral language development is below normal levels for their ages, which small-group activity would be *most* appropriate to develop these skills?
   a. Engaging in group discussion
   b. Producing words that rhyme
   c. Making an oral presentation
   d. Taking turns in telling stories

5. Several students in the same class recently emigrated from an African country where they had no formal schooling. They all speak conversational English competently. They have experience digging wells for their village. Their culture has a strong storytelling tradition. Which of these classroom activities would best build on their backgrounds and strengths?
   a. English vocabulary lists and grammar worksheets prior to any other English assignments
   b. Reading a book in English exposing them to a new subject and writing book reports on it
   c. Researching and writing papers in English about the well-digging process and techniques
   d. Oral class presentations in English explaining the process and techniques of digging wells

6. Relative to language and literacy development, which of the following is accurate?
   a. Most children develop speech and reading sooner than listening and writing skills.
   b. Listening and reading should be taught first, with speech and writing coming later.
   c. Instruction should always include spoken and written language interrelationships.
   d. Reading and writing need direct instruction; oral language skills develop naturally.

7. Which of the following is correct regarding phonological awareness in kindergarteners?
   a. Children with delayed language development have benefited from phonological awareness training.
   b. Researchers into instruction in phonological awareness advise against using SLPs and their methods.
   c. Phonological awareness in kindergarteners requires changing phonemes in words to change meaning.
   d. Phonological awareness instruction for kindergarteners involves only the individual phoneme level.

8. A classroom teacher observes that a new ELL student consistently omits the /h/ sound in words. Of these, what is the *first* factor the teacher should consider?
   a. The student may have an articulation disorder.
   b. The student may be a native Spanish speaker.
   c. The student may need a hearing assessment.
   d. The student may have a respiratory problem.

9. A school has a policy of only permitting administration of its first choice among standardized formal assessments of phonological development twice per school year to conserve money and time. A 1st-grade teacher wanting to inform her instructional planning, implementation, and adjustments appropriately can do which of these?
   a. Stick to the school's policy and do the best she can with the results
   b. Lobby administrators to change policy to giving this test more often
   c. Use informal assessments continually to supplement the formal test
   d. Conduct informal and other formal assessments on an ongoing basis

10. A 1st-grader consistently fronts backed consonants, e.g., saying "I dotta doe" for "I gotta go"; "tat" for "cat"; and additionally substitutes /f/ for /b/ and /p/, e.g., "flue" for "blue" and "fracticing" for "practicing." Based on knowledge of typical phonological and phonemic development, what can his educators most likely assume?
   a. Based on the age for phonological processes to end, this student has normal development.
   b. Based on the age for phonological processes to end, this individual difference is expected.
   c. Based on the age for phonological processes to end, this student needs an SLP's evaluation.
   d. Based on the age for phonological processes to end, this represents errors rare at any age.

11. Which of the following is true about instructional approaches and activities for developing student phonological and phonemic awareness?
   a. Direct, explicit instruction is the only effective method to teach manipulating phonemes in words.
   b. Teachers cannot utilize informal interactions for these purposes because they are not systematic.
   c. One instructional activity that is particularly suited for younger students is playing language games.
   d. For younger students to identify spoken alliteration, they must first identify it in printed language.

12. For teachers to encourage parental collaboration in developing their children's phonological and phonemic awareness, which of the following is most likely to be effective?
 a. Assigning homework to parents that reinforces the lessons given in school
 b. Suggesting or teaching simple, fun games to play during their everyday lives
 c. Warning parents not to demonstrate correct sound production for children
 d. Instructing parents to avoid working on phonemes during bedtime stories

13. According to a large body of research, how is systematic phonics instruction most effective?
 a. For the majority of K-6 students, with the exception of students having difficulty with learning to read
 b. When it is provided to K-6 students as an instructional program separate from any reading instruction.
 c. With pre-K-2 students but not older, and paired with phonemic awareness but not other instruction
 d. In the context of comprehensive reading programs including fluency, vocabulary, and comprehension

14. Of the following, which statement is true about instruction in the alphabetic principle?
 a. Letter-sound relationships with the highest utility should be the earliest ones introduced.
 b. The instruction of letter-sound correspondences should always be done in word context.
 c. Letter-sound relationship practice times should only be assigned apart from other lessons.
 d. Letter-sound relationship practice should focus on new relationships, not going over old ones.

15. Which of the following factors affects ELL students' English-language literacy development?
 a. A Chinese student's L1 is not written alphabetically like English is.
 b. A Spanish student's L1 is more phonetically regular than English is.
 c. Neither one of these has any effects on L2 literacy development.
 d. Both factors affect L1 literacy development, but in different ways.

16. When teaching students relationships between sounds and letters and between letters and words, what practices should teachers best follow?
 a. Use a variety of instructional techniques, but including only the auditory and visual modes
 b. Incorporate multisensory modalities within a variety of instructional strategies and materials
 c. Always adhere to the same exact instructional method and materials to ensure consistency
 d. Introduce similar-looking letters and similar-sounding phonemes together for discrimination

17. What is most accurate about using formal and informal assessments of student alphabetic knowledge and skills?
 a. Individual student skills can only be analyzed via informal assessment.
 b. In order to plan instruction, teachers must utilize formal assessments.
 c. Teachers can monitor daily progress with formal or informal assessment.
 d. Individual student skills can only be analyzed using formal assessment.

18. To get parents to collaborate in supporting their children's alphabetic knowledge and skills development, teachers should observe which principle?
 a. Teachers should focus on any student alphabetic deficits when contacting parents.
 b. Teachers should avoid suggesting specific activities so parents use their own ideas.
 c. Teachers should avoid personalized messages because time constraints limit these.
 d. Teachers should concentrate on quality over quantity in interactions with parents.

19. Which of the following literary elements are most likely to be found in *both* fictional narratives *and* nonfictional informational text?
   a. The writing style of the author
   b. Labeled diagrams and photos
   c. Setting(s) and characters
   d. Themes and plots

20. Regarding these elements of print awareness in literacy development, which is true?
   a. All students with normal development can differentiate printed words from spaces.
   b. To identify initial and final letters in words, students must identify words vs. spaces.
   c. The only students not automatically knowing left-right directionality are certain ELLs.
   d. Being able to identify basic punctuation is not important to reading comprehension.

21. What statement is most accurate regarding the context(s) wherein students develop literacy?
   a. Students develop literacy by reading, writing, listening, and speaking.
   b. Students develop literacy by reading, writing, and listening to speech.
   c. Students develop literacy by reading and writing, not any other ways.
   d. Students develop literacy by reading as the only activity that matters.

22. Among the following, which most represents a print concept that teachers must introduce to young children and/or students who are beginning readers?
   a. How to hold and handle a book
   b. How and where to open books
   c. Table of contents, index, etc.
   d. All of these are print concepts

23. What most accurately identifies the kind(s) of opportunities teachers are expected to give students plenty of with respect to literature?
   a. To read different literary genres independently only
   b. To hear literature read aloud in addition to reading it
   c. To respond to literature by writing and speaking on it
   d. To read, hear, respond, and also interact with others

24. Which of the following arranges steps in teaching author point of view in the correct sequence?
   a. Modeling, whole-class guided practice, explicit or direct instruction, independent practice, paired or small-group guided practice, assessment, comprehension questions to identify POV, further assessment, reteaching and/or enrichment
   b. Explicit or direct instruction, modeling, whole-class guided practice, paired or small-group guided practice, independent practice, comprehension questions to identify POV, assessment, reteaching and/or enrichment, further assessment
   c. Whole-class guided practice, paired or small-group guided practice, explicit or direct instruction, modeling, assessment, reteaching and/or enrichment, independent practice, further assessment, comprehension questions for identifying POV
   d. Independent practice, paired or small-group guided practice, whole-class guided practice, modeling, explicit or direct instruction, reteaching and/or enrichment, assessment, comprehension questions to identify POV, further assessment

25. Among the following, which is NOT a common academic standard for kindergarten students in decoding and identifying words?
    a. Showing knowledge that letter sequences correspond to phoneme sequences
    b. Understanding that word sounds and meanings change along with word letters
    c. Decoding monosyllabic words using initial and final consonant and vowel sounds
    d. Matching letters to consonant sounds; reading simple, monosyllabic sight words

26. Following a typical developmental sequence, which of the following is expected of 2nd-graders in decoding and identifying new or unfamiliar words?
    a. Identifying new words and compound words via phonics, roots, suffixes, and analogies
    b. Identifying new word meanings through knowledge of familiar synonyms and antonyms
    c. Identifying new word meanings by comparing to known homophones and homographs
    d. Identifying new word meanings by roots, prefixes, suffixes, idioms, and dictionary markings

27. When a teacher instructs elementary school students in analyzing phonetically regular words, which of the following would most represent a sequence from simpler to progressively more complex?
    a. Long vowels, short vowels, consonant blends, CVC (consonant-vowel-consonant) and other common patterns, individual phonemes, blending phonemes, types of syllables, onsets and rimes
    b. Onsets and rimes, short vowels, consonant blends, long vowels, blending phonemes, CVC and other common patterns, types of syllables, individual phonemes
    c. Types of syllables, onsets and rimes, CVC and other common patterns, consonant blends, blending phonemes, individual phonemes, long vowels, short vowels
    d. Individual phonemes, blending phonemes, onsets and rimes, short vowels, long vowels, consonant blends, CVC and other common patterns, types of syllables

28. Strategies for teaching word recognition, decoding, and identification skills should follow which of these principles?
    a. Phonics instruction should be systematic, explicit, and match student needs identified by assessment.
    b. Teaching word analysis skills is as effective without following any prescribed sequence or structure.
    c. Once students learn the elements of phonics, they get sufficient practice through everyday activities.
    d. During every lesson in reading, teachers should place primary emphasis on skills for decoding words.

29. To help students decode words of increasing complexity, a teacher instructs them in strategies, including identifying Greek and Latin roots, prefixes, and suffixes to establish meaning. Which of the following does this strategy exemplify?
    a. Alphabetic principle knowledge
    b. Combinations of vowel sounds
    c. Semantic and syntactic context
    d. Structural cues in morphology

30. Teachers should show students how to use dictionaries because good dictionaries can tell students who know how to use them which of the following?

    a. Primarily only the definitions of the literal meanings of words, not connotations or correct usages

    b. Literal definitions, correct spellings, pronunciations, and connotations, but not parts of speech

    c. The correct spellings of words, but only online dictionaries with sound files inform pronunciations

    d. The origins of words, which often inform the meanings of many other words with related origins

31. Which of the following *most* accurately summarizes the relationship of reading fluency and reading comprehension?

    a. As students develop greater reading comprehension, their reading fluency also improves.

    b. When students develop greater reading fluency, their reading comprehension improves.

    c. The relationship between reading fluency and reading comprehension is a reciprocal one.

    d. Reading fluency and reading comprehension are two separate, mainly unrelated skill sets.

32. Which of the following are students in grades 1-3 expected to do?

    a. Regularly read materials at the independent level, i.e., text containing one in 10 or fewer difficult words

    b. Select text to read independently using author knowledge, difficulty estimation, and personal interest

    c. Regularly read materials at the instructional level, i.e., text containing 1 in 20 or fewer difficult words

    d. Read aloud from unfamiliar texts fluently, i.e., with accuracy, phrasing, expression, and punctuation

33. Of the following statements, which is true about the relationship of reading fluency, word decoding, and reading comprehension?

    a. Developing fluency in reading has no relationship to speed and automaticity with decoding words.

    b. Students should have strong word recognition foundations established before fluency instruction.

    c. Reading fluency shows faster information processing speed, but has no impact on comprehension.

    d. Slower, less automatic word decoding decreases reading fluency, but it increases comprehension.

34. Which of these techniques for building reading fluency is NOT necessarily a repeated reading activity?

    a. Tape-assisted reading

    b. Readers theater

    c. Partner reading

    d. Self-correction

35. To select materials for partner reading, which of the following should the teacher do?
    a. Identify materials that are suitable for the higher reader's instructional reading level
    b. Have each student partner in a pair read a different passage from the same material
    c. Select enough materials for every pair of students to read two new passages a week
    d. Identify materials that are suitable for the lower reader's independent reading level

36. Of the following, which is the most appropriate guidance for teachers to help students select text for independent reading?
    a. Match each student to texts that contain roughly five percent of words the student does not know.
    b. Established readability measures and normed comprehension tests have no drawbacks.
    c. Teachers should help students select only texts that fulfill required reading assignments.
    d. Teachers should help students select only texts they want to read that are not assigned.

37. Which of the following involves evaluative reading comprehension?
    a. Identifying an author's point of view
    b. Explaining the author's point of view
    c. Identifying the main idea of the text
    d. Predicting what will happen in a text

38. To determine the subject matter of a section within a text chapter, what should the teacher tell the student to do?
    a. Read the section heading
    b. Read the chapter glossary
    c. Read the index in the text
    d. Read through the section

39. Which statement accurately reflects a principle regarding self-questioning techniques for increasing student reading comprehension?
    a. Asking only what kinds of "expert questions" fit the text's subject matter
    b. Asking only those questions that the text raises for the individual student
    c. Asking how each text portion relates to chapter main ideas is unnecessary
    d. Asking how the text information fits with what the student already knows

40. Among the following reading comprehension strategies, which can be done during and after reading but not before reading?
    a. Previewing
    b. Predicting
    c. Discussing
    d. Rereading

41. The five SCRIP reading comprehension strategies (Pennington, 2008) are *summarize, connect, rethink, interpret,* and *predict.* Connect includes observing a relationship between something in reading text and something in the reader's own personal life experience. What else does it include?
    a. Connecting by comparing but not contrasting parts
    b. Connecting to another text but not to other things
    c. Connecting causes in the text to effects in the text
    d. Connecting cause-and-effect but not sequentially

42. Among Common Core State Standards, which of the following anchor standards is an example for vocabulary development at the 6th-grade level?

    a. Using adjectives and adverbs learned textually and conversationally to describe feelings

    b. Using words and phrases acquired through text-related and conversational experiences

    c. Using grade-level, domain-specific, and general academic words and phrases accurately

    d. Using vocabulary knowledge for words and phrases needed for expression and comprehension

43. Of the following, which represents an indirect way in which students receive instruction in and learn vocabulary?

    a. Being exposed repeatedly to vocabulary in multiple contexts

    b. Being exposed to vocabulary when adults read aloud to them

    c. Being pre-taught specific words found in text prior to reading

    d. Being taught vocabulary words over extended periods of time

44. To support student vocabulary development, which of the following most accurately describes the instructional materials teachers should use?

    a. Teachers should only use literature and expository texts to support student vocabulary development.

    b. Teachers should use newspapers, magazines, etc. in addition to literature and expository textbooks.

    c. Teachers should use trade books, content-specific texts, and technology for vocabulary development.

    d. Teachers should use a broad variety of instructional materials, including all of the above and others.

45. Which of the following is true about what kinds of academic vocabularies students need to learn?

    a. Students who learn general academic vocabulary are able to learn all subject-specific terminologies.

    b. Students must learn subject terminology but know general academic vocabulary without teaching.

    c. Students will need to learn both general academic and specialized vocabularies for school success.

    d. Students learn general and specialized academic vocabularies via direct instruction, not modeling.

46. Among the following reinforcing activities for teaching, monitoring, and assessing student vocabulary knowledge, which one would most help students also understand verb conjugation and noun person and number?

    a. Morphemic analysis

    b. Contextual analysis

    c. Graphic organizers

    d. Word etymologies

47. Which of the following most accurately identifies what teachers should provide students with to promote their vocabulary development?

    a. Direct, explicit vocabulary instruction is the only important factor that teachers should provide.

    b. They should provide instruction and many opportunities to read literature and expository text.

    c. Teachers should provide instruction, reading opportunities, and opportunities to listen to texts.

    d. Teachers should offer instruction and many opportunities to read, listen, and respond to texts.

48. Of the following examples, which one is *not* an open-ended question?

    a. "When does the climax of this story occur?"

    b. "Is this expression a simile or a metaphor?"

    c. "How are similes and metaphors different?"

    d. "What are some reasons we have poetry?"

49. To help students understand abstract concepts in the print materials they read, which instructional aids that teachers provide can students *always* use three-dimensionally?

    a. Examples

    b. Manipulatives

    c. Graphic organizers

    d. Charts, tables, graphs

50. Which of the following ways of presenting information is best for showing change over time?

    a. Tables

    b. Maps

    c. Graphs

    d. Charts

51. Among these instructional strategies that help students understand inquiry and study skills, which is the least structured, generates the largest amounts of information, and contains the most information that may not be used?

    a. Brainstorming

    b. Summarizing

    c. Note-taking

    d. Outlining

52. Which of these is an expectation of 3rd-grade students?

    a. Use technology to record data, see idea relationships, and convert visuals into writing

    b. Use scanning and skimming techniques to identify data by observing textual features

    c. Use text features in picture dictionaries and other references for locating information

    d. Use pictures in combination with writing to document research, with adult assistance

53. Which of the following correctly sequences children's typical developmental phases in writing?
   a. Beginning sounds emerge; letter-like symbols; scribbling; letter strings; initial, middle, and final sounds; consonants represent words; standard spelling; transitional phases
   b. Letter-like symbols; beginning sounds emerge; letter strings; scribbling; initial, middle, and final sounds; transitional phases; standard spelling; consonants represent words
   c. Scribbling; letter-like symbols; letter strings; beginning sounds emerge; consonants represent words; initial, middle, and final sounds; transitional phases; standard spelling
   d. Letter strings; beginning sounds emerge; initial, middle, and final sounds; consonants represent words; letter-like symbols; transitional phases; standard spelling; scribbling

54. After only two or three months into 1st grade, a new substitute teacher gives grades in the 80s to a student who had been receiving 100s from the regular teacher before the teacher had to take emergency leave. The substitute deducts points when the student occasionally reverses a letter or number, or misspells words like *biscuit, butterfly,* and *swallowed.* Which of the following most accurately describes this scenario?
   a. The regular teacher should not have given 100s; the substitute grades errors more thoroughly.
   b. The student should be evaluated for possible dyslexia because she reverses letters and numbers.
   c. The student's writing is developmentally appropriate; the substitute's grading is inappropriate.
   d. The student's occasional reversals are not important, but the misspellings need interventions.

55. Which of the following is the correct sequence of these phases of spelling development?
   a. Semiphonetic, precommunicative, transitional, correct, phonetic
   b. Precommunicative, semiphonetic, phonetic, transitional, correct
   c. Correct, phonetic, semiphonetic, precommunicative, transitional
   d. Phonetic, semiphonetic, transitional, correct, precommunicative

56. A teacher instructing students to develop their spelling skills gives them lessons, worksheets, and exercises for identifying the correct meanings and spellings of words like *air* and *heir, hole* and *whole, ate* and *eight, do* and *due,* etc. These examples are of which of the following?
   a. Homophones
   b. Homographs
   c. Homonyms
   d. Homologs

57. Which of the following reflects expert recommendations for developing children's fine motor skills for writing?
   a. Always have children write using pencil and paper, not finger-writing in the air.
   b. When letting children trace letters for practice, using smooth surfaces is better.
   c. Children should look at three-dimensional letters when they manipulate them.
   d. First teach letters involving similar strokes, progressing from simple to complex.

58. A teacher planning instructional activities to develop student use of writing conventions should teach 4th-grade students to do which of the following?
   a. Capitalize historical events; book, essay, and story titles; use quotation marks and commas
   b. Capitalize names, weekdays, months, letter salutations, and closings; use apostrophes
   c. Capitalize abbreviations, initials, acronyms, organizations; and punctuate quotations
   d. Capitalize the initial letters in sentences and use punctuation at ends of sentences

59. How should teachers best instruct students in writing?
  a. In connection with reading only
  b. By itself to focus student attention
  c. With relation to reading and speaking
  d. Related to listening, reading, and speaking

60. What is the best way for teachers to help students develop larger reading and writing vocabularies?
  a. Give students weekly vocabulary lists to memorize for tests
  b. Assign students to search texts for new vocabulary words
  c. Give students many opportunities for reading and writing
  d. Assign students new-word quotas to include in writing

61. A teacher has a student in her class who is not very motivated to write because he finds it difficult. She observes he has a highly visual learning style, does not like reading books but loves graphic novels, and has considerable artistic drawing talent and interest. Which of the following instructional strategies would best address his individual needs, strengths, and interests?
  a. Giving him audio recordings to accompany and guide his writing homework
  b. Letting him complete all assignments by drawing pictures instead of writing
  c. Having him draw the pictures and write accompanying text in graphic novels
  d. Providing and assigning him to view animated videos on the topic of writing

62. Which of the following is correct regarding the writing process and its stages?
  a. Prewriting is the only stage in the process when the writer generates ideas.
  b. First drafts are usually reader-centered and do not change prewriting plans.
  c. Revising follows the editing stage and makes the document writer-centered.
  d. When editing, spell-checking is the last thing to do before printing the work.

63. A teacher is instructing students in using MS Word as a technology for facilitating written communication. S/he shows them a good way to learn from their previous writing mistakes and the revising and editing processes. What is it?
  a. Turning on Track Changes so they can view all of their markups
  b. Selecting Side-by-Side View to compare rough with final drafts
  c. Exchanging documents with classmates for peer reviews
  d. Printing out rough drafts and revising and editing them by hand

64. Which of the following correctly describes the four purposes and types of writing?
  a. A research paper exemplifies argumentation.
  b. Persuasive writing is often found in editorials.
  c. Exposition is the common purpose of novels.
  d. Character sketches are examples of narrative.

65. Which of the following is *not* an expectation for middle school students?
  a. To interpret and understand visual imagery, meanings, and messages
  b. To conduct analyses and critiques of how visual media are important
  c. To produce visual media representations communicating with others
  d. To get ideas from the environment, and develop and organize them

66. Among four categories of media that teachers instruct students to identify, in which one are books classified?
   a. Media used in one-on-one communication
   b. Media used for entertainment
   c. Media to inform many people
   d. Media for persuading people

67. Among these forms of electronic media, which have the highest level of formality?
   a. Web news articles
   b. Blogs on the web
   c. Email messages
   d. All are the same

68. Which of the following creators of visual images are *most* likely to communicate their messages through satire?
   a. Documentary filmmakers
   b. News photographers
   c. Political cartoonists
   d. Illustrators

69. Line, texture, shape, size, space, and color are examples of which aspect of visual media choices that help to communicate and/or elaborate meaning?
   a. Style
   b. Media
   c. Elements
   d. All of these

70. A teacher shows students a news article and public service announcement, both featuring the same celebrity athlete. The teacher then asks students who produced each message; message purposes, perspectives, and target audiences; and which message uses elements like comparison, repetition, description, and vivid verbs. What does this best help students do?
   a. Compare various celebrity athletes
   b. Compare points of view and ideas
   c. Compare various types of graphics
   d. Compare objectivity to subjectivity

71. To measure children's emergent literacy development, an early childhood teacher informally evaluates their performance and behaviors during daily classroom activities. This is an example of what kind of assessment?
   a. Formative assessment
   b. Summative assessment
   c. Both (a) and (b)
   d. Neither (a) nor (b)

72. Among assessments of reading comprehension, which of these compares student scores to the average scores of a sample of students representing the same population?
   a. A norm-referenced state test
   b. An informal reading inventory
   c. A curriculum-based assessment
   d. A criterion-referenced state test

73. Assessment finds that a student in the 2nd grade follows spoken directions involving a brief sequence of related actions and listens attentively by facing speakers and asking questions for clarification, but does not restate or give others sequenced spoken directions. What does this indicate?
  a. The student meets grade-level expectations.
  b. The student exceeds grade-level expectations.
  c. The student needs help for reaching grade level.
  d. The student's level does not require intervention.

74. A student identifies a text to read independently. According to an informal reading inventory the teacher just conducted, the student understands 48 percent of words in isolation that this text includes; reads words contained in this text with 90 percent accuracy in context; and correctly answers 68 percent of comprehension questions at this text's reading level. What does this indicate to the teacher?
  a. This text is at the student's independent level; the teacher approves the student's selection.
  b. This text is at the student's frustration level; the teacher helps the student find another text.
  c. This text is at the student's instructional level, and the teacher approves it for guided reading.
  d. This text is at some reading level that cannot be identified only from the student information.

75. To ascertain when a student may need specialized reading instruction or classroom intervention and to plan instruction accordingly, what kind of assessment should a teacher use?
  a. Ongoing
  b. Formative
  c. Summative
  d. Both (a) and (b)

Mathematics

1. Mrs. Miller is teaching a unit on number and operations with her sixth grade class. At the beginning of class, she asks the students to work in groups to sketch a Venn diagram to classify whole numbers, integers, and rational numbers on a white board. Which of the following types of assessments has the teacher used?
   a. Summative assessment
   b. Formative assessment
   c. Formal assessment
   d. Informal assessment

2. A teacher is working with her students on a unit on subtraction. She notices that most students are much more successful when working the problems with manipulatives rather than working the problems with numerals. In which stage of development are most of her students operating?
   a. Formal operations stage
   b. Concrete operations stage
   c. Pre-operations stage
   d. Sensory motor stage

3. Ms. Alejo is teaching a unit on fractions to her third grade class. Some students are completing an activity in identifying the parts of a fraction. Others are completing an activity on equivalent fractions. Another group of students is completing an activity on adding and subtracting fractions. Which of the following instruction methods describes the various readiness levels Ms. Alejo is incorporating?
   a. Collaborative learning
   b. Small group instruction
   c. Nonlinguistic representations
   d. Differentiated instruction

4. Mr. Sarver, a second grade teacher, notices that a few of his students are struggling with the concept of borrowing when subtracting two digit numbers. Which of the following activities would best help students understand this concept of borrowing?
   a. The teacher works subtraction problems on the white board.
   b. The students watch a children's video about borrowing.
   c. The students complete a worksheet with subtraction problems.
   d. The students use cardboard manipulatives to model subtraction problems.

5. Which of the following learning goals is most appropriate for a fourth grade unit on geometry and measurement?
   a. The students will be able to use a protractor to determine the approximate measures of angles in degrees to the nearest whole number.
   b. The students will be able to describe the process for graphing ordered pairs of numbers in the first quadrant of the coordinate plane.
   c. The students will be able to determine the volume of a rectangular prism with whole number side lengths in problems related to the number of layers times the number of unit cubes in the area of the base.
   d. The students will be able to classify two-dimensional figures in a hierarchy of sets and subsets using graphic organizers based on their attributes and properties.

6. Which of the following learning goals is most appropriate for a second grade unit on personal financial literacy?
    a. The students will be able to calculate how money saved can accumulate into a larger amount over time.
    b. The students will be able to balance a simple budget.
    c. The students will be able to identify the costs and benefits of planned and unplanned spending decisions.
    d. The students will be able to define money earned as income.

7. During February, the sixth grade teachers at an elementary school decide to work together to teach a unit about the heart. The English teacher will have the students write essays about how the heart functions. The science teacher will teach the basic parts of the heart. The art teacher will have the students build models of the heart. The math teacher will have the students determine the amount of blood that flows through the heart in everyday units of capacity.
The teachers are implementing the concept of which of the following?
    a. Differentiated instruction
    b. Formative assessment
    c. Thematic units
    d. Collaborative learning

8. Which of the following activities would best help first grade students understand the concept of measuring objects?
    a. Measuring the height of the pencil sharpener using a meter stick
    b. Measuring the length of the chalkboard using a tape measure
    c. Measuring the width of their desks using dominoes placed end to end
    d. Measuring the circumference of the trash can using a cloth tape

9. Sophia is at the market buying fruit for her family of four. Kiwi fruit is only sold in packages of three. If Sophia would like each family member to have the same number of kiwi fruits, which of the following approaches can Sophia use to determine the fewest number of kiwi fruits she should buy?
    a. Sophia needs to determine the greatest common multiple of 3 and 4.
    b. Sophia needs to determine the least common multiple of 3 and 4.
    c. Sophia needs to determine the least common divisor of 3 and 4.
    d. Sophia needs to determine the greatest common divisor of 3 and 4.

10. Mr. Mancelli teaches fifth grade math. He is making prize bags for the winners of a math game. If he has eight candy bars and twelve packages of gum, what is the largest number of identical prize bags he can make without having any left-over candy bars or packages of gum?
    a. 2
    b. 4
    c. 6
    d. 8

11. Ms. Chen is instructing her students on divisibility rules. Which of the following rules can be used to determine if a number is divisible by 6?
    a. The last digit of the number is divisible by 2 or 3.
    b. The number ends in 6.
    c. The number is divisible by 2 and 3.
    d. The last two digits of the number are divisible by 6.

12. Which of the following correctly compares the given rational numbers?
    a. $0.2 > 0.0499 > 0.007$
    b. $0 < -2 < 7$
    c. $\frac{1}{5} > \frac{1}{4} > \frac{1}{3}$
    d. $-1 < -4 < -10$

13. A 6th grade math teacher is introducing the concept of positive and negative numbers to a group of students. Which of the following models would be the most effective when introducing this concept?
    a. Fraction strips
    b. Venn diagrams
    c. Shaded regions
    d. Number lines

14. Which of the following options represents equivalency between different representations of rational numbers?
    a. $16 \div (6 - 4)^2 = 64$
    b. $8 - 2(7 - 4) = 18$
    c. $2^3 \div 2 - 2(2) = 0$
    d. $2 + 3(2^2) = 20$

15. Miss Wise asks her students to work in pairs to construct Venn diagrams which classify rational numbers, irrational numbers, real numbers, and integers. As she walks around the room to observe their progress, which of the following criterion could she use to assess the students' understanding of these sets of numbers?
    a. The set of integers should include the other three sets.
    b. The set of rational numbers should include the other three sets.
    c. The set of irrational numbers should include the other three sets.
    d. The set of real numbers should include the other three sets.

16. Which of the following options represents equivalency between mathematical expressions?
    a. $3 + x + 3x + 3 + x = 5x + 6$
    b. $7x - 2x = 9x$
    c. $2y + 2y + 2y = 6y^3$
    d. $2.5(x + 2) = 2.5x + 2$

17. Which of the following problems demonstrates the associative property of multiplication?
    a. $2(3 + 4) = 2(3) + 2(4)$
    b. $(3 \times 6) \times 2 = (4 \times 3) \times 3$
    c. $(2 \times 3) \times 4 = 2 \times (3 \times 4)$
    d. $6 \times 4 = 4 \times 6$

18. A jogger records his distance in meters from his front door as a function of time in seconds on his morning run. If x represents time in seconds, which of the following equations represents the jogger's distance from his front door as a function of time?

Time	0	3	4	6	7
Distance	5.2	25.0	31.6	44.8	51.4

    a. $y = 3x + 25$
    b. $y = 25.0x + 5.2$
    c. $y = 18.4x + 3$
    d. $y = 6.6x + 5.2$

19. Which of the following goals is appropriate in the category of algebraic reasoning for first grade students?
    a. Students represent one- and two-step problems involving addition and subtraction of whole numbers to 1,000 using pictorial models, number lines, and equations.
    b. Students represent real-world relationships using number pairs in a table and verbal descriptions.
    c. Students represent word problems involving addition and subtraction of whole numbers up to 20 using concrete and pictorial models and number sentences.
    d. Students recite numbers up to at least 100 by ones and tens beginning with any given number.

20. Which of the following polynomials is factored correctly?
    a. $3x^2 - 12x + 12 = 3(x - 2)^2$
    b. $x^2 - 9 = (x - 3)^2$
    c. $5x^2 + 5x - 10 = 5(x + 1)(x - 2)$
    d. $4x^2 - 16x = 4(x - 4)$

21. Claus has $20 to spend at the local fun fair. The entrance fee is $2.50 and tickets for the booths are $2 each. Which of the following inequalities represents the number of tickets Claus can afford with his $20?
    a. $2.50x + 2x \leq 20$
    b. $2.50 + 2x \leq 20$
    c. $2x \leq 20 + 2.50$
    d. $2.50 + 2x \geq 20x$

22. Which of the following is the correct solution for x in the system of equations $x - 1 = y$ and $y + 3 = 7$?
    a. $x = 6$
    b. $x = 5$
    c. $x = 4$
    d. $x = 8$

23. Coach Weybright's 6th grade basketball team has played 36 games this season. The ratio of wins to losses is 2:1. If x represents the number of wins, which of the following proportions can be used to determine the number of wins?

a. $\dfrac{x}{36} = \dfrac{2}{1}$

b. $\dfrac{x}{2} = \dfrac{1}{36}$

c. $\dfrac{x}{3} = \dfrac{36}{2}$

d. $\dfrac{x}{36} = \dfrac{2}{3}$

24. Which of the following equations is a linear equation?

a. $y = x^2 + 4$

b. $y = \dfrac{2}{x^3}$

c. $2x - 3y = 5$

d. $x = (y + 2)^2$

25. Marcus, a sixth grade student, is mowing yards and doing odd jobs to earn money for a new video game system that costs $325. Marcus only charges $6.50 per hour. Which of the following equations represents the number of hours Marcus needs to work to earn $325?

a. $6.50x = 325$

b. $6.50 + x = 325$

c. $325x = 6.50$

d. $6.50x + 325 = x$

26. Which of the following best describes an isosceles triangle?

a. A triangle with no sides of equal measurement and one obtuse angle

b. A triangle with three sides of equal measurement

c. A triangle with two sides of equal measurement and two acute angles

d. A triangle with one right angle and two non-congruent acute angles

27. Which of the following describes how to find the formula for the volume of a regular solid prism?

a. Find the perimeter of the base of the prism and multiply by the height of the prism.

b. Find the area of the base of the prism and multiply by the height of the prism.

c. Find the sum of the areas of the faces and multiply by the length of the prism.

d. Find the sum of the areas of the lateral faces and multiply by the number of faces.

28. A teacher is assessing the students' understanding of the appropriate units for length, area, and volume. Which of the following only lists units of area?

a. in², mm², ft²

b. yd, yd², yd³

c. mm, cm, m

d. m², s², km²

29. Which of the following correctly explains one method that may be used to determine the size of each angle in a regular polygon of more than four sides?

    a. Draw all possible diagonals of the polygon. The sum of the angles of the polygon is equal to the product of the number of triangles formed and 180°. Finally, divide this sum by the number of sides of the polygon.

    b. Choose one vertex of the polygon and draw diagonals from that vertex to all nonconsecutive vertices. The sum of the angles of the polygon is equal to the area of the triangles formed. Finally, divide the sum by the number of triangles formed.

    c. Draw all possible diagonals of the polygon. The sum of the angles of the polygon is equal to the product of the number of triangles formed and 180°. Finally, divide the sum by the number of triangles formed.

    d. Choose one vertex of the polygon and draw diagonals from that vertex to all nonconsecutive vertices. The sum of the angles of the polygon is equal to the product of the number of triangles formed and 180°. Finally, divide this sum by the number of sides of the polygon.

30. Mr. Amad draws a line with a slope of $-\frac{2}{3}$ on the white board through three points. Which of the sets could possibly be these three points?

    a. (-6, -2) (-7, -4), (-8, -6)
    b. (-4, 7), (-8, 13), (-6, 10)
    c. (-3, -1), (-6, 1), (0, -3)
    d. (-2, -3), (-1, -3), (0 -3)

31. Which of the following descriptions best fits a hexagonal prism?

    a. 8 faces, 18 edges, 12 vertices
    b. 6 faces, 18 edges, 12 vertices
    c. 8 faces, 16 edges, 8 vertices
    d. 6 faces, 14 edges, 10 vertices

32. During an activity, Mrs. Schwartz instructs her students to place groups of coins in order of decreasing value. Which of the following students correctly completed this activity?

    a. Henry with Group 1: 2 dimes, 2 nickels, and 4 pennies; Group 2: 1 dime, 3 nickels, 2 pennies; Group 3: 1 dime, 2 nickels, 7 pennies

    b. Graham with Group 1: 1 dime, 5 nickels, and 5 pennies; Group 2: 2 dimes, 2 nickels, 8 pennies; Group 3: 1 dime, 2 nickel, 9 pennies

    c. Landon with Group 1: 3 dimes, 4 nickels, and 9 pennies; Group 2: 2 dimes, 4 nickels, 3 pennies; Group 3: 1 dime, 9 nickels, 4 pennies

    d. Elizabeth with Group 1: 2 dimes, 3 nickels, and 6 pennies; Group 2: 2 dimes, 4 nickels, 1 penny; Group 3: 1 dime, 1 nickel, 7 pennies

33. During a unit on geometry, Ms. Nifong instructs her student to sketch two congruent polygons. Which of the following sketches completes this task correctly?

    a. Two rectangles with the same perimeter
    b. Two polygons with the same shape
    c. Two polygons with the same side lengths
    d. Two squares with the same area

34. Given this stem and leaf plot, what are the mean and median?

Stem	Leaf
1	6 8
2	0 1
3	4
4	5 9

    a. Mean = 28 and median = 20
    b. Mean = 29 and median = 20
    c. Mean = 29 and median = 21
    d. Mean = 28 and median = 21

35. Mr. Gomez is a sixth grade teacher presenting a unit on compound probability. He places ten marbles with the digits 0 through 9 in a bowl on his podium. He draws a marble, records the number, and then places the marble back in the bowl. He repeats the process. What is probability that he drew two 5s in a row?
    a. 1/10
    b. 1/5
    c. 1/100
    d. 1/50

36. Ms. Elliott asks her 5th grade students, "Do you prefer chocolate or vanilla ice cream?" If the probability of her students preferring chocolate ice cream is 0.6, what is the probability of her students preferring vanilla ice cream?
    a. 0.6
    b. 0.4
    c. 0.3
    d. 0.5

37. A dart board consists of two concentric circles with radii of 3 inches and 6 inches. If a dart is thrown onto the board, what is the probability the dart will land in the inner circle?
    a. $\frac{1}{4}$
    b. $\frac{1}{2}$
    c. $\frac{1}{3}$
    d. $\frac{1}{5}$

38. The 6th grade teachers at Washington Elementary School are doing a collaborative unit on cherry trees. Miss Wilson's math classes are making histograms summarizing the heights of black cherry trees located at a local fruit orchard. How many of the trees at this local orchard are 73 feet tall?

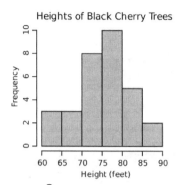

Heights of Black Cherry Trees

a. 8
b. That information cannot be obtained from this graph.
c. 9
d. 17

39. The summary statistics for today's test for Mr. Johnson's 4th grade math class are listed in the table below. Which of the following describes the spread of the test scores?

Mean	86.14
Median	86
Mode	100
Standard Deviation	11.4

a. The mean
b. The median
c. The mode
d. The standard deviation

40. Addison tosses a six-sided die twelve times and records the results in the table below.

Toss	1	2	3	4	5	6	7	8	9	10	11	12
Results	2	5	1	2	3	6	6	2	4	5	4	3

Which of the following statements is true?
a. The experimental probability of tossing a 6 is greater than the theoretical probability.
b. The experimental probability of tossing a 3 is greater than the theoretical probability.
c. The experimental probability of tossing a 1 is greater than the theoretical probability.
d. The experimental probability of tossing a 2 is greater than the theoretical probability.

41. Mr. Carver is teaching his students about deductive reasoning and states the premises listed below. Which of these students has reached a valid conclusion?

| Premise 1 | All primates are mammals. |
| Premise 2 | All lemurs are primates. |

    a. Mia states, "All primates are lemurs."
    b. Carlos states, "All lemurs are mammals."
    c. Xavier states, "All whales are mammals."
    d. Gavin states, "All monkeys are primates."

42. Mr. Orr asks his class to use inductive reasoning as to determine the pattern in this series of numbers. Which number is next in this series?
2, 5, 10, 17, ___
    a. 25
    b. 26
    c. 22
    d. 24

43. Elementary teachers in one school surveyed their students and discovered that 15% of their students have iPhones. Which of the following correctly states 15% in fraction, decimal, and ratio equivalents?
    a. $\frac{3}{20}$, 0.15, 3:20
    b. $\frac{3}{25}$, 0.15, 3:25
    c. $\frac{15}{10}$, 1.5%, 15:10
    d. $\frac{2}{1}$, 1.5%, 2:1

44. Which of the following statements is true concerning the Sumerians?
    a. The Sumerians lived in Africa approximately 20,000 years ago.
    b. The Sumerians included Plato and Archimedes.
    c. The Sumerians are famous for the earliest known written mathematics.
    d. The Sumerians wrote the Rhind papyrus.

45. While teaching the concept of addition, a first grade teacher gives each student two dice to use as manipulatives. Which of the following types of representation is this teacher using to communicate this concept?
    a. Concrete
    b. Verbal
    c. Graphic
    d. Pictorial

46. Mrs. Vories, a fifth grade teacher, asks her class to use compatible numbers to help her determine approximately how many chicken nuggets she needs to buy for a school-wide party. The school has 589 students and each student will be served nine nuggets. Which student correctly applied the concept of compatible numbers?

    a. Madison estimates: $500 \times 10 = 5,000$ nuggets
    b. Audrey estimates: $600 \times 5 = 3,000$ nuggets
    c. Ian estimates: $600 \times 10 = 6,000$ nuggets
    d. Andrew estimates: $500 \times 5 = 2,500$ nuggets

47. A sixth grade teacher askes her students to find the error in this algebra problem. What is the error?

$3x + 4x = (2^2 + 1) + 2(2)$
$7x = 5 + 2(2)$
$7x = 7(2)$
$7x = 14$
$x = 2$

    a. The student incorrectly added before multiplying.
    b. The student incorrectly multiplied before adding.
    c. The student incorrectly applied the exponent.
    d. The student incorrectly combined like terms.

Social Studies

1. How are members of the Federal Judiciary chosen?
    a. They are elected by voters
    b. They are appointed by the President and confirmed by the House of Representatives
    c. They are chosen by a committee
    d. They are appointed by the President and confirmed by the Senate

2. How long can members of the Federal Judiciary serve?
    a. Four years
    b. Eight years
    c. For life
    d. Six years

3. Article III judges who can retire but still try cases on a full-time or part-time basis are called
_____.
    a. Recalled judges
    b. Senior judges
    c. Chief judges
    d. Elder judges

4. Most federal judges have served as local judges, lawyers, and law professors. These are _____
qualifications.
    a. Formal
    b. Required
    c. Informal
    d. Recommended

5. The Supreme Court has nine members. How is this number determined?
    a. It is outlined in the Constitution
    b. Congress determines the number
    c. The President determines the number
    d. The Court decides on the number

6. Criminal cases are tried under:
    I.   State law
    II.   Federal law
    III.   Civil court
    a. I and III
    b. II only
    c. I only
    d. I and II

7. The executive, legislative, and judicial branches of government compose:
    a. The federal government
    b. The state government
    c. Both A and B
    d. None of the above

8. What does the 10th Amendment establish?
   a. Any power not given to the federal government belongs to the states, or the people
   b. The President is responsible for executing and enforcing laws created by Congress
   c. Congress has the authority to declare war
   d. The Supreme Court has the authority to interpret the Constitution

9. How is the jurisdiction of federal courts usually decided?
   a. By the President
   b. By Congress
   c. By the voters
   d. By the Supreme Court

10. How must inferior courts interpret the law?
    a. According to the Supreme Court's interpretation
    b. According to the Constitution
    c. However they choose
    d. According to the political climate

11. How was the Vice President chosen before the 12th Amendment was ratified?
    a. The President chose the Vice President
    b. Congress chose the Vice President
    c. The Vice President came in second in the Electoral College
    d. There was no Vice President

12. What portion of the federal budget is dedicated to transportation, education, national resources, the environment, and international affairs?
    a. Mandatory spending
    b. Discretionary spending
    c. Undistributed offsetting receipts
    d. Official budget outlays

13. The primary expense for most state and local governments is:
    a. Emergency medical services
    b. Transportation services
    c. Police and fire departments
    d. Education

14. Which of the following will result if two nations use the theory of comparative advantage when making decisions of which goods to produce and trade?
    a. Each nation will make all of their own goods
    b. Both nations will specialize in the production of the same specific goods
    c. Each nation will specialize in the production of different specific goods
    d. Neither nation will trade with one another
    e. All of the above

15. Which of the following best defines American GDP?
   a. The value, in American dollars, of all goods and services produced within American borders during one calendar year
   b. The value, in American dollars, of all goods and services produced by American companies during one calendar year
   c. The total value, in American dollars, of all American household incomes during one calendar year
   d. The value, in American dollars, of a "market basket" of goods and services in one year divided by the value of the same market basket in a previous year multiplied by 100
   e. None of the above

16. A country's currency increases in value on foreign currency exchange markets. What will happen as a result?
   I.   Exports will drop
   II.   Imports will rise
   III.   The balance of payments will rise
   a. I only
   b. II only
   c. I and II
   d. II and III
   e. III only

17. Which of the following are true of the demand curve?
   I.   It is normally downward sloping
   II.   It is normally upward sloping
   III.   It is influenced by the law of diminishing marginal unity
   IV.   It is unaffected by the law of diminishing marginal unity
   a. I and III only
   b. I and IV only
   c. II and III only
   d. II and IV only
   e. IV only

18. Which of the following is most likely to benefit from inflation?
   a. A bond investor who owns fixed-rate bonds
   b. A retired widow with no income other than fixed Social Security payments
   c. A person who has taken out a fixed-rate loan
   d. A local bank who has loaned money out at fixed rate
   e. All of the above

19. The impact of a transaction on parties not directly involved in the transaction is known as what?
   a. Social cost
   b. Social benefit
   c. Externality
   d. Marginal social cost
   e. Marginal social benefit

20. Which of the following is associated with market failure?
   - I.   When a firm in a non-competitive industry hires labor at a lower wage
   - II. When the firms in a non-competitive industry create less than the efficient amount of a good or service
   - III. When production of a good creates negative externalities born by third parties
   - IV. Public goods
   - a. I and II only
   - b. II and III only
   - c. I and III only
   - d. I, II, and III only
   - e. I, II, III, and IV

21. Which map describes the movement of people, trends, or materials across a physical area?
   - a. Political Map
   - b. Cartogram
   - c. Qualitative Map
   - d. Flow-line Map

22. Which type of chart is best at representing the cycle of demographic transition?
   - a. Pie chart
   - b. Political map
   - c. Line graph
   - d. Flow-line map

23. What kind of chart would be best for representing the major events of World War I?
   - a. Time line
   - b. Bar graph
   - c. Pie chart
   - d. Political map

24. What is the most common type of volcano on earth?
   - a. Lava dome
   - b. Composite volcano
   - c. Shield volcano
   - d. Cinder cone

25. Which biome features scrubby plants and small evergreen trees and also has a hot, dry summer followed by a wetter winter?
   - a. Taiga
   - b. Coniferous forest
   - c. Chaparral
   - d. Savanna

26. Which type of rock is formed by extreme heat and pressure?
   - a. Limestone
   - b. Metamorphic
   - c. Sedimentary
   - d. Igneous

27. The rocks and landmasses that make up the earth's surface are called the
    a. atmosphere.
    b. biosphere.
    c. hydrosphere.
    d. lithosphere.

28. What causes the motion of glaciers?
    a. Gravity
    b. Erosion
    c. Wind
    d. Temperature change

29. Which of the following is an example of chemical weathering?
    a. Frost wedging
    b. Heat expansion
    c. Acid rain
    d. Salt wedging

30. Which of the following is *not* one of the world's four major population agglomerations?
    a. North Africa
    b. Eastern North America
    c. South Asia
    d. Europe

31. Which of the following locations would be considered a modern cultural hearth?
    a. New York City
    b. Baghdad
    c. Auckland
    d. Edmonton

32. Which of the following is *not* one of the demographic variables?
    a. Fertility
    b. Diversity
    c. Mortality
    d. Migration

33. Which of the following nations is *not* a member of OPEC?
    a. Saudi Arabia
    b. Venezuela
    c. Yemen
    d. Iraq

34. Which of the following is a true statement about the Yucatan Peninsula?
    a. It is densely populated.
    b. It is more mountainous than the rest of Mexico.
    c. It was once inhabited by Aztecs.
    d. It has a number of large sinkholes.

35. What are the Atlantic provinces of Canada?
    a. Labrador, Prince Edward Island, New Brunswick, and Nova Scotia
    b. New Brunswick, Nunavut, Nova Scotia, and Labrador
    c. Prince Edward Island, Nova Scotia, Quebec, and Newfoundland
    d. Manitoba, Nunavut, Ontario, and Saskatchewan

36. Which country controlled Hong Kong before China?
    a. Japan
    b. United States
    c. Great Britain
    d. Korea

37. After the United States, which of the following nations imports the most oil?
    a. China
    b. Brazil
    c. Germany
    d. Japan

38. Which of the following statements is *not* true regarding English expansionism in the 16th century?
    a. England's defeat of the Spanish Armada in 1588 brought a decisive end to their war with Spain.
    b. King Henry VIII's desire to divorce Catherine of Aragon strengthened English expansionism.
    c. Queen Elizabeth's support for the Protestant Reformation strengthened English expansionism.
    d. Sir Francis Drake and other English sea captains plundered the Spaniards' plunders of Indians.

39. Which of the following is *not* true regarding the Virginia Companies?
    a. One of these companies, the Virginia Company of Plymouth, made its base in North America.
    b. One of these companies, the Virginia Company of London, made its base in Massachusetts.
    c. One company had a charter to colonize America between the Hudson and Cape Fear rivers.
    d. One company had a charter to colonize America from the Potomac River to north Maine.

40. Which of the following statements is *not* true regarding the colony of Jamestown?
    a. The colony of Jamestown was established by the Virginia Company of London in 1607.
    b. The colony of Jamestown became the first permanent English colony in North America.
    c. The majority of settlers in early Jamestown died of starvation, disease, or Indian attacks.
    d. John Smith's governance helped Jamestown more than John Rolfe's tobacco discovery.

41. Which of the following conquistadores unwittingly gave smallpox to the Indians and destroyed the Aztec empire in Mexico?
    a. Balboa
    b. Ponce de Leon
    c. Cortes
    d. De Vaca

42. Which of these factors was *not* a direct contributor to the beginning of the American Revolution?

 a. The attitudes of American colonists toward Great Britain following the French and Indian War

 b. The attitudes of leaders in Great Britain toward the American colonies and imperialism

 c. James Otis's court argument against Great Britain's Writs of Assistance as breaking natural law

 d. Lord Grenville's Proclamation of 1763, Sugar Act, Currency Act, and especially Stamp Act

43. Which of the following statements is *not* true regarding the Tea Act of 1773?

 a. The British East India Company was suffering financially because Americans were buying tea smuggled from Holland.

 b. Parliament granted concessions to the British East India Company to ship tea straight to America, bypassing England.

 c. Colonists found that even with added taxes, tea directly shipped by the British East India Company cost less, and they bought it.

 d. American colonists refused to buy less expensive tea from the British East India Company on the principle of taxation.

Science

1. The majority of the solar energy that reaches Earth is absorbed by:
   a. Glaciers.
   b. Landmasses.
   c. Oceans.
   d. The Earth's atmosphere.

2. Tropical climate zones are characterized by:
   a. Extreme temperature variations between night and day.
   b. Extreme temperature variations between seasons.
   c. Frequent rainfall.
   d. All of the above

3. Which of the following statements best describes the physical structure of the universe?
   a. Galaxies are the largest structures in the universe, and they are distributed evenly throughout space.
   b. Superclusters are the largest structures in the universe, and they are distributed evenly throughout space.
   c. Superclusters are the largest structures in the universe, and they are unevenly distributed so that large voids exist in space.
   d. Filaments are the largest structures in the universe, and they surround large, bubble-like voids.

4. Which of the following statements about galaxies is true?
   a. Galaxies are the only structures in the universe that do not contain dark matter.
   b. Galaxies are gravitationally bound, meaning structures within the galaxy orbit around its center.
   c. Galaxies typically contain over one trillion stars.
   d. Galaxies are comprised of clusters and superclusters.

5. The structure of the Milky Way galaxy is best described as:
   a. Spiral.
   b. Starburst.
   c. Elliptical.
   d. Irregular.

6. The distance from the Earth to the Sun is equal to one:
   a. Astronomical unit.
   b. Light year.
   c. Parsec.
   d. Arcsecond.

7. The energy radiated by stars is produced by:
   a. Neutronicity.
   b. Nuclear fusion.
   c. Nuclear fission.
   d. Gravitational confinement.

8. The stream of charged particles that escape the Sun's gravitational pull is best described by which of the following terms?
   a. Solar wind
   b. Solar flare
   c. Solar radiation
   d. Sunspots

9. Which of the following planets in our solar system is NOT a gas giant?
   a. Saturn
   b. Neptune
   c. Venus
   d. Jupiter

10. The asteroid belt in our solar system is located between:
   a. Earth and Mars.
   b. Neptune and Pluto.
   c. Uranus and Saturn.
   d. Mars and Jupiter.

11. Which of the following is a proposed explanation for the formation of black holes?
   a. High-energy collisions
   b. Gravitational collapse
   c. Accretion of matter
   d. A and B

12. Which of the following organelles is/are formed when the plasma membrane surrounds a particle outside of the cell?
   a. Golgi bodies
   b. Rough endoplasmic reticulum
   c. Lysosomes
   d. Secretory vesicles
   e. Endocytic vesicles

13. Which of the following plant organelles contain(s) pigment that give leaves their color?
   a. Centrioles
   b. Cell walls
   c. Chloroplasts
   d. Central vacuole
   e. Golgi apparatus

14. Which of the following is not a characteristic of enzymes?
   a. They change shape when they bind their substrates
   b. They can catalyze reactions in both forward and reverse directions
   c. Their activity is sensitive to changes in temperature
   d. They are always active on more than one kind of substrate
   e. They may have more than one binding site

15. In plants and animals, genetic variation is introduced during
    a. Crossing over in mitosis
    b. Chromosome segregation in mitosis
    c. Cytokinesis of meiosis
    d. Anaphase I of meiosis
    e. Anaphase II of meiosis

16. DNA replication occurs during which of the following phases?
    a. Prophase I
    b. Prophase II
    c. Interphase I
    d. Interphase II
    e. Telophase I

17. A length of DNA coding for a particular protein is called a(n)
    a. Allele
    b. Genome
    c. Gene
    d. Transcript
    e. Codon

18. Which of the following parts of an angiosperm give rise to the fruit?
    a. Pedicel
    b. Filament
    c. Sepal
    d. Ovary
    e. Meristem

19. Which of the following structures is NOT present in gymnosperms?
    a. Leaves
    b. Pollen
    c. Flowers
    d. Stomata
    e. Roots

20. Which of the following plant structures allows for gas exchange?
    a. Xylem
    b. Phloem
    c. Cuticle
    d. Meristem
    e. Stomata

21. Which of the following is an example of the alternation of generations life cycle?
    a. Asexual reproduction of strawberries by runners
    b. Annual plants that live through a single growing season
    c. Ferns that have a large diploid and a diminutive haploid stage
    d. Insects that have distinct larval and adult stages
    e. Reptiles that have long periods of dormancy and metabolic inactivity

22. Which of the following is the major way in which carbon is released into the environment?
   a. Transpiration
   b. Respiration
   c. Fixation
   d. Sedimentation
   e. Absorption

23. What is the largest reservoir of nitrogen on the planet?
   a. The ocean
   b. Plants
   c. Soil
   d. The atmosphere
   e. Sediments, including fossil fuels

24. Which of the following conditions would promote evolutionary change?
   a. Neutral selection
   b. Random mating
   c. A large population
   d. An isolated population
   e. Gene flow

25. Darwin's idea that evolution occurs by the gradual accumulation of small changes can be summarized as
   a. Punctuated equilibrium
   b. Phyletic gradualism
   c. Convergent evolution
   d. Adaptive radiation
   e. Sympatric speciation

26. Which of the following organisms would be most likely to have mercury in their bodies?
   a. Mosquitoes
   b. Carnivorous insects
   c. Frogs
   d. Filter-feeding fish
   e. Fish-eating birds

27. Clear-cutting of rain forests leads to all of the following consequences EXCEPT
   a. Climate change
   b. Erosion
   c. Reduction in species diversity
   d. Air pollution
   e. Desertification

28. Burning fossil fuels releases sulfur dioxide and nitrogen dioxide. These pollutants lead to which environmental problem?
   a. Denitrification
   b. Acid rain
   c. Global climate change
   d. Ozone depletion
   e. Eutrophication

29. Genetic engineering
    a. Is a form of human reproduction
    b. Involves introducing new proteins to a cell
    c. Involves transient expression of genes
    d. Can have no environmental affects
    e. Requires using restriction enzymes to cut DNA

30. Which of the following demonstrations best illustrates Newton's first law?
    a. Giving a billiard ball at rest on a smooth level table a small push and letting it roll on the table.
    b. Dragging a box on a table at a constant speed by exerting a force just enough to overcome the force of friction.
    c. Trying without success to move a heavy bureau or filing cabinet on the floor.
    d. Running a current through two parallel wires.

31. Consider the following statements about Newton's law:
    I.   A newton is a fundamental unit.
    II.   Mass and acceleration are inversely related when the force is constant.
    III.   Newton's first law can be derived from Newton's second law.
    IV.   Newton's second law can be derived from the universal law of gravity.

Which of the following statements are true?
    a. I, II, and III.
    b. II and III only.
    c. III only.
    d. I, II, III, and IV are not true.

32. A box with a weight of 10 newtons is resting on a table. Which statement is true?
    a. The force of the table on the box is the reaction to the weight of the box.
    b. The force of the box on the table is the reaction to the weight of the box.
    c. A 10 newton force on Earth is the reaction force.
    d. There is no reaction force because the system is in equilibrium.

33. You blow up a rubber balloon and hold the opening tight with your fingers. You then release your fingers, causing air to blow out of the balloon. This pushes the balloon forward, causing the balloon to shoot across the room. Which of Newton's laws best explains the cause of this motion?
    a. First law
    b. Second law
    c. Third law
    d. Law of gravity

34. Which has a greater moment of inertia about an axis through its center: a solid cylinder or a hollow cylinder? Both cylinders have the same mass and radius.
    a. Solid cylinder
    b. Hollow cylinder
    c. Both have same moment of inertia.
    d. It depends on how quickly the cylinders are rolling.

35. Two cars driving in opposite directions collide. If you ignore friction and any other outside interactions, which of the following statements is always true?
   a. The total momentum is conserved.
   b. The sum of the potential and kinetic energy are conserved.
   c. The total velocity of the cars is conserved.
   d. The total impulse is conserved.

36. Impulse is measured as the change in an object's momentum. Which statement is correct about the impulse on a ball rolling down a hill? Ignore air resistance and friction.
   a. The impulse is constant.
   b. The impulse only exists for a short time.
   c. The units of impulse are joules per second.
   d. The object's impulse increases.

37. Suppose a moving railroad car collides with an identical stationary car and the two cars latch together. Ignoring friction, and assuming no deformation on impact, which of the following statements is true?
   a. The speed of the first car decreases by half.
   b. The collision is elastic.
   c. The speed of the first car is doubled.
   d. There is no determining the final speed because the collision was inelastic.

38. Which of the following statements about energy is true?
   a. Mechanical energy is always conserved in an isolated system.
   b. Total energy is always conserved in an isolated system.
   c. Energy is never created or destroyed.
   d. You can determine the mechanical energy of an object by using $E = mc^2$

39. Conservative forces are forces that do not lose energy to processes like friction and radiation and where the total mechanical energy is conserved. Which statement best explains why the work done by a conservative force on an object does not depend on the path the object takes?
   a. This is the definition of a conservative force.
   b. The work done by the force of friction on an object depends on the distance the object moves.
   c. Work can be positive, negative, or zero.
   d. If a force is conservative, any component of the force is equal to the change in a potential energy divided by the change in position.

40. Which of the following statements is true about the acceleration of a simple pendulum?
   a. The acceleration is constant.
   b. The magnitude of the acceleration is at a maximum when the bob is at the bottom of the path.
   c. The magnitude of the acceleration is at a maximum when the bob is changing directions.
   d. None of the above.

41. What does it mean when someone says that electric charge is conserved?
   a. Like charges repel, and unlike charges attract.
   b. The net charge of an isolated system remains constant.
   c. Charges come from electrons and protons.
   d. Charge can never be created or destroyed.

42. Which of the following is the correct definition of a conductor?
   a. A metal wire in an electrical circuit.
   b. A material that contains moveable electric charges.
   c. A material that is not a semiconductor or insulator.
   d. Any device that allows electricity to flow.

43. Which of the following devices changes chemical energy into electrical energy?
   a. battery
   b. closed electric circuit
   c. generator
   d. transformer

44. Which of the following statements about electricity flowing through a circuit can be correctly derived from Ohm's law?
   a. Increasing the voltage decreases the current if the resistance remains unchanged.
   b. Increasing the current and the resistance decreases the voltage.
   c. Increasing the current increases the voltage if the resistance is unchanged.
   d. Increasing the resistance increases the current if the voltage remains unchanged.

45. How is energy generated in a nuclear reaction?
   a. Matter is converted into energy.
   b. Photon excitation and emission.
   c. Kinetic collision of highly energetic hydrogen atoms.
   d. Gravitational energy is converted into electromagnetic radiation.

46. Which of the following statements about isotopes of an element is true?
   a. They have the same number of nucleons.
   b. They have the same number of neutrons, but different numbers of protons.
   c. They have the same number of protons, but different numbers of neutrons.
   d. They have a different number of electrons.

47. An inch is approximately equivalent to which of the following?
   a. 25.4 mm
   b. 25.4 cm
   c. 2.54×10^{-4} km
   d. 2.54×10^{2} m

48. Which of the following statements is true about the physical properties of liquids and gases?
   I.   Liquids and gases are both compressible
   II. Liquids flow, but gases do not
   III. Liquids flow, and gases are incompressible
   IV. Liquids flow and gases are compressible
   V.   Gases flow and liquids are incompressible
   a. I and III
   b. II and IV
   c. III and V
   d. IV and V

49. What would be the best analytical tool for determining the chemical structure of an organic compound?
    a. NMR
    b. HPLC
    c. IR
    d. Mass spec

50. Proteins are made up of which of the following repeating subunits?
    a. Sugars
    b. Triglycerides
    c. Amino acids
    d. Nucleic acids

The Arts, Health, and Fitness

1. By correctly rendering proportion in her work, an artist can create which of the following artistic effects?
   a. Emotion
   b. Energy
   c. Realism
   d. Rhythm

2. Imagination would be the best source of inspiration for which of the following types of paintings?
   a. A portrait of a nude subject painted from a photograph
   b. An oil painting of the artist's hometown
   c. A copy of an original artwork
   d. An abstract sculpture

3. Visual literacy can best be described as the
   a. ability to communicate through images and comprehend the messages contained in images.
   b. ability to construct three-dimensional images.
   c. incorporation of literary text into works of art.
   d. incorporation of art into literary texts.

4. Traditionally, visual artists have participated in performing arts in all but which of the following ways?
   a. Designing costumes
   b. Applying makeup
   c. Designing sets
   d. Casting performers

5. An art teacher wants to incorporate the subjects students are learning in their general education classes into his art lesson. Which of the following lessons could be incorporated into his art class?
   a. A social studies lesson on political propaganda
   b. A math lesson on data analysis
   c. An English lesson about haiku
   d. All of the above

6. Which of the following activities would be most appropriate for helping high school students develop an appreciation for the value and role of art in U.S. society?
   a. Having students create a PowerPoint presentation about a famous American artist
   b. Asking students to create a time line showing when famous works of American art were created
   c. Taking students on a field trip to an art museum
   d. Asking students to write an essay comparing and contrasting the influence that two famous American artists or artworks had on U.S. society

7. Which of the following strategies would be the most effective way to support high school students when teaching them to identify the main idea in a work of art?
    a. Giving them a "bank" of possible main ideas to choose from
    b. Preteaching the background knowledge about the artwork that is needed to correctly find the main idea
    c. Explaining the concept of a main idea in art
    d. Allowing students to work in groups to find the main idea

8. In order to teach a safety technique to students, the best method for a teacher to use is to
    a. show how to execute the technique while explaining it verbally, and then closely supervise students as they begin to practice it themselves.
    b. demonstrate the consequences of not executing the technique properly.
    c. verbally explain the technique to students.
    d. give students written instructions to follow while they perform the technique themselves.

9. An art teacher is planning to teach her seventh-grade class how to create drawings that accurately render perspective using a single vantage point. Which of the following lesson plans would be most appropriate?
    a. Giving students an exemplar drawing and asking them to copy it
    b. Delivering a mini lesson in which the terms "perspective" and "vanishing point" are defined, and then asking students to create their own drawings using these concepts
    c. Asking students to observe while the teacher composes an entire drawing with a single vanishing point
    d. Briefly modeling the technique for incorporating perspective into a drawing, having students attempt to replicate the example with the teacher's guidance, and then having students attempt to create their own drawings using the technique

10. Which of the following is not true of careers in the art industry?
    a. The majority of artists are self-employed.
    b. Few artists bother earning postsecondary degrees or certificates.
    c. Competition is keen for salaried jobs in the art industry.
    d. Annual earnings for artists vary widely.

11. Artists often use portfolios to
    a. demonstrate their capabilities to potential employers.
    b. display at art shows.
    c. teach their students.
    d. document their progress over time.

12. As it relates to set design and scenery, a flat is:
    a. A set that resembles a European apartment
    b. A portion of flat scenery usually framed in wood and wrapped in canvas
    c. A small piece of flat scenery hinged to another piece of flat scenery
    d. A hinged metal plate used for suspending scenery

13. Fill in the blank: A batten can best be described as ____:
    a. A long metal pole or pipe from which lighting, scenery, or curtains can be hung
    b. A painted canvas or backcloth hung at the back of the stage
    c. A hidden door in the stage where actors can enter and exit
    d. A piece of cloth used to separate the stage from the audience

14. A chart that lists characters that will be onstage, what they will be wearing, and possible wardrobe difficulties for every scene is called what?
    a. Costume plan
    b. Costume sketch
    c. Costume plot
    d. Costume script

15. How do most high schools obtain costumes for theatrical productions?
    a. High schools typically rent their costumes
    b. A costume designer makes the costumes
    c. Costumes are usually donated by students
    d. Costumes can be rented, made, or donated

16. According to most manufacturers of theatrical makeup, cosmetic products contain preservatives. What is the purpose of these preservatives?
    a. To prevent the transmission of infection due to makeup sharing
    b. To prolong the shelf life of the product
    c. To protect the product from color fading
    d. To prevent discoloration under theatrical lighting

17. Foam urethane and latex are standard materials used for making:
    a. Scenery backdrops
    b. Simple prosthetics
    c. Costume undergarments
    d. Non-slip pads for actors' shoes

18. Set construction, sound mixing and recording, light hanging, and prop procurement are all aspects of:
    a. Process-centered theatre
    b. Practical theatre
    c. Technical theatre
    d. Artistic theatre

19. Which genre of theatre pokes fun at current events and/or noteworthy people?
    a. Farce
    b. Comedy
    c. Satire
    d. Slapstick

20. A prime example of how live theatre has impacted society in the United States by creating jobs and attracting mass consumerism in a concentrated location is:
    a. Broadway
    b. West End
    c. Experimental theatre
    d. Comedy clubs

21. Which theatrical term best describes a dramatic outburst or a release of strong emotion by an actor or an audience member?
   a. Catharsis
   b. Alienation effect
   c. Performance purification
   d. Ablution

22. What is the difference between a musical and an opera?
   a. A musical is sung in English; an opera is sung in Italian.
   b. Dance is typically incorporated in an opera; there is usually no dancing in musicals.
   c. An opera is usually sung all the way through (without dialogue); musicals contain spoken dialogue between songs.
   d. During an opera, a live orchestra fills the time between songs; during a musical, dance fills the time between songs.

23. In order to effectively educate students of diverse backgrounds, a drama teacher might do which of the following?
   a. Seek out plays and scripts written by minorities
   b. Single out students of diverse backgrounds and make them do oral reports on their culture
   c. None of the answers are appropriate. It is never a drama teacher's responsibility to educate students about diversity
   d. Assign minority roles to Caucasian students

24. Which situation would be an example of a junior high drama teacher using her knowledge of a student's prior experiences and interests to encourage participation and involvement in her classroom?
   a. She asks the quarterback of the football team to play the lead in the popular play about baseball, *Damn Yankees*
   b. She asks the shiest girl in class to sing a song of her choosing in front of the class
   c. She asks the star of the baseball team to recite the poem, "Casey at the Bat"
   d. She asks the class clown to play the very serious lead role in *The Crucible*

25. Although every audience is different, it is important to teach students audience etiquette. All of the following are universally appropriate rules to follow when attending a performance except:
   a. Avoid speaking under all circumstances
   b. Do not bring electronic gadgetry into a performance
   c. Avoid falling asleep
   d. Do not unwrap candy

26. Students in a high school drama class are told to partner up and create an original script that is based on the personal experiences of both partners. This activity is designed to promote what?
   a. A better understanding of interpersonal relationships
   b. Creative problem solving
   c. Self-confidence while performing in front of others
   d. Exploration of content-related material

27. Which of the following would not be considered a professional developmental resource for a high school drama teacher?
a. Other theatre teachers
b. Community theatre actors
c. The World Wide Web
d. A local art museum

28. Which portion of a daily class lesson would be the best for teaching concentrated, fundamental lessons in voice training?
a. at the beginning of class
b. between the periods designated for learning and rehearsing specific pieces
c. at the end of class
d. Such teaching is not appropriate, since instructional time is limited and the appropriate place for voice training would be private lessons

29. Which of the following statements is true of vocal changes in developing adolescents?
a. It is largely a myth and can be kept in check by teaching proper technique.
b. Girls' singing voices do not change, although boys' singing voices do change.
c. Because their voices change in unpredictable ways, boys should stop singing during the middle school years and then resume in high school.
d. Girls' singing voices change just as boys' voices do.

30. Which of the following statements is true of the oboe?
a. Young students should always begin playing an easier woodwind instrument prior to transitioning to oboe.
b. Typically, the oboe is held nearly 90 degrees from the body.
c. It uses a double reed.
d. It is assembled in three parts.

31. Which of the following statements is true of program notes typically given to audience members during a performance?
a. They are optional, at best.
b. They only should include the names of the pieces and the composers.
c. They should include the lyrics of vocal pieces.
d. They should include the arrangers of the pieces rather than merely the composers.

32. Which of the following statements is true about a band or choir director's conducting style?
a. A band or choir director's conducting style is mostly for show.
b. He or she should practice conducting in front of a mirror along with taped or recorded music in order to make sure his or her conducting style is rhythmic and appropriate.
c. Conducting styles should be forceful and dynamic, since they bring out the most in students. Furthermore, the audience's attendance is due in part to see the conductor's work.
d. Conducting style can help an ensemble keep time, but it rarely influences dynamics, and style.

33. Which of the following statements is *not* true about a school's musical instrumental practice rooms?
a. Practice rooms are relatively expensive to build and maintain.
b. Practice rooms should include indirect lighting or lighting projected from the rear.
c. Practice rooms should include an electronic tuner.
d. Practice rooms are among the most frequently used rooms after classrooms.

34. Which of the following statements is true regarding the piccolo?
    a. Even skilled flutists cannot play the piccolo without relearning another instrument.
    b. The D-flat piccolo is today's standard instrument.
    c. The piccolo uses less air, but the musician must blow that air more rapidly.
    d. The piccolo has the same flexibility in pitch as the flute.

35. Which of the following characteristics do the baritone and the euphonium have in common?
    a. The music for both instruments requires beginning players to read treble and bass clef equally.
    b. Both instruments are pitched to B-flat.
    c. Most models of both instruments sold and used in the United States come with four valves.
    d. Both instruments have the same size mouthpiece and bore.

36. Which of the following statements is true of the tuba?
    a. The number of tuba players in a band is entirely up to the number of players who want to play it and the desires of the band director.
    b. A tuba is the perfect instrument for a player who doesn't have a good ear.
    c. The best tuba players are the largest students.
    d. The tuba is made only in one key, F.

37. Which of the following is true of extrinsic motivation in a music classroom?
    a. There are no uses for extrinsic motivation; all motivation from student musicians should come from within.
    b. Should be limited to routine, well-earned behaviors.
    c. Should be given for solving complex tasks related to music.
    d. Extrinsic motivation is banned by most school districts.

38. Which of the following is generally not true of a march?
    a. It has a lively, "up-beat" accompaniment.
    b. It is written in 2/4 time.
    c. It should feature slowed-down tempos when playing piano dynamics.
    d. It has an independent bass line.

39. Which is true of the amount of practice a student instrumentalist or singer should do every day?
    a. From the beginning, student musicians should practice at least an hour a day.
    b. Student musicians should not be expected to practice at first, especially if they are younger. There will be plenty of time to practice once they have more mastery.
    c. Students should practice a half-hour or so each day, then ideally work up to more than an hour every day.
    d. Practice time should vary, according to the difficulty of the class' repertoire and the student's mood.

40. Competitions for chair positions in a student band or orchestra:
    a. should be held daily
    b. have no place in a the rehearsal space of an enlightened music educator in charge of developing musicians' self-esteem
    c. should be held at the beginning and end of the semester only
    d. should be held both unannounced and on a scheduled basis, at the instructor's discretion

41. The most common method of vibrato for trumpet—and the easiest to develop—is
    a. voice vibrato
    b. hand vibrato
    c. jaw vibrato
    d. embouchure vibrato

42. Which of the following statements is true of a *diagnostic* assessment?
    a. It is performed at the beginning of the semester, and it includes auditions.
    b. It is performed in the middle of the semester, and is an important component of a student musician's midterm letter grade.
    c. It is another term for summative assessment.
    d. It never should be reserved for students college age and above.

43. Which of the following assessment scales would be appropriate for a teacher measuring progress of her second grade music students?
    a. letter grades, A to F
    b. percentages
    c. second graders are too young for assessments; the focus should be on an introduction to music without judgment or pressure
    d. a simple system such as checks and plusses

44. Involuntary body functions such as breathing, digestion, heart rate, and blood pressure are controlled by the:
    a. somatic nervous system.
    b. autonomic nervous system.
    c. central nervous system.
    d. cerebrum.

45. What is generally the best emergency procedure to control bleeding?
    a. Apply a tourniquet
    b. Apply pressure to the carotid artery
    c. Cover the wound in a clean cloth and apply direct pressure
    d. Clean the wound and apply a sterile bandage

46. Which of the following blood pressure readings would most likely be treated with medication?
    a. 90/75
    b. 110/70
    c. 135/85
    d. 140/90

47. According to social learning theory, what is one way of motivating students to engage in physical activity?
    a. Let the class choose which physical activities to participate in.
    b. Provide appropriate role models who engage in physical activity.
    c. Have students discuss in small groups the benefits of physical activity.
    d. Talk with students to select appropriate fitness goals and appropriate rewards.

48. Which of the following is NOT a basic principle in managing equipment in a physical education class?
    a. transportation of equipment
    b. use of student "managers"
    c. safe use of equipment
    d. distribution of equipment

49. What which of the following is NOT a good way to maximize participation in a physical education class?
    a. Let each student choose his or her own activity, as long as it is physical.
    b. Group the students according to skill level.
    c. Set up different activity stations for students to use.
    d. Change the rules of games to suit different skill levels.

50. Which of the following BEST describes how participation in physical education can improve a student's self-esteem?
    a. It can teach students new or improved skills.
    b. It can foster a sense of wonder at human athleticism.
    c. It can teach students to take turns when playing sports/games.
    d. It can cause the release of endorphins, natural "feel good" chemicals.

51. Which of the following social skills is NOT a possible benefit of participating in physical education activities?
    a. communication
    b. self-esteem
    c. cooperation
    d. respecting diversity

52. What is a good way of preventing shin splints?
    a. Continue exercise even after feeling shin pain.
    b. Wear shin guards while exercising.
    c. Exercise on a relatively soft surface, such as grass.
    d. Walk up hills but run down them.

Answers and Explanations

Reading and English Language Arts

1. C: The example has an error in subject-verb agreement, which is a component of syntax (sentence structure and word order). Phonology (a) involves recognition and production of speech sounds and phonemes, including differentiation, segmentation, and blending. Semantics (b) involves the meanings of words. Pragmatics (d) involves the social use of language to communicate and meet one's needs.

2. A: Basic interpersonal communication skills (BICS) are language skills required in everyday social communication. These are less cognitively demanding, do not involve specialized vocabulary, typically take place in meaningful social contexts, and are necessary for social interaction. Cognitive academic language proficiency (CALP) is formal academic subject content language learning. CALP is more cognitively demanding, involves specialized subject vocabularies, takes place in academic contexts, and is necessary for school success. ELL students typically take 6 months to 2 years to develop adequate BICS, but at least 5-7 years to develop adequate CALP. If they had no formal education in their native languages and/or no second-language acquisition support, development may take 7-10 years.

3. A: The /p/ sound is among the earliest phonemes to develop, from ages 1.5 to 3 years old. The /ʒ/ phoneme (b) has the oldest age norm for normal development—5.5 years to 8.5 years old is a typical range for children to acquire correct production of this sound. The /v/ sound (c) typically develops in most children from the ages of 4 to 8 years. Most children develop correct articulation of the /s/ sound (d) by 2.5 to 4 years old. Hence not all kindergarteners, who are typically around 5 years old, are expected to master phonemes with acquisition norm ranges older than 5-8 years. A 5-year-old is *most* likely to be referred for SLP evaluation if s/he does not correctly produce /p/, which children normally develop by around 3 years old.

4. B: Producing words that rhyme, which involves some phonemic awareness, is developmentally most appropriate for preschool-aged children, particularly if their oral language skills are below normal developmental levels. Group discussions (a), oral presentations (c), and storytelling (d) require more advanced levels of language development, involving grammar; syntax; connected sentences; pragmatics (e.g., turn-taking in discussions or storytelling); more formal language in presentations; and skills for organizing, sequencing, and expressing narratives.

5. D: Assigning oral presentations builds on the strong oral tradition of these students' culture, and using a topic with which they have personal life experience builds on their backgrounds and strengths. Research shows that students learn new languages best in the contexts of topics meaningful to them, not through studying vocabulary words and grammatical rules in isolation (a). While exposing students to new subjects expands their experience and knowledge, reading a book in English and writing book reports on it (b) does not access the students' oral storytelling strengths or background knowledge. It is also likely too difficult for students with no previous formal schooling, who are unlikely to read and write their L1 well, let alone English. While (c) addresses their life experience, it ignores their lack of formal education by requiring researching and writing papers in English.

6. C: Because the spoken and written aspects of language are so closely interrelated, teachers should always demonstrate these relationships in their instruction so that student proficiency in listening, speaking, reading, and writing all develop concurrently and students recognize their interrelatedness. Receptive language and literacy skills for listening and reading typically develop sooner than expressive speaking and writing skills (a). However, this does *not* mean they should be taught separately at different times (b). Instead, they should all be incorporated, and at appropriate developmental levels for each. Although many children acquire oral language skills naturally from adults and older children in their environments, not all do; for those who do, this does not preclude the need for instruction (d).

7. A: Multiple research studies have found that teaching phonological awareness skills to kindergarteners with delayed language development has enhanced their language development. Researchers also recommend involving speech-language pathologists (SLPs) and their instructional methods as effective in teaching phonological awareness skills (b). Phonological awareness involves being able to recognize and change phonemes (speech sounds) without any reference to meanings (c) of words, syllables, or morphological units. Researchers and others instructing kindergarteners in phonological awareness skills have provided training at both the individual phoneme level (identifying and differentiating phonemes, matching initial and final phonemes, deleting phonemes, blending phonemes, etc.) and above (d) the phoneme level (syllable, word, and rhyme awareness).

8. B: In the Spanish language, the letter *h* is typically silent. Because the student is an ELL and the USA has many people—both immigrants and those born here—whose first and/or only language is Spanish, this is the first factor to consider among the choices. An articulation disorder (a) is possible, but the teacher should not assume this first with an ELL student. (An SLP evaluation can determine the difference.) While hearing assessment (c) is always a good idea, if /h/ omission were due to hearing loss the student would likely omit or distort other unvoiced fricatives like /f/, /s/, /ʃ/, and /θ/. If the student had a breathing problem (d), other symptoms would occur in addition to not articulating /h/.

9. D: The most practical, thorough, and effective solution is to conduct informal assessments, as well as formal assessments other than the one the school has selected for biannual administration, to obtain continuing data on student phonological development to inform instructional planning, implementation, and adjustments according to student responses. Limiting assessment to the biennial formal test (a) will not provide enough information for individualizing instruction to each student's needs timely enough. Lobbying administrators to change policy (b) could work with some teachers and some administrators, but in many other cases would waste energy and time—and could strain teacher-administrator relations—without succeeding. Using informal assessments continually (c) is a good but not complete solution, whereas using both informal and other formal assessments continually (d) is.

10. C: Phonological processes common during early speech development include fronting backed consonants, hence (d) is incorrect as such errors are *not* rare at any age. However, these processes should end around 5 years of age, whereas this student is in 1st grade. Also, his substitutions of /f/ are for /p/ and /b/—consonants typically acquired by around ages 3 and 4 years, respectively, whereas this student is 6-7 years old; hence his errors do *not* represent normal development (a), not even considering individual differences (b). Because the errors are consistent throughout his speech and persist beyond age norms both for easier consonants and for phonological processes to end, evaluation by an SLP (c) is indicated as these are signs of an articulation disorder.

11. C: Playing language games helps younger students to develop phonological and phonemic awareness while having fun, which better motivates them to learn. For example, teachers can ask children to see how many different rhyming words they can produce by changing the initial sound of a given word (e.g., cat, hat, mat, fat, sat, pat, bat, rat, vat, etc.). Hence manipulating phonemes in words not only can be taught in different ways, making (a) incorrect; moreover, it *should* be taught using a variety of approaches and materials. Such approaches include utilizing informal interactions (b): these provide a meaningful context for learning, which is more important than systematically controlling their occurrence. Younger students are more apt to identify alliteration they hear before they can read (d). (They may be taught visual recognition of the same letter beginning multiple words in a sentence, but this does not develop phonemic awareness, which develops and/or can be taught even earlier.)

12. B: Most parents are eager to help their children and may simply need some suggestions and ideas of how to do it. For example, teachers can suggest using an "I Spy" game during everyday life wherein the parent and child both look for things in the home, outdoors, in stores and other public places whose names start with a target phoneme. While more practice to reinforce classroom lessons is good, "assigning homework" to parents (a) is likely to alienate them. Teachers should encourage parents to model correct phoneme production for children rather than warm them against it (c). Teachers can also suggest to parents including bedtime stories as opportunities for identifying target phonemes in words, not avoiding this (d), as the parent and/or child reads aloud.

13. D: According to the National Reading Panel (NRP, 2000), multiple and replicated research studies conducted over time confirm that systematic phonics instruction is most effective when taught as part of a comprehensive reading program that also includes phonemic awareness, vocabulary, reading fluency, and reading comprehension. Hence (b) and (c) are incorrect regarding teaching phonics separately (b) or only with phonemic awareness (c). The research also finds this instruction effective for both K-6 students and students having difficulty with learning to read. This makes (a) incorrect, as well as (c) regarding student age and grade levels.

14. A: While there is no consensus among experts as to any universal sequence of instruction for teaching the alphabetic principle through phonics instruction, they do agree that, to enable children to start reading words as soon as possible, the highest-utility relationships should be introduced earliest. For example, the letters *m, a, p, t,* and *s* are all used frequently, whereas the *x* in *box*, the sound of *ey* in *they*, and the letter *a* when pronounced as it is in *want* have lower-utility letter-sound correspondences. Important considerations for the alphabetic principle are to teach letter-sound correspondences in isolation, not in word contexts (b); to teach them explicitly; to give students opportunities to practice letter-sound relationships within their other daily lessons, not only separately (c); and to include cumulative reviews of relationships taught earlier along with new ones in practice opportunities (d).

15. D: The Chinese written language is ideographic rather than alphabetic (a)—i.e., its written symbols represent concepts visually rather than being letters representing speech sounds. Also, the fact that Spanish is much more phonetically regular than English (b)—i.e., many more words are pronounced the same way as they are spelled than in English—contribute different effects to ELL students' English-language literacy development. Therefore, (c) is incorrect.

16. B: Teachers should apply a variety of instructional techniques to enable students with different strengths, needs, and learning styles to understand sound-letter and letter-word relationships, but they should not restrict the instructional modalities to auditory and visual (a) simply because

sounds are auditory and letters are visual. Multisensory modalities (b) are more effective because different students use different senses to learn; redundancy is necessary for learning; and input to multiple senses affords a more multidimensional learning experience, promoting comprehension and retention. While some aspects of this instruction should be consistent (e.g., starting with high-frequency letters and with phonemes children can produce more easily), sticking to only one method and set of materials (c) prevents using variety to reach all students. Visually similar letters and auditorily similar phonemes should *not* be introduced together (d) before students can discriminate among them; teachers should begin with more obvious differences.

17. C: Standardized formal assessments are available for testing alphabetic principle knowledge and skills that equal informal assessments for ease and speed of administration (e.g., the Dynamic Indicators of Basic Early Literacy Skills [DIBELS] for grades K-6, including the Nonsense Word Fluency [NWF] and other measures, all administered in about one minute each). Many formal assessments can be administered to individual students, so (a) is incorrect. Teachers can inform their instructional planning using results from both formal and informal assessments, so (b) is incorrect. Teachers also use informal assessment to analyze the skills of individual students, so (d) is incorrect.

18. D: Research finds student achievement benefits more from the quality of teacher-parent interactions than their quantity. Researchers recommend that, while teachers most frequently contact parents about student problems, it is better to communicate positive student progress and accomplishments to parents first (a), facilitating parental responsiveness to teacher communications about any problems and parental willingness to collaborate by helping children at home with alphabet knowledge. Experts advise teachers to provide practical information like resources for understanding school curriculum and specific suggestions of activities (b) parents can do with children to reinforce and augment alphabetic learning. Although they realize time is scarce for teachers to send personalized messages to all students' parents, experts still recommend including personal messages (c) whenever they can because this increases parent-teacher collaboration.

19. A: In both the fictional narrative genre and the nonfictional informational genre, the author will demonstrate some individual writing style; even very factual and objective expositional writing will reveal some personal stylistic characteristics. Labeled diagrams and photos (b) are more likely to be found in informational nonfiction. The majority of books with settings and characters (c) are fictional narratives (some informational nonfiction books are presented in narrative form and include characters, especially in children's literature, but these are the minority). Themes and plots (d) are also literary elements associated with fictional narrative.

20. B: Students must be able to distinguish between printed words and the spaces between them to identify the first and last letters of each word, as spaces are the boundaries between words. It is not true that all normally developing students can tell words from spaces (a): those not exposed to or familiar with print media may need to be taught this distinction. Although left-to-right directionality is more of a problem for ELL students whose L1s have different writing or printing directions (e.g., some Asian languages are written vertically, some can be written vertically or horizontally, and some Semitic languages like Hebrew and Arabic are written right-to-left), again, children unfamiliar with print or writing may also not know writing, print, or book directionality either (c). Identifying basic punctuation is important to reading comprehension as it affects meaning. For example, consider "Let's eat, Grandma" vs. "Let's eat Grandma"—one comma differentiates an invitation to dinner from a cannibalistic proposal.

21. A: Students develop literacy within multiple contexts by learning to listen to, speak, read, and write language. Therefore it is inaccurate to say that only reading, writing, and listening (b) are activities for developing literacy. Literacy development is not confined to reading and writing (c) as some non-educators may believe. Some may even have the mistaken impression that reading is the only activity important for literacy development (d). However, literacy develops through all activities using language.

22. D: With young children and older students lacking exposure to or familiarity with print, teachers need to teach them basic print concepts that adults usually take for granted, including how to hold and handle a book properly (a); how to open a book and where to open it (b); the orientation and directionality of print and pages; the title page, table of contents, chapters, headings, epilogue, index, and in some books, glossaries, references, bibliographies, etc. (c)—i.e., the parts of a book. The alphabetic principle (letter-sound relationships) is also a vital print concept.

23. D: Teachers are expected to give students plenty of opportunities not only to read different literary genres independently (a), but also to listen to literature read aloud (b), live, and/or recorded; to attend or view productions of dramatic literature; to express their responses to literature in writing and speech (c); and to interact with others (d) in class and group discussions, pairs, cooperative learning projects, conversations, etc.

24. B: In explicit (or direct) instruction, teachers introduce the strategy for author point of view (POV) identification using personal experience(s) or real-life example(s). Then teachers model the strategy using a text. Whole-class guided practice in identifying author POV in another text is the third step. Step four is giving students guided practice in pairs or small groups. In step five, teachers provide text, time, and directions for students to practice identifying author POV independently. To connect the POV identification strategy to reading comprehension, the teacher's sixth step is to have students identify author POV in their answers to comprehension questions the teacher asks them. Step seven is assessment: teachers evaluate student effectiveness in applying the strategy. Teachers follow step eight of reteaching and/or enrichment by assigning students with performance *greater than or equal to* 80 percent to small groups to identify author POV in leveled texts of increasing complexity; and students with *less than or equal to* 80 percent to repeat previous steps as needed with leveled texts, continuing to monitor their strategy understanding and application. Step nine, further assessment, repeats step seven using different, leveled, or other text.

25. C: Decoding monosyllabic words by referring to the initial and final consonant, short vowel, and long vowel sounds represented by their letters is a common academic standard for 1st-grade students. Typical academic standards for kindergarten students include demonstrating knowledge of letter-sound correspondences (a); understanding the alphabetic principle (b); matching letters to their corresponding consonant (and short vowel) sounds; and reading simple, monosyllabic sight words (d), i.e., high-frequency words.

26. B: According to many academic standards, 2nd-graders should be able determine the meanings of new or unfamiliar words by comparing them to synonyms (words with similar meanings) and antonyms (words with opposite meanings). First-graders are expected to use phonics (letter-sound correspondences), word roots, word suffixes, and analogies (a) to decode words for reading. It is expected of 3rd-graders to use not only known synonyms and antonyms, but additionally homophones (words sounding the same with different meanings) and homographs (words spelled the same but with different meanings) they know to discern new or unfamiliar word meanings (c).

Determining word meanings by referring to word roots, prefixes, suffixes, idiomatic expressions, and familiar diacritical marks used in dictionaries (d) is expected of 4th-graders.

27. D: To instruct students in word analysis following a sequence progressing from simpler to more complex, teachers would first introduce individual phonemes (speech sounds); then the blending of two or more individual phonemes; then onsets and rimes, i.e., phonograms and word families (e.g., *-ack, -ide, -ay, -ight, -ine,* etc.); then the easier short vowels, followed by the more difficult long vowels; then blends of individual consonants; then CVC (consonant-vowel-consonant) words (e.g., *bag, hot, red, sit,* etc.) and other common patterns of consonants and vowels in words; and then the six most common types of syllables (closed, VCe, open, vowel team, r-controlled, and C-le).

28. A: Before teaching phonics, decoding, or word analysis skills, teachers should assess students' phonics skills. They should then plan instruction that matches each student's assessed needs, is systematic in nature and delivery, and teach all concepts and skills explicitly. Another principle to follow in word analysis instructional strategies is organization: teachers should either adopt an existing structured, phonics-based teaching program or follow a defined skills sequence for effectiveness (b). An additional principle is to give students controlled vocabulary tests and/or other opportunities to practice the elements of phonics after learning them. If they do not, they will not get enough practice (c) to apply this knowledge. Experts also advise incorporating all the component skills for reading in every lesson rather than focusing exclusively or primarily on decoding skills (d).

29. D: Word roots, prefixes, and suffixes are all morphological units, i.e., the smallest structural or grammatical units of words that carry meaning (e.g., the *–s* ending added to regular nouns changes them from singular to plural in number, and the *–ed* ending added to regular verbs changes them from present to past tense). Identifying morphological word parts gives students structural cues to determine word meaning. Option (a) is the knowledge that letters correspond to speech sounds. Option (b) enables word decoding by using (a) and phonics to connect combinations of vowel letters with their combined sounds. Option (c) enables decoding unknown words by considering the meaning of the surrounding phrase, sentence, paragraph, etc., i.e., semantic context; and/or the surrounding sentence structure and word order, i.e., syntactic context.

30. D: A good dictionary identifies the original word, country, language, year or century, original definition or meaning, and languages or countries it passed through historically en route to its arrival in our contemporary language. Knowing the derivation of a word or root often informs the meanings of many other related words. Good dictionaries not only give literal word definitions, but often also provide their connotations and examples of correct usages (a); correct spellings; which part(s) of speech a word can be (b); and correct pronunciations, which do not require sound files (c) but are indicated in print dictionaries by syllable divisions, accent marks showing short or long vowels, boldface, italics, apostrophes and/or accent marks indicating stressed syllables and phonetic spellings. Many dictionaries additionally offer synonyms, antonyms, related words, and sentence examples using different meanings and parts of speech of a word.

31. C: Researchers and educators have found that reading fluency and reading comprehension have a reciprocal relationship: the more fluently a student can read, the more able the student's brain is to process the meaning of text. For example, developing automaticity of word identification enhances comprehension. Conversely, the better a student can understand the text, the more fluently s/he can read it. Therefore, while (a) and (b) are both true, each represents only half of the relationship whereas (c) indicates the relationship's mutual nature; and (d) is incorrect as reading

fluency and reading comprehension are interrelated components in deriving meaning from text and not separate.

32. B: 1st- to 3rd-graders are expected to read materials regularly at the independent level, which is defined as text where approximately one in 20 words or fewer are difficult for the student—not one in 10 (a). Students are also expected to select text to read independently, informed by their knowledge of authors, text genres and types; their estimation of text difficulty levels; and their personal interest (b). They should also read text regularly that is at the instructional level, which they define as including no more than one in 10 words the reader finds difficult—not one in 20 (c). Finally, students are expected to read aloud fluently from familiar texts, not unfamiliar ones (d).

33. B: Before beginning fluency instruction, typically not before halfway through the 1st grade at the earliest, teachers should ensure that students have strong word recognition skills to provide the necessary foundation. Student speed and automaticity in decoding individual words are directly related to developing reading fluency (a): rapid, automatic word decoding is the precursor to fluent reading. Reading fluency not only indicates faster information processing, it also has a direct impact on comprehension (c) because the faster a student can process information, the better the student can comprehend what s/he reads. When a student must decode words more slowly and less automatically, both reading fluency and comprehension are decreased (d): slow, conscious decoding does not increase comprehension by being more careful or thoughtful; instead, laborious student efforts to decode separate words for meaning divert the attention they could devote to overall comprehension if they could decode rapidly, effortlessly, and automatically.

34. D: Self-correction is an important and useful student behavior in reading. Teachers are advised to observe self-corrections during reading fluency screening, but not to mark them as errors. Although self-correction can certainly be incorporated into repeated reading activities, it is not necessarily a repeated reading activity per se. Tape-assisted reading (a) or computer-assisted reading, readers theater (b) activities, and partner reading (c) are all types of repeated reading activities wherein students read the same text repeatedly until they attain fluency.

35. C: To select materials suitable for partner (paired) reading, the teacher should identify materials that are suitable for the *lower* reader's instructional reading level, not the higher reader's (a). Instructional level equals no more than one reading error per 10 words. Therefore (d) is incorrect: the independent reading level equals no more than one reading error per 20 words. Each student partner in a pair should read the *same* passage from the same text, not different ones (b) to enable modeling by the more fluent reader for the lower reader and repeated reading. The teacher should select enough reading materials for every pair of students to read two new passages each week (c).

36. A: To determine whether books are at reading levels appropriate for a student, teachers should match texts to the student that have approximately five percent of words the student does not know. A lower percentage makes the text too easy, and a higher percentage makes it too difficult. Experts (cf. Pennington, 2009) provide an easy formula to determine four to six percent by counting words on a page x 3, counting unknown words; doing this for a page near the book's beginning, middle, and end respectively; and dividing total unknown words by total words. Readability measures, standardized comprehension tests, and leveled individual reading inventories can help, but do have drawbacks (b) including being time-consuming; limited practical application due to individual reader and text differences; and difficulty of interpretation, even for trained reading specialists. Teachers should help students select not only assigned texts (c) or only students' choices (d), but a balance between these.

37. B: Identifying point of view (a) is an example of *literal* reading comprehension. Explaining the point of view (b) is an example of *evaluative* reading comprehension. Identifying the main idea of a text passage (c) is an example of *literal* reading comprehension. Making predictions about what will happen in a text (d) is an example of *inferential* reading comprehension.

38. A: Students need to know why and how to use text features to inform their reading. Reading headings above sections within chapters (a) help students determine the main subject matter of each section. Reading the glossary for a chapter (b) gives students definitions of terms used in the chapter. Reading the index in a text (c) is a way to locate page numbers of references to subjects or authors in the text. Whether they will be reading the entire section or not, students need not read through the whole thing (d) only to determine its subject matter when its heading will typically indicate this. Headings inform students of topics in advance if they will be reading the section; if they are doing research or choosing what to read, headings can help them decide.

39. D: When students ask themselves how the information in a text they are reading fits with what they already know, they are relating the text to their own prior knowledge, which increases their reading comprehension. Students should not only ask themselves what kinds of "expert questions" fit the subject matter of the text (a)—e.g., classification, physical, and chemical properties are typical question topics in science; genre, character, plot, and theme are typical of literature questions; sequence, cause-and-effect, and comparison-contrast questions are typical of history— but also what questions the material brings up for them personally (b). It is necessary and important for students to ask themselves continually how each text portion relates to its chapter's main ideas (c) as they read to optimize their reading comprehension and retention.

40. D: Previewing (a) a text is done before reading to get a general idea of its author, subject, publication year, length, chapters, etc. Predicting (b) what will come next in a text before reading further is done during but not after reading, and may also be done before reading. Discussing (c) text is an obvious choice after reading, but students can also discuss text during reading, i.e., exchanging and comparing their responses so far when they are in the middle of the same text. Rereading (d) can be done after reading to reinforce comprehension and retention, and during reading (e.g., rereading parts of text to clarify understanding or memory) either immediately after reading them or going back to reread earlier portions.

41. C: In addition to connecting something in text to something in one's own life experience, the SCRIP Connect reading comprehension strategy includes connecting parts of text not only by comparison but also by contrast (a); connecting parts of text to other texts; connecting parts of text to movies, TV programs, or historical events as well as to other texts (b); connecting parts of text to other parts of text to identify cause-and-effect relationships (c); and connecting parts of text as a sequence (d) of ideas or events.

42. D: Reviewing their accumulated vocabulary knowledge to consider words or phrases that are important for expressing or comprehending meaning is an example of a standard for 6th-grade vocabulary development. Using adjectives and adverbs learned through textual and conversational experiences for description, e.g., of feelings like happy or sad (a) is an example of a standard for 2nd-grade vocabulary development. Simply using words and phrases learned through textual and conversational experiences (b) is an example of a standard for kindergarten vocabulary development. Accurately using grade-level, domain-specific, and general academic words and phrases (c), including those defining precise states of being, actions, or emotions and those fundamental to specific topics, is an example of a standard for 4th-grade vocabulary development.

43. B: Indirect ways in which students receive instruction and learn vocabulary include through daily conversations, reading on their own, and being read aloud to by adults. Direct instruction and learning in vocabulary include teachers' providing extended instruction exposing students repeatedly to vocabulary words in multiple contexts (a), teachers' pre-teaching specific words found in text prior to students' reading it (c), and teachers' instructing students over extended time periods (d) and having them actively work with vocabulary words.

44. D: Teachers should use a broad variety of instructional materials to support student vocabulary development, including not only literature and expository texts (a) but also newspapers, magazines (b), trade books, content-specific texts, technology (c), and other sources of vocabulary words to provide students with the richest and most authentic array of contexts possible for the greatest quantity and quality of exposure to and learning of vocabulary.

45. C: Students need to learn both general academic vocabulary that applies across school subjects and specialized vocabularies used in each respective subject to succeed. It is not true that knowing general academic vocabulary will enable them to understand specialized subject terminologies (a), which are different for each subject. It is also not true that students will simply know general academic vocabulary without instruction (b). Younger students and those having no previous experience with general academic vocabulary especially need instruction in general academic language, which differs from everyday conversational language. Teachers should teach general and specialized academic vocabularies not only via direct instruction, but also by modeling (d) their use for students.

46. A: Morphemic analysis enhances vocabulary knowledge by enabling students to differentiate among different forms of words, like verb tenses and noun person and number, by observing and recognizing plural endings, past tense endings, auxiliary verbs with progressive and perfect tenses, etc. Contextual analysis (b) helps students determine unknown vocabulary word meanings by observing their surrounding sentence or phrase contexts for semantic (meaning) and syntactic (sentence structure) cues. Graphic organizers (c) help students understand and organize vocabulary concepts and relationships by making them more visual. Word etymologies (d) help students expand their vocabulary knowledge by enabling them to relate new words to known words sharing common roots, prefixes, etc.

47. D: Teachers should not only give students explicit, direct instruction in vocabulary (a), but also many opportunities for reading literature and expository text (b), multiple opportunities to listen to text read aloud (c), and multiple opportunities for responding to (d) the text that they read and listen to for optimal promotion of their vocabulary development.

48. B: This is an example of a closed question because it asks either/or and the student can only answer "simile" or "metaphor" without needing to elaborate unless asked to explain the answer. In contrast, (c) is an open-ended question because the student must both define simile and metaphor and explain the difference between them. Option (a) is an open-ended literature question because the student cannot answer with yes, no, or some other single word or short phrase; s/he has to describe the action or events in a story that represent its climax, which requires understanding story structure, story elements, knowing the definition of a story's climax, reading the story, and understanding it. Option (d) is a very open-ended question, as students have considerable latitude in giving the reasons each of them perceives for having poetry.

49. B: Manipulatives are three-dimensional concrete objects that students can not only look at, but also touch, move, dismantle and reassemble (in some cases), rearrange, etc.—i.e., manipulate as the name indicates. Examples (a) may be three-dimensional objects, demonstrations, or (more often) verbal descriptions given orally, printed, or written. Graphic organizers (c) are diagrams (e.g., Venn diagrams), charts, timelines, concept maps, word webs, etc. which are two-dimensional, visual, graphic materials. Charts, tables, and graphs (d), though less pictorial and conceptual and more linear and numerical than graphic organizers, are also two-dimensional in print, online, or on screen.

50. C: Depending on their type, graphs can be used to compare quantities or values at the same point in time (or irrespective of time), or to show changes in quantities or values over time. For example, a bar graph can show different numbers of students in different categories, different test scores, etc. next to each other for comparison, or different numbers yearly, monthly, weekly, daily, etc. Line graphs only show changes in values over time. Tables (a) are good for organizing information into categories, but do not show linear changes over time. Maps (b), when cartographic (actual maps), depict geographical locations and can include other information (e.g., population totals, percentages, income, domestic or national product figures, annual rainfall, temperatures, etc.) via color-coding and other graphics. Other map types used in education, including concept maps for students, curriculum maps and resource maps for educators, etc. do not show linear chronological change. Charts (d), e.g., pie charts, which show percentages or proportions of a whole quantity divided by categories, do not show change over time.

51. A: Brainstorming is not meant to be structured or overly controlled. Its purpose is to generate the largest amounts of information related to the identified topic without advance censoring or editing. Hence large parts of brainstorming results may not actually be used, but they give students and teachers more material from which to choose for further study or development. Summarizing (b) produces less information because its purpose is to condense more extensive material down to its gist to identify its main ideas or essential elements. Note-taking (c) typically reflects the structure and amount of information in the teacher's lesson or lecture. Outlining (d) reduces information to its essential components similarly to summarizing, except outlines have more overt structure, either reflecting the information's innate structure or imposing another structure upon it.

52. B: 3rd-graders are expected to be able to scan and skim textual features, e.g., boldface, italics, key words, captions, etc. to identify data. Using available technology (e.g., word processing or spreadsheet software programs) to record data, visualize relationships among ideas and concepts, and convert visual representations into written language (a) is an expectation of 5th-grade students in this category. Using text features like the table of contents, headings, alphabetical index, etc. in picture dictionaries and other age-appropriate reference sources for locating information (c) is an expectation of 1st-grade students in this category. Using pictures in combination with writing to document research with adult assistance (d) is an expectation of kindergarten students.

53. C: *Scribbling*: not printing, random; but significantly, representing ideas with written or drawn marks. *Letter-like symbols:* Forms resembling letters alternating with numbers, seldom with spacing. *Letter strings:* Some letters are legible, typically capitals, still not spaced; students mostly do not match letters to sounds yet but are developing phonological awareness. *Beginning sounds emerge:* Children still may not space between words, but begin distinguishing letters from words. Words match pictures, particularly with topics children choose. *Consonants represent words:* Children begin spacing between words, may mix upper-case and lower-case letters, start punctuating, and typically express ideas through written sentences. *Initial, middle, and final sounds:* Children may correctly spell familiar names, environmental print, and some sight words, but

otherwise use spell phonetically; writing is much more readable. *Transitional phases:* Children's writing approximates conventional spelling. *Standard spelling:* Children spell most words correctly; they develop understanding of word roots, compound words, and contractions, increasing correct spelling of related words. (J. Richard Gentry, Ph.D., 1982, 2006, 2010)

54. C: It is normal for students to reverse letters and numbers occasionally not only in 1st grade, but through the end of 2nd grade. Thus they do not indicate possible dyslexia (b) at this age. The words cited are above 1st-grade spelling level, particularly so early in the school year, so misspelling them is normal, should not be marked incorrect, and does not require intervention (d). Also, teachers should not deduct points for misspelling in written compositions unless the misspelled words are included in weekly class spelling lists. First-graders are frequently in transitional phases of writing when phonetic spelling is not only common but desirable. The student's writing is developmentally appropriate; the substitute's grading is inappropriate. Hence (a) is incorrect.

55. B: Based on Charles Read's (1975) research into invented and phonetic spelling, Richard Gentry (1982, 2006, 2010) identified five phases of spelling. *Precommunicative:* Alphabetic symbols without letter-sound correspondences, complete alphabet knowledge, spelling directionality, or uppercase and lowercase letter distinctions. *Semiphonetic:* Letter-sound correspondence understanding emerges; students frequently spell words with single letters or abbreviated syllables. *Phonetic:* Not all spellings follow standard conventions, but students systematically represent all phonemes with letters. Misspellings are typically accurate in terms of articulatory placement (*e* for short *i*, *a* for short *e*, *i* for short *o*, etc.) *Transitional:* Students move from phonetic to conventional, visual spellings, informed by their growing understanding of word structure. "Higheked" for "hiked" and "egul" for "eagle" are examples of their more approximate spellings. *Correct:* Students have learned the fundamental rules of English orthography, including irregular and alternative spellings, silent consonants, prefixes and suffixes, etc. and identify misspellings.

56. A: The examples in this question are all of homophones, i.e. they sound the same but have different meanings and spellings. Homographs (b) are words that are spelled the same but have different meanings (e.g., *bear* meaning to give birth, to support weight, or an animal). Homonyms (c) are words that are spelled and sound the same but have different meanings (e.g., *stalk* meaning a plant stem or the act of following and harassing someone). Homologs (d) are not words, but things that are biologically homologous, i.e., they have the same relative value, structure, or position (e.g., chromosomes). (Homologous has a somewhat different meaning in chemistry.)

57. D: When giving children writing implements, it is best to teach them letters involving similar strokes first, and progress from simpler to more complex strokes and letters; then teach combining letters into short words; then teach writing sentences; and eventually have children write independently. While the ultimate goal is writing with pencil and paper, having a young child extend her or his arm at eye level and write in the air with a finger (a) is actually a good exercise for developing fine motor control before writing on paper (pencils and paper can slip). Tracing letters is another way to develop fine motor skills for writing; providing textured surfaces increases the tactile awareness needed for writing (b). Another way to develop tactile awareness is to blindfold children and have them manipulate three-dimensional letters (c).

58. A: One of the expectations of 4th-grade students is to capitalize the names of historical events and documents and book, essay, and story titles; to use quotation marks; and to use commas in compound sentences. 2nd-grade students are expected to capitalize names, weekdays, months, letter salutations and closings; and to use apostrophes (b) to indicate contraction and possession.

Capitalizing abbreviations, initials, acronyms, and organization names; and using correct punctuation in quotations (c) is an expectation for 5th-grade students. Capitalizing initial letters in sentences and punctuating the ends of sentences (d) is an expectation for kindergarten students.

59. D: Teachers should instruct students in writing not in isolation (b), not relating writing only to reading (a) or reading and speaking (c), but by showing students the interrelationships of listening, speaking, reading, and writing. In addition, teachers should not just teach writing as a rote chore or drill, but give students lessons and assignments that demonstrate legitimate purposes for writing and provide topics to write about that are meaningful to students.

60. C: The best way for teachers to help students develop larger reading and writing vocabularies is simply to provide them with as many opportunities as possible for reading and writing. The more they read and write, the bigger their reading and writing vocabularies will grow, more effectively than from having to memorize vocabulary lists and being tested on them weekly (a). Having students search for new vocabulary words in texts (b) does not let them actually read, which is superior for learning new words within meaningful contexts as well as developing all other reading skills. Students learning new words in isolation will not learn their appropriate use. Rather than assigning minimum numbers of new words to include in their writing (d), teachers should give students actual opportunities to write, which both develops all writing skills and increases writing vocabulary. Also, (b) involves reading vocabulary but not writing vocabulary, and (d) involves writing vocabulary but not reading vocabulary, in addition to the fact that neither one involves actual reading and writing.

61. C: Because this student loves reading graphic novels and has both talent and enjoyment in drawing, having him create his own graphic novels is a good way to motivate him to write by using his visual style, ability, and interest to access writing activity. Giving audio recordings (a) to a highly visual student is not as appropriate to his strengths and interests. Letting him substitute drawing pictures for all writing assignments (b) would address his strengths and interests, but not his needs for learning to write. Having him watch animated videos about writing (d) would suit his visual learning style, but would not give him the actual writing practice he needs.

62. D: While ideas figure prominently in the first stage, writers also generate ideas throughout the entire writing process, not only during prewriting (a). First drafts are typically writer-centered, not reader-centered—the writer is telling himself (or herself) what he knows and thinks about the topic of the writing—and no matter how much we plan during prewriting, giving words to ideas affects them; the specific words we choose evoke further implications and/or ideas (b). The revision stage precedes the editing stage, not vice versa, and makes the document reader-centered (c). Writers devote more attention to reader expectations and needs, supporting evidence necessary for persuading readers, terms to define for the intended audience, and whether their writing is effectively organized. After revision, the final stage of editing involves checking grammar, spelling, and mechanics. Experts advise spell-checking as the last step before printing a document (d).

63. A: Track Changes is a highly valuable feature of MS Word that enables writers, including students, to see every deletion, insertion, substitution, rearrangement, and other changes they make to a draft in red to contrast with the black of unaltered text. It can be easily turned off for viewing, printing, and sharing a clean final copy. Word also features a Side-by-Side View option (b) that enables seeing and reading two documents together in the same window; however, it does not make revisions as readily visible as Track Changes. Peer review (c) is a useful learning exercise for students; however, though it gives the advantage of another's perspective when the writer cannot

view his (or her) work objectively, classmates may not be any more accurate than the writer, and he learns more about revising and editing his own work by doing it. Also, peer review can but does not necessarily involve technology use. Hand-writing changes on printouts (d) defeats the purpose of using word-processing technology, which makes revising and editing far easier to do and read.

64. B: The four main purposes of writing also determine its four basic types: narration, description, exposition, and persuasion. Persuasive writing aims to express opinions and/or convince readers to agree with or believe something. Examples of persuasion, also called argumentation, include editorials, advertising, literary essays, book reviews, movie reviews, and music reviews. Research papers are not examples of persuasive writing (a), but of exposition. The purpose of expository writing is to give information and/or explain. In addition to research papers, examples include news reports, instruction manuals, and encyclopedias. Novels do not commonly have the purpose of exposition (c); they tell stories, which is the purpose of narrative. Additional examples of narration include biographies, anecdotes, short stories, and personal narratives.

65. D: Expectations of high school and middle school students include interpreting and understanding visual imagery, meanings, and messages (a); analyzing and critiquing the importance of visual media (b); and evaluating the ways that various media inform and influence people (c). Developing and organizing ideas from the environment (d) is an expectation, but *not* for the Viewing and Representing strand or even from the English Language Arts subject area; it is an expectation for middle school students in the Fine Arts subject area.

66. C: When teaching students about various media types, the four categories listed as choices are ways to classify them. Option (a) includes emails, phone calls, and letters but not books. Option (b) includes movies, TV shows, video games; and novels are included, but not the wider class of books. (Note that there are many more kinds of books than novels.) Option (c) includes books, newspapers, websites, and radio news broadcasts. Option (d) includes advertising, direct mail marketing, telemarketing calls, and infomercials.

67. A: News articles published on the worldwide web are more formal in their content and language than blogs on the web (b), which are written from a more personal, less journalistic perspective; or than email messages (c), which can be even more casual than blogs as they involve communications between individuals rather than writing intended for larger audiences like blogs and news articles. Hence these are not all the same in formality level (d).

68. C: Satire is a common technique used by political cartoonists to communicate messages that criticize politicians, governmental administrations, political groups, etc. through the use of humor. Documentary filmmakers (a) focus on recording aspects of the lives, careers, or activities of individuals, groups, movements, etc. As the name implies, their purpose is to document; while filmmakers often present documentaries from perspectives that are not completely objective, neither are documentaries fictional or satirical in nature. News photographers (b) also document real-world events; while their photos can also communicate subjective messages, they are less likely to use satire than political cartoonists and more likely to provide journalistic records. Illustrators (d) typically create drawings, paintings, or other visual media as pictorial representations, either to accompany print text or independently; they are less often satirical, more often artistic and interpretive.

69. C: The properties listed are all elements of visual art media that help to communicate and/or elaborate meaning. Although visual artists may make use of these elements characteristic of certain styles (a), the elements themselves are not style, which depends on the form of media. For example,

surrealism is a style found in both paintings and films. Media (b) are what artists use to create products, e.g., film in still photography and cinematography; watercolor paint, oil paint, charcoal, pastels, ink, mixed media, etc. in paintings and drawings; clay, stone, wood, metal, fabric, etc. in sculptures; digital imagery in websites, computer programs, movies, TV; and many more. Thus (d) is incorrect.

70. B: By asking students to analyze these elements of the two pieces of media, the teacher is helping students to compare the points of view and ideas they communicate. They are not comparing various celebrity athletes (a) as both media products feature the same celebrity athlete. They are not comparing different types of graphics (c) as the question does not indicate each used a different kind. They are not comparing objectivity to subjectivity (d) as both products likely contain elements of both, and the elements the teacher asks students to identify do not specifically address these.

71. A: This is an example of formative assessment, which can be formal or informal but is more often informal; it is conducted during instruction to inform teachers of student progress and enable them to adjust instruction if it is not effective enough; this is done on an ongoing basis. Summative assessment (b) is typically formal; it is conducted after instruction to measure final results for grading, promotion, accountability, etc. and inform changes to future instruction, but does not enable adjusting the current instruction. Therefore, it is not an example of (c) or (d).

72. A: Norm-referenced tests compare student scores to the average scores of a normative sample of similar students that represents the target population. Informal reading inventories (b) use graded word lists, reading passages from authentic texts, and comprehension questions to identify student reading levels, strengths, and instructional needs rather than comparing student scores to normative group scores. Curriculum-based assessments (c) test student knowledge of the specific material included in the school's curriculum rather than comparing scores. Criterion-referenced tests (d) compare student performance against pre-established criteria for mastery of specific skills, not other students' performance.

73. C: The student needs additional help or intervention to reach grade-level expectations for listening in the Listening and Speaking knowledge and skills area for grade 2 ELA and reading. The skills the student demonstrates are expectations for the kindergarten grade level. The additional skills the student does not demonstrate are listening expectations for the grade 1 and grade 2 levels. Therefore, the student is two years below grade level and does not meet (a) or exceed (b) grade-level expectations. This gap is too significant to preclude intervention (d).

74. B: One set of criteria suggested for use with informal reading inventories (Pumfrey, 1976) equates the independent reading level (a) to knowing 95-100 percent of words in isolation, 99-100 percent accuracy reading words in context, and answering comprehension questions 90-100 percent correctly; the instructional level (c) to knowing 60-94 percent of words in isolation, 95-98 percent accuracy reading words in context, and answering comprehension questions 70-89 percent correctly; and the frustration level with knowing below 50 percent of words in isolation, reading below 95 percent of words accurately in context, and answering below 70 percent of comprehension questions correctly. Hence the text described is at the student's frustration level and too difficult. Because the student information identifies reading levels below these suggested criteria for the frustration level, (d) is incorrect.

75. D: Student reading skills and progress are not necessarily constant relative to grade-level standards over time, so teachers should use ongoing (a), i.e., formative (b) assessment to ascertain

when a student might need specialized instruction or classroom intervention and plan instruction accordingly. Summative (c) assessment is conducted after instruction is over, which does not enable ongoing evaluation or planning of current instruction.

Mathematics

1. B: This is a formative assessment because she is assessing students while she is still teaching the unit. Summative assessments are given at the end of the unit. Formal assessments are usually a quizzes or tests. Informal assessments includes asking individual students questions. Therefore, the correct choice is B.

2. B: The students are more successful with physical objects. They can understand the concept of conservation. They can grasp subtraction in terms of concrete operations. Typically, 7-11 year olds are in the concrete operations stage. In this stage, the formal code is too abstract for their understanding. Therefore, the correct choice is B.

3. D: Ms. Alejo is using different activities to meet the various readiness levels of her students. This aspect is described by differentiated instruction. Collaborative learning and small group instruction describe the aspect that the students are in groups. The question does not address nonlinguistic representations such as charts and visual aids. Therefore, the correct choice is D.

4. D: Of the available options, choice D is the most learner-centered activity since it includes hands-on activities with the use of manipulatives. Choices B and C are learner-centered but do not include hands-on activities. Choice A is teacher-centered. Therefore, the correct choice is D.

5. A: Choice A is correct because the fourth grade students should be able to use a protractor to determine the approximate measures of angles in degrees to the nearest whole number. Choices B, C, and D are expectations for fifth grade students. Therefore, the correct choice is A.

6. A: Choice A is correct because second grade students should be able to calculate how money saved can accumulate into a larger amount over time. Choice D, which is expected of first grade students, is too basic for second grade. Choice C is expected of third grade students. Choice B is expected of fifth grade students. Therefore, the correct choice is A.

7. C: Since all of the teachers implementing a theme about the heart, this is a thematic unit. Collaborative learning typically involves students working in groups. Formative assessments are ways teachers assess learning while working on a unit. Differentiated instruction is the use of multiple methods when teaching a unit. Therefore, the correct choice is C.

8. C: Choice C matches the goal for first grade students which states, "Illustrate that the length of an object is the number of same-size units of length that, when laid end-to-end with no gaps or overlaps, reach from one end of the object to the other." The other three choices are too difficult for a first grade student. Therefore, the correct choice is C.

9. B: Sophia needs to find multiples of 3 (3, 6, 9, 12, 15...) and multiples of 4 (4, 8, 12, 16,...) and find the least common multiple between them, which is 12. The greatest common divisor of 3 and 4 is 1. The least common divisor between two numbers is always 1. The greatest common multiple can never be determined. Therefore, the correct choice is B.

10. B: Since Mr. Mancelli has eight candy bars, he can make at most eight identical bags, each containing a single candy bar and a single package of gum; in this case, however, he will have four packages of gum remaining. To determine the greatest number of prize bags he can make so that no candy bars or packages of gum remain, he needs to find the greatest common divisor (or greatest common factor) of 8 and 12. Factors of 8 include 1, 2, 4, and 8. Factors of 12 include 1, 2, 3, 4, 6, and

11. C: A number that is divisible by 6 is divisible by 2 and 3. For example, the number 12 is divisible by 2 and 3. A number ending in 6, a number with the last two digits divisible by 6 and a number with the last digit divisible by 2 or 3 is not necessarily divisible by 6; for example, 16 and 166 are not divisible by 6. Therefore, the correct choice is C:

12. A: In choice A, a comparison of the digits in the tenths place shows that 0.2 is greater than both 0.0499 and 0.007. Then, a comparison of the hundredths place shows that 0.0499 is greater than 0.007. Choice B should read $-2 < 0 < 7$. Choice C should read $\frac{1}{3} > \frac{1}{4} > \frac{1}{5}$. Choice D should read $-10 < -4 < -1$. Therefore, the correct choice is A.

13. D: Number lines can help students understand the concepts of positive and negative numbers. Fraction strips are most commonly used with fractions. Venn diagrams are commonly used when comparing groups. Shaded regions are commonly used with fractions or percentages. Therefore, the correct choice is D.

14. C: Only choice C correctly applies the order of operations. The left side of choice A is equivalent to 4. The left side of choice B is equivalent to 2. The left side of choice D is equivalent to 14. Therefore, the correct choice is C.

15. D: Real numbers include all rational and irrational numbers. Rational numbers include all integers. The set of real numbers include the other three sets. Therefore, the correct choice is D.

16. A: Choice A correctly shows how the combination of like terms on the left side of the equation results in the expression on the right side of the equation. Choice B incorrectly combines like terms by adding the coefficients rather than subtracting. Choice C incorrectly adds the exponents of like terms instead of just adding the coefficients of like terms. Choice D incorrectly distributes the 2.5 across by parentheses by neglecting to multiply the 2.5 with the last term in the expression. Therefore, the correct choice is A.

17. C: The associative property of multiplication states that when three or more numbers are multiplied, the product is the same regardless of the way in which the numbers are grouped. Choice C shows that the product of 2, 3, and 4 is the same with two different groupings of the factors. Choice A demonstrates the distributive property. Choice B shows grouping, but the factors are different. Choice D demonstrates the commutative property of multiplication. Therefore, the correct choice is C.

18. D: The general form for this linear equation is
$y = mx + b$ in which m is the jogger's rate and b is the jogger's distance from his front door at the beginning of his run. The rate can be found by (25.0-5.2)/(3-0),which reduces to 6.6 meters per second. The starting distance from the door is 5.2 meters. The linear equation that represents this situation is y=6.6x+5.2.

Therefore, the correct choice is D.

19. C: Only choice C is the appropriate level for first grade students. Choices A and B are appropriate for third grade students. Choice D is appropriate for kindergarten. Therefore, the correct choice is C.

20. A: Choice A first factors to $3(x^2 - 4x + 4)$, which further factors to $3(x - 2)^2$. Choice B of $x^2 - 9$ factors to $(x - 3)(x + 3)$. Choice C first factors to $5(x^2 + x - 2)$, which further factors to $5(x + 2)(x - 1)$. Choice D factors to $4x(x - 4)$. Therefore, the correct choice is A.

21. B: Since Claus has at most $20 to spend, the amount he spends must be less than or equal to ($\leq$) $20, which eliminates choice D: Since the entrance fee of $2.50 is only charged once, it should not be multiplied by x, so choice A is also incorrect. The cost of the entrance fee ($2.50) and the cost of the tickets ($2x) should be added together to find the Claus's total cost of the fun fair. This eliminates choice C: The correct inequality is 2.50+2x≤20.

Therefore, the correct choice is B.

22. B: The equation $y + 3 = 7$ is solved by subtracting 3 from both sides to yield $y = 4$. Substituting
$y = 4$ into $x - 1 = y$ yields $x - 1 = 4$. Adding 1 to both sides of this equation yields $x = 5$.
Therefore, the correct choice is B.

23. D: This problem can be represented using the proportion $\frac{number\ of\ wins}{total\ games} = \frac{number\ of\ wins}{total\ games}$. If
the ratio of wins to losses is 2:1, then the ratio of wins to total games is 2:3. The proportion to determine the number of wins is x/36=2/3.

Therefore, the correct choice is D.

24. C: A linear equation is an equation of the first degree. That means that the highest exponent of any term or variable is one, so it follows that an exponent cannot be variable. Choice C is a linear equation. Choices A and D are quadratic equations. Choice B is neither linear nor quadratic. Therefore, the correct choice is C.

25. A: Marcus needs $325 for the new gaming system. If he earns $6.50 an hour, the number of hours he needs to work can be determined by dividing $325 by $6.50 which is written as
$\frac{325}{6.50} = x$. Multiplying both sides of the equation by 6.50 yields $6.50x = 325$. Therefore, the correct choice is A.

26. C: Triangles can be classified as scalene, isosceles, or equilateral. Scalene triangles have no equal side measurements and no equal angle measurements. Isosceles triangles have two sides of equal measurement and two angles of equal measurement. Equilateral triangles have three sides of equal measurement and three angles of equal measurement. A right triangle is isosceles only if its two acute angles are congruent. Therefore, the correct choice is C.

27. B: A regular solid prism is a solid, three-dimensional shape which has length, width, and height. The bases are of the same shape, and the shape of the other faces depend on the shape of the bases. The volume of a regular solid prism can be determined by multiplying the area of the base by the height of the prism. For example, the volume of a rectangular prism is found by
$Volume = Area\ of\ base \times Height$ which is more commonly known as $Volume = Length \times Width \times Height$. Therefore, the correct choice is B.

28. A: Since area is two dimensional, the units for area have an exponent of two such as in², yd², cm², or m². Choice B includes a unit of length (yd) and a unit of volume (yd³). Choice C includes only units of length. Choice C includes a square unit of time (s²). Therefore, the correct choice is A.

29. D: A polygon may be decomposed into triangles by drawing all possible diagonals from one of the vertices. The sum of the degrees of a polygon is equal to the sum of the degrees of the triangles formed. Then the angle of the polygon is equal to that sum divided by the number of sides. For example, in a hexagon, four triangles are formed. The sum of the angles of a hexagon is equal to 4(180°) or 720°. Each angle of a regular hexagon measures $\frac{720°}{6}$, or 120°. Therefore, the correct choice is D.

30. C: The slope of a line can be found from any two points by the formula $slope = \frac{y_2 - y_1}{x_2 - x_1}$.

A quick sketch of the point in Choice C reveals a line with a negative slope. Substituting the last two points into the formula yields slope= (-3 -1)/(0-(-6)) which reduces to (-4)/6 or (-2)/3.The points in Choice A form a line with a positive slope. The points in Choice B form a line with a negative slope of (-3)/2.

The points in Choice D form a horizontal line. Therefore, the correct choice is C.

31. A: A hexagon has six ides. A hexagonal prism has 8 faces consisting of two hexagonal bases and six rectangular lateral faces. This results in 18 edges and 12 vertices. Therefore, the correct choice is A.

32. B: Graham has placed Group 1 with 40¢, Group 2 with 38¢, and Group 3 with 29¢. Henry has placed Group 1 with 34¢, Group 2 with 27¢, and Group 3 with 27¢. Landon has placed Group 1 with 59¢, Group 2 with 43¢, and Group 3 with 59¢. Elizabeth has placed Group 1 with 41¢, Group 2 with 41¢, and Group 3 with 22¢. Therefore, the correct choice is B.

33. D: Congruent figures have the same shape and the same size. Two squares have the same shape. If the areas are the same, they also have the same size and are congruent. Choice A is incorrect because two rectangles can have the same perimeter but not the same shape. Choice B is the incorrect because two polygons of the same shape are not necessarily the same size. Choice C is incorrect because two polygons can have the same side lengths but different shapes. Therefore, the correct choice is D.

34. C: The mean is the average of the data and can be found by dividing the sum of the data by the number of data: $\frac{16 + 18 + 20 + 21 + 34 + 45 + 49}{7} = 29$. The median is the middle data point when the data are ranked numerically. The median is 21. Therefore, the correct choice is C.

35. C: This is a compound event. Since the marble is replaced after the first draw, the probability of each event is $\frac{1}{10}$. The probability of drawing two 5s in a row is $\frac{1}{10} \cdot \frac{1}{10}$ or $\frac{1}{100}$. Therefore, the correct choice is C.

36. B: Since the events are mutually exclusive, the sum of their individual probabilities is 1.0. Subtracting 0.6 from 1.0 yields 0.4. Therefore, the correct choice is B.

37. A: The probability that the dart will land in the inner circle is equal to the ratio of the area of inner circle to the area of the outer circle, or $\frac{\pi 3^2}{\pi 6^2}$. This reduces to $\frac{1}{4}$. Therefore, the correct choice is A.

38. B: The histogram only shows that there are eight trees between 70 and 75 feet tall. It does not show the individual heights of the trees. That information cannot be obtained from this graph. Therefore, the correct choice is B.

39. D: The standard deviation is a measure of spread. The mean, median, and mode are measures of central tendency. Therefore, the correct choice is D.

40. D: The theoretical probability of tossing any particular number is $\frac{1}{6}$. Since she tosses a two $\frac{3}{12}$, or $\frac{1}{4}$, times, the experimental probability of tossing a 2 is greater than the theoretical probability. The experimental probability should grow closer to the experimental probability as she tosses the die more times. Therefore, the correct choice is D.

41. B: If all primates are mammals, and all lemurs are primates, then all lemurs are mammals. All primates are not lemurs. Since neither whales nor monkeys are mentioned in the premises, they cannot be included in the conclusion. The conclusion can only be based on the information given in the premises. Therefore, the correct choice is B.

42. B: This series lists the sum of the squares of natural numbers and 1. For example, $1^2 + 1$ is 2, and $2^2 + 1$ is 5. The next number in the series can be determined by $5^2 + 1$ which is 26. Note also that the differences between consecutive numbers in the series are consecutive odd integers starting at 3; for example, $2 + 3$ is 5, $5 + 5$ is 20, and $10 + 7$ is 17, so the next number in the series is $17 + 9$, or 26. Therefore, the correct choice is B.

43. A: To a convert a percent to a fraction, remove the percent sign and place the number over 100. That means 15% can be written as $\frac{15}{100}$, which reduces to $\frac{3}{20}$. To covert a percent to a decimal, remove the percent sign and move the decimal two places to the left. To convert a percent to a ratio, first write the ratio as a fraction, and then rewrite the fraction as a ratio. Therefore, the correct choice is A.

44. C: The Sumerians were Babylonians who lived in Mesopotamia a few thousand years ago. Plato and Archimedes were Greeks. The Egyptians wrote the Rhind papyrus. Therefore, the correct choice is C.

45. A: Since the students are using manipulatives, this is a concrete representation. Therefore, the correct choice is A.

46. C: The number 589 can be estimated to be 600. The number 9 can be estimated to be 10. The number of chicken nuggets is approximately 600×10, which is 6,000 nuggets. Therefore, the correct choice is C.

47. A: In the third line of the problem, the student incorrectly added the 5 and 2 rather than multiplying 2(2). According to the order of operations, the student should multiply before adding. Therefore, the correct choice is A.

Social Studies

1. D: According to Article III of the Constitution, Justices of the Supreme Court, judges of the courts of appeals and district courts, and judges of the Court of International Trade are appointed by the President with the confirmation of the Senate. The judicial branch of the government is the only one not elected by the people.

2. C: Article III judges are appointed for life and can retire at 65. They can only be removed from their posts by impeachment in the House and conviction in the Senate. Having judges serve life terms is meant to allow them to serve without being governed by the changing opinions of the public.

3. B: Judges who are eligible to retire but still work are called senior judges. Retired judges who occasionally hear cases are called recalled judges. Both senior and recalled judges handle about 15-20 percent of district and appellate court caseloads.

4. C: There are no formal qualifications for members of the judicial branch. However, having a background in law is an informal qualification that is considered when appointing Article III judges.

5. B: Congress has the authority to shape the judicial branch. The Supreme Court once operated with only six members. Nine has been the standard number since 1869.

6. D: Criminal cases are tried under both state law and federal law. The nature of the crime determines whether it is tried in state court or federal court.

7. C: State governments follow the example of the federal government and have executive, legislative, and judicial branches of their own, and elected governors who head the executive branch.

8. A: The 10th Amendment establishes that any power not given to the federal government in the Constitution belongs to the states, or the people. The federal and local governments share many responsibilities.

9. B: Congress normally chooses the jurisdiction of federal courts. The Supreme Court has original jurisdiction in certain cases, which Congress cannot revoke. For example, the Supreme Court has the right to settle a dispute between states.

10. A: The Supreme Court interprets law and the Constitution. The inferior courts are bound to uphold the law as the Supreme Court interprets and rules on it.

11. C: The 12th Amendment passed in 1804 gave each member of the Electoral College one vote for the President and another for the Vice President. Previously, the runner-up in the Presidential election became Vice President.

12. B: Discretionary spending is dedicated to transportation, education, national resources, the environment, and international affairs. State and local governments use this money to help finance programs. Mandatory spending covers entitlements such as Medicare, Social Security, Federal Retirement, and Medicaid.

13. D: Free public education has been a U.S. tradition since the 18th century. State constitutions govern the education issues of each state, although federal, state, and local governments all work together on educational issues.

14. C: When a nation follows the theory of comparative advantage, it specializes in producing the goods and services it can make at a lower opportunity cost and then engages in trade to obtain other goods.

15. A: Answer B is a definition of gross national product, and answers C and D define other economic measures.

16. C: If a country's currency increases in value, foreigners will have to give up more of their own currency to get the original country's currency in order to buy the original country's goods and services. This will cause a drop in exports. At the same time, it will be less expensive for people in the original country to exchange their currency for foreign currencies, causing the price of imported goods to drop and the total value of imports to rise.

17. A: As people have more and more of something, they value it less and less. This is the law of diminishing marginal utility, and it is what causes the downward slope of the demand curve.

18. C: A person who has taken out a fixed-rate loan can benefit from inflation by paying back the loan with dollars that are less valuable than they were when the loan was taken out. In the other examples, inflation harms the individual or entity.

19. C: The impact of a transaction on third parties not involved in the transaction is known as an externality. An externality can be positive, in which case it's a positive externality or social benefit. An externality can also be negative, in which case it's a negative externality or a social cost.

20. E: A market failure is any situation in which the production of a good or service is not efficient. In the cases listed, non-competitive markets allow for the underpayment of labor and the underproduction of a good or service; externalities are negative consequences assumed by parties not involved in a transaction; and public goods are an example of a good the market will not produce at all, or at efficient levels.

21. D: A flow-line map describes the movement of people, trends, or materials across a physical area. The movements depicted on a flow-line map are typically represented by arrows. In more advanced flow-line maps, the width of the arrow corresponds to the quantity of the motion. Flow-line maps usually declare the span of time that is being represented. A political map depicts the man-made aspects of geography, such as borders and cities. A cartogram adjusts the size of the areas represented according to some variable. For instance, a cartogram of wheat production would depict Iowa as being much larger than Alaska. A qualitative map uses lines, dots, and other symbols to illustrate a particular point. For example, a qualitative map might be used to demonstrate the greatest expansion of the Persian Empire.

22. C: The cycle of demographic transition is best illustrated by a line graph. Demographic transition is a phenomenon in which a region's growth rate increases rapidly, peaks, and then decreases slowly over a long time. In the early phase of a region's development, both the birth and death rates are high, which can cause the population to fluctuate. As the people of the region become settled, the growth rate calms down, and the region enters a period of rapid increase. Political maps are better at depicting borders and the locations of cities, while pie charts are better

at representing proportions. Flow-line maps are good for illustrating the movement of people, goods, or trends across a physical area.

23. A: A time line would be the best way to represent the major events of World War I. Time lines place events in chronological order, with the distance between the events correlated to their interval on the line. A time line can run in any direction. A thematic map or a flow-line map might also be good at representing this subject, but a political map is restricted to borders and cities; therefore, it would not be able to suggest the changes caused by the war. Bar graphs and pie charts are used to depict quantities and proportions rather than sequences of events.

24. B: The composite volcano, sometimes called the stratovolcano, is the most common type of volcano on earth. A composite volcano has steep sides, so the explosions of ash, pumice, and silica are often accompanied by treacherous mudslides. Indeed, it is these mudslides that cause most of the damage associated with composite volcano eruptions. Krakatoa and Mount Saint Helens are examples of composite volcanoes. A lava dome is a round volcano that emits thick lava very slowly. A shield volcano, one example of which is Mt. Kilauea in Hawaii, emits a small amount of lava over an extended period of time. Shield volcanoes are not known for violent eruptions. A cinder cone has steep sides made of fallen cinders, which themselves are made of the lava that intermittently shoots into the air.

25. C: The chaparral biome features scrubby plants and small evergreen trees and also has a hot, dry summer followed by a wetter winter. This biome is mainly found around the Mediterranean Sea, though there are also chaparrals in Australia, South Africa, and the American Southwest. The taiga is a colder biome found primarily in northern Europe and Asia. The vegetation of the taiga is mainly scattered stands of coniferous trees. A coniferous forest, meanwhile, is a warmer forest composed of trees that have needles and cones rather than leaves. These trees are better suited for a cold climate than are deciduous trees. A savanna is a tropical grassland with only a few trees. Savannas are clustered around the equator.

26. B: Metamorphic rock is formed by extreme heat and pressure. This type of rock is created when other rocks are somehow buried within the earth, where they are subject to a dramatic rise in pressure and temperature. Slate and marble are both metamorphic rocks. Metamorphic rocks are created by the other two main types of rock: sedimentary and igneous. Sedimentary rock is formed when dirt and other sediment is washed into a bed, covered over by subsequent sediment, and compacted into rock. Depending on how they are formed, sedimentary rocks are classified as organic, clastic, or chemical. Igneous rocks are composed of cooled magma, the molten rock that emerges from volcanoes. Basalt and granite are two common varieties of igneous rock.

27. D: The rocks and land formations that make up the earth's surface are collectively known as the lithosphere. The lithosphere does not include the core or mantle of the earth. The atmosphere is the air, water, and particles that are above the surface of the earth. The biosphere encompasses all the living things of the earth, such as animals, plants, fungi, and bacteria. The hydrosphere is all the water on and beneath the surface of the earth, including all the lakes, oceans, rivers, and creeks.

28. A: Glaciers move because they are incredibly heavy, and the force of gravity slowly pulls them lower. Erosion is a result rather than a cause of glacier movement. Although large glaciers may only move a few inches a year or may not move at all, some valley glaciers in Europe move as much as 600 feet annually. The result is a rounded valley and a trail of rock and soil debris known as a moraine. The Great Lakes in the United States were formed by the passage of glaciers long ago.

29. C: Acid rain is an example of chemical weathering. When acidic chemicals are evaporated and fall as rain, they can have devastating effects on plant and animal life. Although human activity is the primary cause of acid rain, weathering chemicals can also get into the atmosphere through oceanic bacteria and volcanoes. The other three answer choices are examples of mechanical weathering. Frost wedging occurs when water seeps into a narrow space within a rock formation and then freezes. Because water takes up more space as ice and frost than it does in its liquid state, this process can cause structural damage to the rock. Heat expansion occurs when rapid changes in temperature cause rocks to expand, leading to cracks and fissures. Salt wedging occurs when water flowing into a rock brings salt in with it. The water evaporates, but the salt is left behind, and over time the deposits of salt can create pressure within the rock.

30. A: North Africa is not one of the world's four major population agglomerations. These are eastern North America, South Asia, East Asia, and Europe. The largest of these is East Asia, which encompasses Korea, Japan, and the major cities of China. The second-largest population agglomeration is South Asia, which includes India and Pakistan. Most of the population in this area is near the coasts. The European agglomeration is spread across the largest piece of land, while the much smaller agglomeration in eastern North America is primarily focused on the string of cities from Boston to Washington, DC.

31. A: Of the four answer choices, New York City is the most likely to be considered a modern cultural hearth. A cultural hearth is an area from which cultural trends emanate. Geographers suggest that there were seven original cultural hearths, including Mesoamerica and the Indus River Valley. The modes of living that originated in these areas emanated out into the rest of the world. These days, the cultural hearths tend to be the cities and countries with the most economic power. Of the four answer choices, New York City is clearly the wealthiest and the most influential. The styles and trends that originate in New York City find their way into communities all around the world.

32. B: Diversity is not one of the demographic variables. Demographers, or those who study population, rely on fertility, mortality, and migration to determine the number of people in a region. The general equation is *Total Population = Original Population + Births – Deaths + Immigration – Emigration*. The natural increase, on the other hand, is calculated only with the number of births and deaths. The diversity of a population may be relevant to subsequent research performed by the demographer, but it is not considered one of the essential three demographic variables.

33. C: Yemen is not a member of OPEC, the Organization of Petroleum Exporting Countries. Yemen has some deposits of oil, but the nation has only recently begun developing them. This, along with a desperate water shortage, accounts for Yemen's position as the poorest nation in the Middle East. OPEC was established in 1960 to set oil prices and production. Until the formation of OPEC, many oil-producing nations felt they were being exploited by Western oil companies. This organization has obtained a great deal of power and is held responsible for the gas shortages that wracked the United States during the late 1970s.

34. D: One of the unique features of the Yucatan Peninsula in Mexico is its collection of sinkholes created by the collapse of limestone caverns beneath the surface. Unlike most of the rest of Mexico, which has firm bedrock, the Yucatan is supported by porous limestone. When this limestone becomes too weak, it creates deep sinkholes that can be used as wells. The other answer choices are all false statements about the Yucatan Peninsula. This region of Mexico is relatively unpopulated; the largest city, Merida, has only about 500,000 citizens. The Yucatan is much flatter than the rest of Mexico; indeed, it is this absence of prehistoric volcano sites that accounts for the difference in soil.

Finally, the Yucatan was once inhabited by Mayans, not Aztecs. Some scholars believe that the modern name of the peninsula is derived from the Mayan words for "I do not understand your words," which was merely the unrelated reply to questions from Spanish explorers.

35. A: The Atlantic provinces of Canada are Labrador, Prince Edward Island, New Brunswick, and Nova Scotia. All of these provinces have a coastline on the Atlantic Ocean. Although these four provinces represent only about 5 percent of Canada's total landmass, they have played a major role in the development of the nation. In particular, the fishing industry off the coasts of Nova Scotia and Newfoundland has long been a solid component of the Canadian economy. There is also a great deal of agriculture in Nova Scotia and Prince Edward Island.

36. C: Before China took control of Hong Kong in 1997, the island was administrated by Great Britain. This transfer of power had been planned for a long time. One of the conditions for the transfer was that Hong Kong will retain political and economic independence from China. Hong Kong is referred to as a Special Administrative Region of China, and its citizens are given much more leeway than other Chinese citizens. To date, China has been successful in harnessing the economic power of Hong Kong and allowing two systems of governance to coexist within one nation.

37. D: Japan imports the second-highest amount of oil after the United States. Following World War II, Japan rapidly became one of the foremost industrial powers. Despite thriving economically, however, Japan is not especially rich in natural resources. Only slightly more than 10 percent of the nation's land can be farmed, and there are no significant oil deposits. For this reason, Japan must import most of the raw materials it needs for its manufacturing base.

38. A: It is not true that England's defeat of the Spanish Armada in 1588 ended their war with Spain. It did establish England's naval dominance and strengthened England's future colonization of the New World, but the actual war between England and Spain did not end until 1604. It is true that Henry VIII's desire to divorce Catherine of Aragon strengthened English expansionism (b). Catherine was Spanish, and Henry split from the Catholic Church because it prohibited divorce. Henry's rejection of his Spanish wife and his subsequent support of the Protestant movement angered King Philip II of Spain and destroyed the formerly close ties between the two countries. When Elizabeth became Queen of England, she supported the Reformation as a Protestant, which also contributed to English colonization (c). Sir Francis Drake, one of the best known English sea captains during this time period, would attack and plunder Spanish ships that had plundered American Indians (d), adding to the enmity between Spain and England. Queen Elizabeth invested in Drake's voyages and gave him her support in claiming territories for England.

39. B: The Virginia Company of London was based in London, not Massachusetts. It had a charter to colonize American land between the Hudson and Cape Fear rivers (c). The other Virginia Company was the Virginia Company of Plymouth, which was based in the American colony of Plymouth, Massachusetts (a). It had a charter to colonize North America between the Potomac River and the northern boundary of Maine (d). Both Virginia Companies were joint-stock companies, which had often been used by England for trading with other countries.

40. D: It is not true that John Smith's governance helped Jamestown more than John Rolfe's discovery that a certain type of East Indian tobacco could be grown in Virginia. Smith's strong leadership from 1608-1609 gave great support to the struggling colony. However, when Smith's return to England left Jamestown without this support, the future of the colony was again in question. In 1612, however, when John Rolfe found that an East Indian tobacco strain popular in

Europe could be farmed in Virginia, the discovery gave Jamestown and Virginia a lucrative crop. Therefore, both Smith's time in office and Rolfe's discovery were beneficial to Jamestown. Jamestown was established by the Virginia Company of London in 1607 (a), and it became the first permanent settlement by the English in North America (b). It is also true that Jamestown survived in spite of the fact that most of its early settlers died from starvation, disease, and Indian attacks (c). It is also true that many of Jamestown's settlers came from the English upper class and were unwilling to farm the land, while others came hoping to find gold or other treasures, and persisted in their search for these instead of working to make the land sustainable.

41. C: Hernando Cortes conquered the Mexican Aztecs in 1519. He had several advantages over the Indians, including horses, armor for his soldiers, and guns. In addition, Cortes' troops unknowingly transmitted smallpox to the Aztecs, which devastated their population as they had no immunity to this foreign illness. Vasco Nunez de Balboa (a) was the first European explorer to view the Pacific Ocean when he crossed the Isthmus of Panama in 1513. Juan Ponce de Leon (b) also visited and claimed Florida in Spain's name in 1513. Cabeza de Vaca (d) was one of only four men out of 400 to return from an expedition led by Panfilio de Narvaez in 1528, and was responsible for spreading the story of the Seven Cities of Cibola (the "cities of gold"). Hernando de Soto led an expedition from 1539-1541 to the southeastern part of America.

42. A: The attitudes of American colonists after the 1763 Treaty of Paris ended the French and Indian War was not a direct contributor to the American Revolution. American colonists had a supportive attitude toward Great Britain then, and were proud of the part they played in winning the war. Their good will was not returned by British leaders (b), who looked down on American colonials and sought to increase their imperial power over them. Even in 1761, a sign of Americans' objections to having their liberty curtailed by the British was seen when Boston attorney James Otis argued in court against the Writs of Assistance (c), search warrants to enforce England's mercantilist trade restrictions, as violating the kinds of natural laws espoused during the Enlightenment. Lord George Grenville's aggressive program to defend the North American frontier in the wake of Chief Pontiac's attacks included stricter enforcement of the Navigation Acts, the Proclamation of 1763, the Sugar Act (or Revenue Act), the Currency Act, and most of all the Stamp Act (d). Colonists objected to these as taxation without representation. Other events followed in this taxation dispute, which further eroded Americans' relationship with British government, including the Townshend Acts, the Massachusetts Circular Letter, the Boston Massacre, the Tea Act, and the resulting Boston Tea Party. Finally, with Britain's passage of the Intolerable Acts and the Americans' First Continental Congress, which was followed by Britain's military aggression against American resistance, actual warfare began in 1775. While not all of the colonies wanted war or independence by then, things changed by 1776, and Jefferson's Declaration of Independence was formalized. James Otis, Samuel Adams, Patrick Henry, the Sons of Liberty, and the Stamp Act Congress also contributed to the beginning of the American Revolution.

43. C: Colonists did find that tea shipped directly by the British East India Company cost less than smuggled Dutch tea, even with tax. The colonists, however, did not buy it. They refused, despite its lower cost, on the principle that the British were taxing colonists without representation (d). It is true that the British East India Company lost money as a result of colonists buying tea smuggled from Holland (a). They sought to remedy this problem by getting concessions from Parliament to ship tea directly to the colonies instead of going through England (b) as the Navigation Acts normally required. Boston Governor Thomas Hutchinson, who sided with Britain, stopped tea ships from leaving the harbor, which after 20 days would cause the tea to be sold at auction. At that time, British taxes on the tea would be paid. On the 19th night after Hutchinson's action, American protestors held the Boston Tea Party, dressing as Indians and dumping all the tea into the harbor to

destroy it so it could not be taxed and sold. Many American colonists disagreed with the Boston Tea Party because it involved destroying private property. When Lord North and the British Parliament responded by passing the Coercive Acts and the Quebec Act, known collectively in America as the Intolerable Acts, Americans changed their minds, siding with the Bostonians against the British.

Science

1. C: The majority of the solar energy that reaches Earth is absorbed by the oceans, which make up 71 percent of the Earth's surface. Because of water's high specific heat capacity, oceans can absorb and store large quantities of heat, thus preventing drastic increases in the overall atmospheric temperature.

2. C: Tropical climate zones are characterized by frequent rainfall, especially during the monsoon season, and by moderate temperatures that vary little from season to season or between night and day. Tropical zones do experience frequent rainfall, which leads to abundant vegetation.

3. D: The physical structure of the universe is thought to consist of filaments (walls of superclusters, clusters, and galaxies) that surround large, bubble-like voids. Filaments are the largest structures in the universe, with some forming huge structures like the Great Wall and the Sloan Great Wall.

4. B: It is true that galaxies are gravitationally bound so that structures within them orbit around the center. Galaxies do contain dark matter, and only the largest "giant" galaxies contain over one trillion stars. The smallest "dwarf" galaxies contain as few as 10 million stars. Clusters and superclusters are comprised of many galaxies.

5. A: The structure of the Milky Way galaxy is spiral, meaning it has curved "arms" stretching out from a central point. While spiral galaxies have a flat, disc-like appearance, elliptical galaxies are three-dimensional and appear to be roughly the same shape regardless of the viewing angle.

6. A: The distance from the Earth to the Sun is equal to one astronomical unit. An astronomical unit (AU) is equal to 93 million miles, and is far smaller than a light year or a parsec. A light year is defined as the distance light can travel in a vacuum in one year, and is equal to roughly 64,341 AU. A parsec is the parallax of one arcsecond, and is equal to 206.26×10^3 astronomical units.

7. B: The energy radiated by stars is produced by nuclear fusion. This is the process whereby the nuclei of individual atoms bind together to form heavier elements and release energy outward. By the time this energy, which is created in the star's core, reaches the outer walls of the star, it exists in the form of light.

8. A: The stream of charged particles that escape the Sun's gravitational pull is called solar wind. Solar wind is comprised primarily of protons and electrons, and these particles are deflected away from the Earth by its magnetic field. When stray particles do manage to enter the atmosphere, they cause the aurorae (Northern and Southern Lights) and geomagnetic storms that can affect power grids.

9. C: Venus is not a gas giant. The four gas giants are Jupiter, Saturn, Uranus, and Neptune. While these "gas giants" are larger than Earth and are comprised mostly of gases, Venus is a terrestrial planet that is comparable in size to the Earth.

10. D: The asteroid belt in our solar system is located between Mars and Jupiter. The asteroid belt is populated by asteroids and dwarf planets that are distributed thinly enough that spacecraft can pass though the belt with relative ease.

11. D: Gravitational collapse and high-energy collisions are both proposed explanations for the formation of black holes. Gravitational collapse occurs when the outward pressure exerted by an

object is too weak to resist that object's own gravity. Collisions that produce conditions of sufficient density could also, in theory, create black holes. The accretion of matter is considered observational evidence for the existence of black holes.

12. E: Endocytosis is a process by which cells absorb larger molecules or even tiny organisms, such as bacteria, than would be able to pass through the plasma membrane. Endocytic vesicles containing molecules from the extracellular environment often undergo further processing once they enter the cell.

13 C: Chloroplasts contain the light-absorbing compound chlorophyll, which is essential in photosynthesis. This gives leaves their green color. Chloroplasts also contain yellow and red carotenoid pigments, which give leaves red and yellow colors in the fall as chloroplasts lose their chlorophyll.

14. D: Enzymes are substrate-specific. Most enzymes catalyze only one biochemical reaction. Their active sites are specific for a certain type of substrate and do not bind to other substrates and catalyze other reactions.

15. D: In anaphase I, homologous chromosome pairs segregate randomly into daughter cells. This means that each daughter cell contains a unique combination of chromosomes that is different from the mother cell and different from its cognate daughter cell.

16. C: Although there are two cell divisions in meiosis, DNA replication occurs only once. It occurs in interphase I, before M phase begins.

17. C: Genes code for proteins, and genes are discrete lengths of DNA on chromosomes. An allele is a variant of a gene (different DNA sequence.. In diploid organisms, there may be two versions of each gene.

18. D: The ovary houses the ovules in a flower. Pollen grains fertilize ovules to create seeds, and the ovary matures into a fruit.

19. C: Gymnosperms reproduce by producing pollen and ovules, but they do not have flowers. Instead, their reproductive structures are cones or cone-like structures.

20. E: Stomata are openings on leaves that allow for gas exchange, which is essential for photosynthesis. Stomata are formed by guard cells, which open and close based on their turgidity.

21. C: Alternation of generations means the alternation between the diploid and haploid phases in plants.

22. B: Carbon is released in the form of CO_2 through respiration, burning, and decomposition.

23. D: Most nitrogen is in the atmosphere in the form of N_2. In order for it to be used by living things, it must be fixed by nitrogen-fixing bacteria. These microorganisms convert N_2 to ammonia, which then forms NH_4^+ (ammonium).

24. E: Options A-D all describe conditions that would lead to genetic equilibrium, where no evolution would occur. Gene flow, which is the introduction or removal of alleles from a population, would allow natural selection to work and could promote evolutionary change.

25. B: Phyletic gradualism is the view that evolution occurs at a more or less constant rate. Contrary to this view, punctuated equilibrium holds that evolutionary history consists of long periods of stasis punctuated by geologically short periods of evolution. This theory predicts that there will be few fossils revealing intermediate stages of evolution, whereas phyletic gradualism views the lack of intermediate-stage fossils as a deficit in the fossil record that will resolve when enough specimens are collected.

26. E: Mercury is a fat-soluble pollutant and can be stored in body tissues. Animals higher up the food chain that eat other animals are most likely to accumulate mercury in their bodies.

27. D: Air pollution would not be a direct result of clear-cutting forests. It would result in increased atmospheric CO_2, however, as well as localized climate change. Transpiration from trees in the tropical rain forest contributes largely to cloud formation and rain, so rainfall decreases because of clear-cutting, resulting in desertification.

28. B: When sulfur dioxide and nitrogen dioxide mix with water and other substances in the atmosphere, they produce sulfuric acid and nitric acid. These acids kill plants and animals when they reach the surface of the earth.

29. E: Genetic engineering is a general term to describe altering DNA sequences through adding or removing pieces of DNA from a native sequence. Restriction enzymes perform this "clipping" function.

30. A: Newton's first law (inertia) says an object in motion stays in motion, and an object at rest stays at rest, unless external forces act on them. I is an excellent demonstration because it shows the ball at rest and in motion. At rest, the ball stays at rest until a force acts on it. When the ball is moving, there is no force acting on the ball in the direction of motion. Thus, the natural state of the ball is to be at rest or moving with a constant speed. Ans. C is not a good demonstration because the force of friction is what makes it hard to move the heavy object. Ans B is a good demonstration of equilibrium and friction. Ans D, running a current through wires, has nothing to do with Newton's first law.

31. B: The newton is defined in terms of the fundamental units meters, kilograms, and seconds (N = kg $\times$ m/s^2), so it is not a fundamental unit. II is a verbal statement of $F = ma$, Newton's second law, which is true. If $F = 0$ N, then the acceleration is 0 m/s^2. If the acceleration is 0 m/s^2, then the speed is 0 m/s or a nonzero constant. This is a nonverbal statement of Newton's first law, meaning Newton's first law can be derived from his second law. Newton's second law cannot be derived from the universal law of gravity.

32. A: Newton's third law is that if object A exerts a force on object B, then object B exerts and equal and opposite force on object A. This means for every action (force) there is a reaction (force in opposite direction). The box is in equilibrium because the force of the table on the box is equal and opposite to the force of gravity (weight) of the box pushing against the table. Since the force of the box against the table is an action force (caused by gravity), the reaction force would be the table pushing back against the box.

33. C: All three laws are operating, but the third law (forces come in equal and opposite pairs) best explains the motion. The first law (inertia) is shown from the fact that the balloon doesn't move until a force acts upon it. The second law (F = ma) is shown because you can see the force and the

acceleration. The force comes from the contraction of the rubber balloon. The stretched rubber exerts a force on the air inside the balloon. This causes the air to accelerate in accordance with the second law. You can't see this acceleration because the air is invisible and because it is all the air in the room that the balloon is exerting a force on. However, the air in the room exerts and equal and opposite force on the balloon (this is Newton's third law), which causes the balloon to accelerate in the direction it did.

34. B: The moment of inertia of a point mass about any axis is given by mR^2, where R is the distance from the axis. The moment of inertia of a solid object is calculated by imagining that the object is made up of point masses and adding the moments of inertia of the point masses. The average radius of the particles in a hollow cylinder will be R (all the mass is at radius R). For a solid cylinder, however, the average radius is less than R, meaning the overall moment of inertia will be smaller, which means Answer B is correct. To actually calculate the moment of inertia of a cylinder of thickness $R_2 - R_1$ is $\frac{1}{2}m(R_1^2 + R_2^2)$. For a solid cylinder, R_1 = 0 meters. For a hollow cylinder, $R_1 = R_2$.

35. A: In a closed system (when you ignore outside interactions), the total momentum is constant and conserved. The total energy would also be conserved, although not the sum of the potential and kinetic energy. Some of the energy from the collision would be turned into thermal energy (heat) for example. Nor is the total velocity conserved, even though the velocity is a component of the momentum, since the momentum also depends on the mass of the cars. The impulse is a force over time that causes the momentum of a body to change. It doesn't make sense to think of impulse as conserved, since it's not necessarily constant throughout a collision.

36. D: Impulse is the change in an object's momentum (mv), which is in units of kg x m/s. An object's impulse can change, depending on the forces acting upon it. For a ball rolling down a hill, gravity provides a constant force, which causes the ball to accelerate. This creates an impulse that increases as the ball gets faster and faster. This impulse does not exist for a short time, but will continue as long as the ball is accelerating.

37. A: A collision is considered elastic when neither object loses any kinetic energy. Since the cars latch together, this can't be the case. You could easily prove this by calculating the cars' KE = $\frac{1}{2}mv^2$. If the railroad cars had bumpers instead of couplers, the moving car would stop and transfer all its momentum and kinetic energy to the stationary car, causing an elastic collision. In a closed system like this one, however, the conservation of momentum is an absolute law, where an objects' momentum is its mass times its velocity. There are no external forces acting on the two cars. The only forces are between the two cars themselves. The momentum before the collision is the same as the momentum after the collision: $mv_{initial} + m(0 \text{ m/s}) = mv_{final} + mv_{final}$. So $mv_{initial} = 2mv_{final}$, and $v_{initial} = 2v_{final}$. Thus the final velocity is half the initial velocity.

38. B: The total energy of an isolated system is always conserved. However the mechanical energy may not be, since some mechanical energy could be converted into radiation (light) or heat (through friction). According to Einstein's famous equation E = mc^2, energy is (occasionally, like in nuclear reactions!) converted into mass, and vice versa, where c is the speed of light. This does not affect the conservation of energy law, however, since the mass is considered to have an energy equivalent. This equation does not tell anything about the mechanical energy of a particle; it just shows how much energy would be generated if the mass was converted directly into energy.

39. D: Answers A, B, and C all shed light on what conservative forces are but do not answer the question of why the work on an object doesn't depend on its path. Friction is a force that causes

kinetic energy to be lost and where the amount of loss depends on the path taken. Work can be expressed in multiple ways, including as the sum of potentials, and all that matters is the beginning and ending position. Think of this in terms of gravity, gravitational potential energy, and the work done by gravity. In this case, $W = \Delta PE = mg\Delta h$, where h is an objects height. Dividing work by the change in position shows $mg = \Delta PE/\Delta h$. Since mg is a force, you can say $F = \Delta PE/\Delta h$, or the force equals the work/change in potential energy divided by its change in position.

40. C: Although the acceleration of a falling object is constant (9.8 m/s^2), this is not true for a pendulum. The total force on a simple pendulum is the resultant of the force of gravity on the bob acting downward and the tension in the string. When the pendulum is at the bottom of its swing, the net force is zero (tension = weight), although the bob does have a velocity. At the top of its swing, when it's changing direction, the tension is least. Therefore, the net force is greatest here, too. The bob is stationary momentarily at its highest level. Since F = ma, a large force means that the acceleration here is highest, too.

41. B: Although Answer A is also true, Answer B correctly states the law of conservation of charge. Answer C is only partially true because there are other elementary particles with a charge. Answer D is false because a photon will produce an electron-positron pair. There is also the example of a proton and electron combining to form a neutron.

42. B: Answer B correctly states the definition of a conductor. Answer C is incorrect because a current will also flow in an insulator, for example, although that current will be very low. In metals, the current flow caused by an electric field is much greater than in an insulator or semiconductor because the electrons are not bound to any particular atom, but are free to move. Answer D is incorrect because a vacuum tube is a device that electrons can flow in, butut a vacuum tube is not considered a conductor.

43. A: In a Zn-Cu battery, the zinc terminal has a higher concentration of electrons than the copper terminal, so there is a potential difference between the locations of the two terminals. This is a form of electrical energy brought about by the chemical interactions between the metals and the electrolyte the battery uses. Creating a circuit and causing a current to flow will transform the electrical energy into heat energy, mechanical energy, or another form of electrical energy, depending on the devices in the circuit. A generator transforms mechanical energy into electrical energy and a transformer changes the electrical properties of a form of electrical energy.

44. C: Ohm's law is that $V = IR$. Answer C is the only relation that holds true using this equation. If the resistance doesn't change, increasing the current on the right side must cause the voltage to also increase on the left side.

45. A: In a nuclear reaction, be it fission or fusion, matter is converted into energy. Einstein first postulated the law of energy-mass conservation using the equation $E = mc^2$, where m is mass, E is energy and c is the speed of light. Looking closely at this equation shows that a tiny amount of matter can produce a large amount of energy, which is why nuclear reactions are so energetic.

46. C: Protons and neutrons are both considered nucleons. The number of nucleons in a nucleus is called the *mass number.* Isotopes of the same element have different mass numbers. But since they are the same element, they must have the same atomic number, which is equal to the number of protons. Thus, only the number of neutrons changes, since electron's mass is so low that it doesn't have much effect on the mass number of an element. Unless they are also ionized, they would have the same number of protons and electrons.

47. A: An inch is about 2.54 cm = 25.4 mm = 2.54×10^{-5} km = 2.54×10^{-2} m.

48. D: Both liquids and gases are fluids and therefore flow, but only gases are compressible. The molecules that make up a gas are very far apart, allowing the gas to be compressed into a smaller volume.

49. A: NMR, or nuclear magnetic resonance, allows one to determine the connectivity of atoms in an organic molecule, by "reading" the resonance signals from the attached hydrogen atoms. IR, or infrared spectroscopy, can help to identify the functional groups that are present, but does not give much information about its position in the molecule. Mass spectrometry breaks apart a large molecule and analyzes the masses of the fragments. It can be useful in analyzing protein structure. HPLC, or high performance liquid chromatography, is a method used to separate a mixture into its components.

50. C: Proteins are large polypeptides, comprised of many amino acids linked together by an amide bond. DNA and RNA are made up of nucleic acids. Carbohydrates are long chains of sugars. Triglycerides are fats and are composed of a glycerol molecule and three fatty acids.

The Arts, Health, and Fitness

1. C: By correctly rendering proportion in her work, an artist can achieve a sense of realism. Correctly rendering proportion involves depicting the size relationships within and among objects as they are actually perceived by the human eye. For example, objects in the foreground of a painting should generally be larger than objects in the background (even if they are smaller in real life), since this is how the human eye perceives them.

2. D: Imagination would be a more appropriate source of inspiration for an abstract sculpture than for a still life, a portrait, or a copy of an original work. The nude portrait would be primarily inspired by the original photograph, rather than imagination, and the copy would be inspired by the original artwork. In the case of the painting of an artist's hometown, the inspiration would be memory, rather than imagination.

3. A: Visual literacy can best be described as the ability to communicate through images and comprehend the messages contained in images. In visual literacy education, students are taught not only to create images that appropriately communicate information, but also to interpret and derive meaning from both artistic and informational images.

4. D: Traditionally, visual artists have participated in the performing arts by creating costumes and applying makeup for performers and by painting sets; however, they have not typically participated in the casting of performers, as this process is not directly related to the visual arts.

5. D: all of the above. A social studies lesson on political propaganda could be incorporated into an art class by asking students to evaluate political propaganda posters or create their own. A math lesson on data analysis could be incorporated by asking students to use the principles and elements of art to create the most effective data displays possible. An English lesson about haiku could be incorporated by asking students to illustrate a haiku poem.

6. D: Assigning students to write an essay comparing and contrasting the influence that two famous American artists or artworks had on U.S. society would be most appropriate for helping high school students develop an appreciation for the value and role of art in U.S. society. The other activities mentioned, including having students create a PowerPoint presentation about a famous American artist, asking students to create a time line showing when famous works of American art were created, and taking students on a field trip to an art museum, would not necessarily achieve this learning goal because they do not include it explicitly.

7. B: Preteaching the background knowledge about the artwork that is needed to correctly find the main idea would be the most effective way to support high school students when teaching them to identify the main idea in a work of art. Giving them a "bank" of possible main ideas from which to choose would give too much support for this grade level, and explaining the concept of a main idea in art should be unnecessary at this level because students should have learned it in earlier grades. While allowing students to work in groups to find the main idea may be an appropriate lesson activity, it does not provide the level of targeted instructional support that preteaching does.

8. A: In order to teach a safety technique to students, the best method for a teacher to use would be to show how to execute the technique while explaining it verbally, and then closely supervising students as they begin to practice the technique themselves. Demonstrating the consequences of not executing the technique properly could be dangerous for the teacher and does not help the students learn to perform the technique properly. Both verbally explaining the technique to

students and giving the students written instructions to follow while they perform the technique are useful strategies, but they should be accompanied by direct modeling and guided practice by the teacher so that students who are visual and kinesthetic learners can comprehend the technique.

9. D: The teacher should briefly model the technique for incorporating perspective into a drawing, give students a chance to replicate the example with the teacher's guidance, and then allow students to create their own drawings using the technique. This method is most appropriate because it incorporates the strategy of "gradual release," in which students see the teacher model the process, practice it themselves with close guidance from the teacher, and then practice it independently.

10. B: In fact, the majority of artists hold postsecondary degrees or certificates. More than half of artists are self-employed, and competition is keen for salaried jobs in the art industry. Annual earnings for artists vary widely, according to the Bureau of Labor Statistics.

11. A: Artists often use portfolios to demonstrate their capabilities to potential employers. Portfolios can often act as a sort of resume, showing potential employers the range of the artist's abilities. Since they are usually in book form, portfolios are not appropriate for display at art shows, and they are rarely used for teaching purposes. An artist would not use a portfolio primarily to document his or her work, because art portfolios are product oriented as opposed to progress oriented.

12. B: A flat is a portion of a set, not a *type* of set. Therefore, answer choice A is incorrect. A small piece of scenery that is hinged to another piece of flat scenery is known as a *flipper*, so answer choice C is incorrect. A metal plate that is hinged and used for scenery suspension is called a *flying iron*, so answer choice D is incorrect. A flat is a piece of flat scenery that is framed in wood and usually wrapped in cloth or canvas.

13. A: A painted canvas or backcloth hung at the back of the stage is called a *backdrop*, so answer choice B is incorrect. A hidden door in the stage where actors can enter and exit is called a *trap*, so answer choice C is incorrect. A piece of cloth used to separate the stage from the audience is called a *curtain* or *grand drape*, so answer choice D is also incorrect.

14. C: Similar to a lighting plot, a costume plot is a chart or document created by the designer to inform her team of costuming directions. It lists each costume with accessories, which character will be wearing each costume, and when exactly they will appear onstage. While a costume plot is a *plan* that can be *sketched* or written out like a *script*, the technical term used by professionals in the industry is costume *plot*.

15. D: Theatre costumes can come from anywhere. There is no set standard with respect to how a high school should obtain costuming. Renting costumes can be more cost effective than hiring a seamstress or costume designer to make each wardrobe piece. Donated costumes are obviously even more cost effective than rented ones. Sometimes, when costumes are donated, a seamstress will add accessories to make an old costume or article of clothing more unique or more suitable for a specific performance.

16. B: The preservatives in theatrical makeup are added to prolong the shelf life of the product. There are no other benefits of preservatives in makeup. They do not prevent the transmission of infection caused by sharing product. The only way to prevent infections is to refrain from sharing

makeup. Preservatives will not prevent against color fading, nor will they prevent discoloration under bright theatre lights. Therefore, answer choices A, C, and D are all incorrect.

17. B: A simple prosthetic can be a scar, a wound, or a fake nose. Simple prosthetics are typically made from foam urethane and latex. Scenery backdrops might contain foam or other materials typically found in prosthetics, but answer choice B is not the best answer. Costume undergarments are typically made from cloth, so answer choice C is incorrect. Non-slip pads may be constructed out of latex, but answer choice D is not the *best* choice.

18. C: Process-centered *drama*, not *theatre*, is a learning technique, not a type of production. Therefore, answer choice A is incorrect. Practical theatre is a term rarely used in the theatre industry today, so answer choice B can be eliminated. Artistic theatre focuses on the actors and the dramatic performance, whereas technical theatre focuses on set construction, sound mixing and recording, light hanging, prop procurement, and all other aspects of theatre that are undetected by the audience.

19. C: A farce can be recognized by its outlandish, physical nature. Plots are fast-paced and typically involve improbable circumstances, so answer choice A is incorrect. The term *comedy* is too broad to be the *best* choice here, so answer choice B is incorrect. Slapstick can be identified by exaggerated, sometimes violent gestures, so answer choice D is incorrect. Satire is the only genre that regularly pokes fun at famous people and/or current events.

20. A: Broadway has impacted society by bringing countless jobs and mass consumerism to the United States, specifically New York. The West End has done the same thing. The West End, however, is in London, England. Therefore, answer choice B is incorrect. Experimental theatre has done little in terms of job creation and mass consumerism, mainly because it appeals to audiences and producers on a budget. Therefore, answer choice C is incorrect. Comedy clubs have created some jobs and generated some consumerism, but their impact is small compared to Broadway. Therefore, answer choice D is not the best choice.

21. A: As it relates to theatre, catharsis is a term that means "to purge the emotions." The terms *purification* and *ablution* have similar connotations, meaning "to cleanse or purify," but neither term is commonly used in the theatre industry. Therefore, answer choices C and D are incorrect. The alienation effect is when a director wants to distance the audience from the characters so they can be observed and critiqued from a non-emotional standpoint. Therefore, answer choice B is incorrect.

22. C: Operas and musicals can be sung or performed in any language, so answer choice A is incorrect. There is typically no dancing in operas, whereas there is almost always dancing in musicals, so answer choice B is incorrect. The time between songs can be filled with an orchestra *and* dancing in musicals, so answer choice D is incorrect. The main difference is that operas are usually sung all the way through, while musicals contain spoken dialogue between songs.

23. A: To effectively stress diversity in the classroom, a teacher should introduce scripts containing multicultural themes and characters of all ethnic backgrounds. It would never be a good idea to single out a student of a different race or cultural heritage for any reason, so answer choice B is incorrect. Teaching diversity is indeed part of most curriculums, so answer choice C is incorrect. Assigning minority roles to Caucasian students would be more closely related to nontraditional casting, not diversity in education, so answer choice D is incorrect.

24. C: The operative phrase in the question is *prior experience*. Answer choice A gives no indication that the football player has prior baseball experience, so answer choice A is incorrect. If a student is known for being shy, and not necessarily her singing skills, she is unlikely to feel comfortable singing in front of the class. Therefore, answer choice B is incorrect. Given his prior experience with comedy, a class clown would be more likely to take on a comedic role than a serious role. Therefore, answer choice D is incorrect.

25. A: Bringing electronic gadgetry into a performance, falling asleep, and unwrapping candy with noisy wrappers should be avoided when watching a theatre performance. It is very important to stress these rules of etiquette to students so they will be able to show respect for the actors onstage. If a student did not hear something, it is perfectly acceptable to quietly ask a neighbor for clarification. There are also times when performers interact with audience members, so speaking back would be necessary.

26. A: Partnering students is a great way to promote a better understanding of interpersonal relationships. While problems may arise that need creative problem solving, that is not the focus of the activity, so answer choice B is not the *best* choice. A student may become more confident after being partnered up with another student, but the focus of the activity is on understanding partnerships and relationship building, so answer choice C is incorrect. Exploration of content-related material is not relevant in the scenario, so answer choice D is incorrect.

27. D: There are many professional development resources available to high school teachers today. One of the best resources to tap into would be other theatre teachers, whether they are in the same school or in another part of the country. Theatre teachers should familiarize themselves with local community actors and conduct research online. An art museum might inspire a lesson plan, but it would be a better professional resource for an art teacher. Therefore, answer choice D is the one that does not belong.

28. A: At the beginning of class. While all of a vocal performance class should be considered voice training, all classes should start with warm-ups. During this time, teachers should reinforce the fundamentals of singing, such as breath and posture, range, and intonation. Because the quality of student singing is likely to be poor without adequate preparation, answer B is incorrect, as is answer C, as an entire class period of poorly performed pieces would make the vocal training at the end of class largely moot. Since most students in a general classroom setting do not receive private voice training and are in classes, ostensibly, to obtain such training, answer D is incorrect. Indeed, all young singers can benefit from the fundamentals of voice training, regardless of whether or not they are taking private lessons.

29. D: Girls' singing voices change just as boys' do. While the change may begin earlier—as is the case with most of a girl's adolescent development—and is subtler, it does indeed take place. Girls who wish to sing through early adolescence and beyond will need the coaching of a good, patient instructor. Because girls' voices change, answers A and B are incorrect. Also incorrect is answer c. Boys, like girls, can make good music in elementary and middle school, regardless of the changes taking place in their voices.

30. C: The oboe uses a double reed. The oboe, along with the bassoon, uses a double reed system to produce its distinctive sound. While playing the instrument can present a challenge to younger, more inexperienced players, it is possible for a student in even in the elementary grades to begin playing the oboe with a little extra help from his or her teacher. Only if extra time is impossible should an aspiring oboist be guided toward the clarinet or saxophone first. Therefore, answer A is

- 182 -

incorrect. Also incorrect is answer B, because an oboe properly played should be held between 30 and 45 degrees from the body. Finally, since the oboe is assembled in four parts, not three, answer D is incorrect.

31. D: Program notes should include the names of the arrangers of instrumental and vocal pieces, not just the names of composers. In addition, more complete program notes could provide brief information about the music contained in the program in order to give the audience a greater understanding and appreciation for the musical selections they are about to hear. As such, answer A, that notes are optional, is incorrect. Answer B is also incorrect, since notes showing only the names and composers of the pieces are incomplete in almost all performances. While program notes certainly should engage the audience, excessively long notes containing pages of information or song lyrics would be too much for most audiences and not add anything to the performance.

32. B: A conductor should practice his or her conducting style in front of a mirror along with taped or recorded music in order to make sure his or her conducting style is rhythmic and appropriate. As awkward as this practice may seem, conductors should practice their batons in much the same way their students practice their instruments: regularly, so their performance adds to the work of the group. Additionally, a conductor *does* add to the quality of the ensemble's musical performance. A good conductor can signal information to musicians regarding a wide variety of musical output including the tempo, rhythm, *and* style, which means that answer D is incorrect. For the same reasons, answer A is incorrect, because conductors' performances are not for show and help the ensemble to perform. Still, the conductor's style is not the audience's primary focus; therefore, answer D is incorrect.

33. D: Practice rooms are rarely used, except for before and after school and, as such, run the risk of being used for storage or becoming eyesores. They have value, however, and should be used, despite their considerable cost to build and maintain. Answer B is incorrect, because practice rooms should use indirect lighting, or lighting projected from the rear, to aid the reading of music without eyestrain. Answer C is incorrect because practice rooms should always include an electronic tuner.

34. C: The piccolo uses less air, but the musician must blow that air more rapidly. The piccolo is smaller than its lower-pitch cousin, the flute; therefore, the piccolo requires less air to work. Nonetheless, since that air is going to be generating notes that are higher in pitch, the air must move with greater speed. Although the piccolo is different from the flute in many ways both subtle and overt, it is similar enough that a flutist with sufficient skill should be able to play it. Therefore, answer A is incorrect. Also incorrect is answer B, because the instrument widely in use today is the C piccolo; the D-flat instrument was used long ago. Finally, the piccolo is known for having *less* pitch flexibility than its larger cousin, so answer D is incorrect.

35. B: Both instruments are pitched to B-flat. While the euphonium and baritone have many features in common, they are different instruments, making the other three possible answers to this question incorrect. First, answer A is incorrect on its face, as both the euphonium and baritone use bass clef, not treble. Secondly, most euphoniums come with four valves, and while four-valve baritone models are made, most baritones in this country come with three valves. Therefore, answer C is incorrect, as is answer D, because the euphonium requires a larger mouthpiece than the baritone.

36. A: The number of tuba players in a band is entirely up to the number of players who want to play it and the desires of the band director. While there are disagreements, as always, regarding the "ideal" number of tubas in an ensemble, the number should depend entirely on the type of sound

for which the band director is looking, plus the number of students willing to play this instrument. Anyone who is interested can play the tuba, regardless of size, so answer C is incorrect. Also incorrect is answer B, because while size is unimportant in deciding which students should play the tuba, its sound demands a player who can discern the differences between the lower tones. Finally, modern tubas are made in several keys including F, E-flat, CC, and BB-flat. So, answer D is incorrect.

37. B: Extrinsic rewards (such as prizes and certificates) should be awarded only to routine tasks, such as cleaning a rehearsal space or learning more scales than were assigned. Rewards for accomplishing more complex, musically related tasks should be more *intrinsic*, which is to say, from within. Praise, especially in front of a student's peers, would count as intrinsic motivation, as would the sense of satisfaction a student should feel upon solving a complex task. Yet, extrinsic motivation does have a place in most classrooms, so answer A is incorrect. Answer C also is incorrect, as previously stated. Finally, answer D is incorrect, since systems of rewards generally are left to the teacher's discernment and are rarely banned if they do not detract from the learning environment.

38. C: Because a march should *not* feature slowed down tempos when playing softer dynamics. The rest of the answers—up beat accompaniment, 2/4 time, independent bass line—are all characteristics of a march that band directors should know.

39. C: Students should practice a half-hour a so a day, then ideally work up to more than an hour every day. All students, regardless of age and experience, should learn the value and importance of daily practice; a shorter time period, such as a half hour, can start good habits without being overwhelming. By the time the student has gotten older and gained more experience, an hour or more a day of practice would be ideal. Nonetheless, because an hour a day from the beginning will seem overwhelming to a beginner, answer A is incorrect. Also incorrect is answer B, because practice from the beginning of a musical career will help ensure that the career in question will continue to grow, regardless of age or experience. Finally, answer D is incorrect, as inconsistent amounts and qualities of practice will quickly break down. The amount of practice every day should be roughly the same, regardless of the student's mood or repertoire.

40. D: Competitions for chair placement should be held both with advance notice and at unannounced times. Periodic competitions for first chair and so on keep more advanced students playing at their best level; many students further down the row will strive to improve their play in order to catch up. The result is a better orchestra. Therefore, answer B is incorrect; while a student's self-esteem is important, all musicians should be able to withstand the pressure of demonstrating their skills to their peers and their instructor. Accordingly, both announced and unannounced competitions have their place in this process. Daily competitions, answer A, would obviously be excessive in a student orchestra's busy schedule. Answer C, conversely, would not put *enough* motivation or pressure on the students to improve.

41. B: Hand vibrato. Beginning trumpet players can be taught easily to add vibrato to the tone their instruments make. All they need to do is move their thumb back and forth as they use their hand to brace their fingers on the valves. Answer A, voice vibrato, is incorrect, as one does not use the vocal cords when playing the trumpet. Answer C, jaw vibrato also is incorrect, because moving the jaw is not used commonly as a technique for achieving vibrato with the trumpet. Moving the lips, or embouchure, is an accepted technique for achieving vibrato, but it takes more practice and skill than using the hand. As a result, answer D is not the best method for a beginning trumpet player to use in order to achieve vibrato in his or her tone.

- 184 -

42. A: Diagnostic assessment is performed at the beginning of a semester and includes auditions for select ensembles. While diagnostic assessment can be used to assess a student's skill level and to judge whether he or she is prepared to enter a more advanced band or choir, it also can be used to determine one or more students' skill levels before the teacher begins selecting the semester's music and planning its lessons. Answer B, an assessment performed in the middle of the semester, would be better termed as a *formative* assessment. Answer B is incorrect. Answer C, a *summative* assessment, would be performed at the end of the semester in order to give a summary assessment of skills the student has been expected to know. Since diagnostic assessments are key to students of virtually every age, answer D, reserving them for college age students, is incorrect.

43. D: A simple system such as checks (for meeting the standard) and plusses (for exceeding them). A third symbol, such as an O for approaching the standard, also would be appropriate. Answer A, assigning letter grades, would be appropriate only for older students, and then only as an overall grade. Therefore, answer A is incorrect. Also incorrect is answer B, percentages, since they would be overly detailed and unnecessary to assess the basic process of students so young. Conversely, answer C, which asserts that second graders are too young for assessment, is incorrect, as state and national standards exist for students as young as those of pre-school age.

44. B: The autonomic nervous system maintains homeostasis in the body. For the most part, it is not subject to voluntary control.

45. C: Direct pressure constricts the blood vessels and stems blood flow. Pressure on the carotid artery can cause brain damage. Tourniquets can damage nerves and blood vessels. Attempting to clean a deep wound may increase bleeding.

46. D: A reading of 140/90 is the minimal definition of hypertension. Choices A and B represent normal blood pressure, while choice C would be characterized as high-normal, or prehypertension, and would probably be observed for a period of time before medication would be deemed appropriate.

47. B: The theory of social learning focuses on the idea that people learn through observing and imitating each other (therefore, learning is essentially social in nature). Providing a role model – someone a student might admire and who successfully participates in physical activity – provides a model for students to imitate, potentially motivating the student to engage in physical activity. Options A, C, and D do not touch upon observation or imitation and can all be rejected on that basis.

48. B: Basic principles of managing equipment in a physical education class include knowing how to transport and distribute equipment and ensure the safe use of equipment (principles described in options A, C, and D). Using student managers is one way a teacher might decide to transport and/or distribute equipment; it is a method of carrying out a basic principle of managing equipment. However, it is not a basic principle itself, and can therefore be rejected. In other words, using student managers is not a fundamental concern of managing equipment, but rather a way of addressing a fundamental concern.

49. A: Each other option correctly identifies a good way of maximizing participation in a physical education class. One way is grouping students according to skill level (for instance, having skilled students play with skilled students, or arranging teams so that they have a mix of beginning and more advanced students); therefore option B can be rejected. Option C can be rejected because another way to maximize participation is to offer different specific activities at individual stations, making the most use of equipment and appealing to a range of interests. Option D – changing the

rules of games to better suit student skill levels – is also a good way to ensure more student participation. The problem with letting each student choose his or her own physical activity without any further guidelines is that such an approach lacks organization, which can inadvertently suggest that the class is not to be taken seriously and make it more difficult to teach important specific content or skills.

50. A: When students learn new skills or improve existing skills, they tend to feel a sense of accomplishment, which can lead to improved self-esteem (higher regard of oneself). This is the best answer. Option B makes a true statement, but wonder at human athleticism is not as clearly linked to improved self-esteem as learning new skills or improving one's skills (a student might feel wonder at a person who is athletically gifted and feel inferior in comparison). Option C can be rejected because there is no clear connection between learning to take turns and improved self-esteem. Option D can be rejected because endorphins, which can be released in the course of exercise, make a person feel good in the sense of being in a good mood, rather than fostering the general condition of improved self-esteem.

51. B: Although participating in physical education activities can help foster self-esteem, self-esteem itself is not a social skill, but rather a personal quality (a person can have high self-esteem but lack all social skills). All of the other options identity a possible benefit of participating in physical education activities. Playing games and sports often involves communication (option A) and cooperation (option C), such as discussing and agreeing on a given strategy and then working together to carry it out. Sports and games can also involve respecting diversity (option D), especially in the context of teamwork, as different team members will have different, but similarly valuable, strengths. In addition, students will often work with different classmates they might not normally know or like and possibly develop positive relationships with those classmates, despite having differences with them.

52. C: Shin splints is pain in the shins, often caused by strenuous, high-impact activities such as running. One way of preventing shin splints is simply by strengthening the shins; another way is to reduce the impact on the body, such as by walking, swimming, or by walking or running on a relatively soft surface. Option A can be rejected because continuing to exercise even after feeling pain in the shin is likely to worsen shin splints, not prevent them. Option B does not describe a way of preventing shin splints, and neither does option D (running down hills is a possible cause of shin splints rather than a way of preventing them).